PENGUIN BOOKS

# ILL FARES THE LAND

Susan George, an American living in France, holds degrees from Smith College, the Sorbonne and the École des Hautes Études en Sciences Sociales of the University of Paris, where she took her doctorate. She is Associate Director of the Transnational Institute (TNI), Amsterdam, the international wing of the Institute for Policy Studies (IPS), Washington, DC, and has been a Fellow of TNI since 1974. The Institute's work 'addresses the fundamental disparities between the rich and poor peoples and nations of the world, investigates their causes and develops alternatives for their remedy'. She participated in the TNI report *World Hunger: Causes and Remedies* for the 1974 World Food Conference and subsequently published *How the Other Half Dies: The Real Reasons for World Hunger* (Penguin, 1976); *Feeding the Few: Corporate Control of Food* (IPS, 1979); *Les Stratèges de la faim* (her doctoral dissertation, Éditions Grounauer, Geneva, 1981); *Food for Beginners* (Writers & Readers 'Beginners' series, 1982) and *A Fate Worse than Debt* (Penguin, 1988), which won the Judges Award (book category) in the 1988 US World Hunger Media Awards. She has written numerous articles in English and French and her work has been translated into a dozen languages. She has acted as a consultant to Unesco, the United Nations University, the Economic Commission for Europe of the UN, the International Union of Food Workers, the Government of Nicaragua; she serves on the International Advisory Board of the UN Economic Commission for Africa. She has worked closely with several European, North American and Australian non- governmental organizations concerned with Third World development and frequently acts as adviser to the media, most recently for the Channel Four/Yorkshire TV four-part series *The Politics of Food* and the BBC2 film entitled *A Fate Worse than Debt*.

SUSAN GEORGE

# ILL FARES THE LAND

### ESSAYS ON
### FOOD, HUNGER
### AND POWER

**PENGUIN BOOKS**

PENGUIN BOOKS

Published by the Penguin Group
27 Wrights Lane, London w8 5tz, England
Viking Penguin Inc., 40 West 23rd Street, New York, New York 10010, USA
Penguin Books Australia Ltd, Ringwood, Victoria, Australia
Penguin Books Canada Ltd, 2801 John Street, Markham, Ontario, Canada l3r 1b4
Penguin Books (NZ) Ltd, 182–190 Wairau Road, Auckland 10, New Zealand

Penguin Books Ltd, Registered Offices: Harmondsworth, Middlesex, England

First published in the USA by the Institute for Policy Studies, Washington, DC 1984
First published in Great Britain by Writers & Readers Publishing Cooperative
Society 1985
This revised and expanded edition first published by Penguin Books 1990
2 4 6 8 10 9 7 5 3 1

Filmset in 10/12½ pt Photina

Made and printed in Great Britain by
Richard Clay Ltd, Bungay, Suffolk

HD
9000.5
.G385
1990

FOR MY FATHER AND FOR LAURA,
HIS GREAT-GRANDDAUGHTER, WHO MAY WITNESS AN END TO HUNGER,
WITH LOVE

# CONTENTS

*Ill fares the land, to hastening ills a prey,*
*Where wealth accumulates, and men decay;*
*Princes and lords may flourish, or may fade;*
*A breath can make them, as a breath has made.*
*But a bold peasantry, their country's pride,*
*When once destroyed, can never be supplied.*

Oliver Goldsmith,
'The Deserted Village', 1770

# AUTHOR'S FOREWORD

The publication by Penguin Books of this new and expanded edition of *Ill Fares the Land* gives me the greatest pleasure. I'm particularly attached to this book. Before introducing the essays it contains, however, a word about its publishing history and a short explanation of how the pieces came to be written are perhaps in order.

Half of these essays, the six written from 1979 to 1982, appeared initially under this same title with the Institute for Policy Studies (Washington, DC, 1984) and Writers & Readers (London, 1985). Shortly thereafter, Writers & Readers declared bankruptcy, leaving in its wake a wretched legal mess and legions of unpaid authors. For this author at least, going unpaid is disagreeable; going unread – so long as people want to read you – is intolerable.

Writers & Readers had also published my *Food for Beginners*. The hapless publishers who attempted to retrieve the 'Beginners' series from the ruins eventually informed me that, for reasons too boring to explain here, *Food*, like other titles in the series, would never see the light of day again. I long feared a similar fate for *Ill Fares the Land*. Before its demise, Writers & Readers had somehow contrived to sell out the first printing and had managed to get the book reviewed sufficiently often for most publishers to turn down the risk of reissuing a title not entirely new and not wholly their own.

Not so Penguin. Penguin are both reissuing the older pieces and letting me add a half-dozen others written between 1983 and 1985, the year I started working full time on *A Fate Worse than Debt.* My deep gratitude goes to my previous Penguin editor for *Fate,* Andrew Franklin, who made the decision to reissue *Ill Fares the Land* (and then got promoted – I like to think the two events are causally linked!) and to my present one, Jon Riley, who saw it through to publication.

Some readers like to know something of the background to the books they read, and here I don't mind giving it. Should they wonder why I wrote the essays in this collection, the honest answer would be, almost invariably, 'because someone asked me to'. With two short exceptions ('SNOB' and 'Ordering the World') none of these papers emerged from any particular need to communicate or to express myself; rather, they happened because someone convinced me I could make myself useful by writing them.

Books like *How the Other Half Dies* or *A Fate Worse than Debt* reflect my own agenda; *Ill Fares the Land* corresponds on the whole to other people's. Naturally the two agendas mesh, or we wouldn't have cooperated in the first place. As far as my working life goes, however, the real difference between these three books is that the first two were written thanks to refusals, whereas this collection emerged from acceptances. Other writers may have a different experience; mine is that producing anything sustained means I must clear my calendar, say 'No' to everyone and everything and live a cloistered life. Writing a book is an activity so lonely, so frustrating and so basically unfair to one's entourage that I am wary of younger people who say gushingly to me, 'Oh, I just love writing!' Generally I restrain myself from replying, 'That must be because you haven't done very much.' What *I* like is to have written something.

Although the subjects of the essays collected here are serious ones, I usually find writing shorter and self-contained pieces like these more enjoyable and certainly less lonely, particularly because they are often linked to the more sociable aspects of life. Many of these papers were the consequence – sometimes the cause – of friendships; most, too, were related to travelling somewhere for an event or a conference: to Washington, Bangladesh, Yugoslavia, Senegal, Geneva, Bruges, Canada. Mine is a full and fortunate life.

I was paid something for the essays that comprise Chapters 1, 2 and 7 (by UN agencies) and 12 (an endowed lecture), but nothing for the others. An author/speaker simply cannot write a paper for, and then attend without honorarium, several conferences a year unless someone provides a minimum material base. The Institute for Policy Studies (IPS) in Washington and the Transnational Institute (TNI), its sister in Amsterdam, have long provided this for me; both know how grateful I am. *Un grand merci* as well to the French *Comité Catholique contre la Faim et pour le Développement* whose grant I spent on working expenses between 1979 and 1982, including the trip to Bangladesh. Most of all, my husband, Charles-Henry George, made it possible for me to embark on and then to stick with this indefinable career of mine.*

The first and shorter edition of *Ill Fares the Land* appeared when stories of starvation in Ethiopia and other African countries were filling the media. It seemed an important time to publish this work, for, as I said at the time in the Introduction:

> Visible famine is once again pushing the issues of hunger and underdevelopment into the forefront of public consciousness. It's not that hunger had ever gone away – it had merely receded from the television screen, due to the temporary absence of victims spectacular enough to photograph. Now, God help them, and us, the victims are

---

*I mention these material aspects, burdened as I am at present with fund-raising for TNI. It is amazing how many organizations want, indeed expect, people like me to provide lectures, seminars, articles, etc., for their constituencies (usually free of charge) yet do not seem to recognize that our presentations do not fall from heaven but result from years of hard work. Somehow, someone has to pay for this work, before the books come out (assuming they do) and their authors are invited to hold forth. If organizations want the product, they should also contribute to the process.

back for all to see. Perhaps such needless suffering will at least compel serious discussion of their plight and what might – must – be done about it. Such a debate should be carried on by as many people as possible, and, I would submit, forced upon those who do not care to participate, either from bureaucratic inertia or because it is not in their economic or political interests to do so.

With this book, I hope to contribute to such a debate. The pieces collected here all run along the lines of my previous work: they examine questions of power. Some fit into the 'food systems and hunger' category, others are more concerned with how we *think* about food systems and hunger; all deal with the means by which some groups gain authority and ascendancy over others. Control over the world food system ... the subject of much of my earlier writing and of some that appears here – implies control over technology and ideology, scholarship and culture as well. Such areas are not peripheral to the horrors of hunger.

I still hope to contribute to such a debate, which is more needed today than ever: the new essays expand on these same themes. The first edition of this book contained two basic 'food system' essays; to these are now added, in Part I, a piece concerned specifically with famine (not the same thing as hunger) and how we could avoid it; another suggests what Europe could do to combat chronic hunger in Africa and why it would be in her interests to do so.

If I had another life, I'd devote much of it to a better understanding of science. In Part II, I take one path open to the non-scientist, and make an attempt at least to examine the social conditions in which scientific and technological activity takes place. The 1982 essay on the 'transfer' of technology and its impact on Third World societies is now accompanied by one, written in 1984, on corporate control of biotechnology.

Part III, on ideology, scholarship and culture, now contains more chapters than any other. Among the questions explored: What are the present conditions of the production of knowledge about hunger and poverty? Who actually benefits from research done on them? How do the laws of cultural imitation ensure that Third World societies will follow the mass consumption patterns of the West? What sort of a university do we need if we want it to contribute to authentic development? Where do the categories which we use to think about all these things come from – that is, what are our unstated prior assumptions? In the Introduction to the first edition I wrote that these issues are 'not peripheral to the horrors of hunger': I now believe they are absolutely central.

The concluding chapter, from 1985, concerns food as a human right. It provides a bridge between the food and justice issues I began working on fifteen years ago (particularly in *How the Other Half Dies*), and the human consequences of Third World debt, the subject of the book I'd begun to work on in 1985 and which became *A Fate Worse than Debt*.

Though the reader must be his or her own judge, on re-reading I found the pieces collected here – both the older and the more recent ones – nearly impervious to the passage of time. This is due not to my perspicacity but to the unchanging nature of power. The poor may always be with us but so, surely, will the powerful – ever seeking to expand their freedoms at the cost of ours; to deny justice unless it serves their ends; to persuade us that theirs is the natural and beneficent order of things. It is the consistency of their actions that keeps my words from seeming too dated. Timely or not, these essays are published here almost exactly as they first appeared. Though I've made some stylistic changes, I've not touched the texts themselves except when repetitions or excess detail required deletions. Remaining repetitions are intentional and useful to the arguments. The few textual additions appear in footnotes.

The situation we face at the outset of the 1990s, though in many ways constant, is undeniably different from that of the previous decade. Five years after the great famines of the 1980s – and as many of us foresaw – 'compassion fatigue' has set in with a vengeance. Amid general indifference, chronic hunger – especially in Africa – has grown more severe with each passing year. Throughout the Third World, austerity measures designed to ensure repayment of crushing debts threaten the food security and the lives of millions. The power of the rich countries, and often that of Third World elites, has been entrenched by the debt phenomenon, as I have tried to show in detail elsewhere.

In the past decade furthermore, the southern half of the globe has become less important to the northern half. If the poorest continents dropped off the map, it is not certain that everyone in the rich countries would notice. Latin America now represents a mere 4.1 per cent of the value of world trade; Africa 2.4 per cent (with South Africa responsible for a fifth of that). Any two of the four Asian 'dragons' (Korea, Taiwan, Singapore, Hong Kong) account for a higher proportion of world trade value than all the countries of Africa taken together.

Except for these dragons and a few apprentice dragons, the major industrial countries no longer look much to the Third World as a trading partner or a source of cheap labour – they've found an alternative. Though splendid developments in themselves, *glasnost* and *perestroika* in the USSR and Eastern Europe may have unforeseen consequences as the State socialist countries move closer to the parliamentary democracies.

And yet, in the year 2000, the Third World, broadly defined, will contain nearly 90 per cent of humanity – much of it poor, hungry and young. For the rich, industrialized countries (North America, Eastern and Western Europe, perhaps Australia and a few others) the temptation may be overwhelming to unite along more or less racialist lines in order to keep this seething mass under control. The South will be perceived as dangerous, a threat to the power, the profits and (to some extent) the values of the North in general. The response from the said seething mass will most likely manifest itself in different sorts of fundamentalism and terrorism born of despair, though employing far more sophisticated methods and weapons than present-day ones.

Just as hunger is likely to grow, so the rape and plunder of the planet will continue unless today's promising environmental movement grows exponentially and becomes the political context within which all leaders must work or perish. To escape the destructive logic of our century we must build stronger political coalitions, regrouping forces separate today: Greens, trade unionists, farmers, women, churches, youth, etc. Demands for democracy world wide must focus on the powerful – not just on States but also on corporations, banks, national and inter-national bureaucracies – and force them to change course. Most important, we must make new international alliances, from North to South, between democratic forces and dissident elites – those who have not sold out to greed.

In the last analysis, I wrote the essays which follow because I believe (without sufficient proof, it is true) that the world is ultimately subject to rationality. Perhaps it isn't; perhaps we're up against not just the terrible logic of our century but the lunacy of our species as well. In that case there is no hope at all. But until proven irrevocably wrong, I intend to stand on the side of reason and in the hope of justice, with my countless comrades fighting innumerable battles; muttering occasionally under my breath, 'All that is required for evil to triumph is that good men and women do nothing.'

Lardy
Essonne
September 1989

# PART I

# FAMINES, FOOD SYSTEMS AND SOLUTIONS

# I
# OVERCOMING HUNGER:
## STRENGTHEN THE WEAK,
## WEAKEN THE STRONG

*The Food and Agriculture Organization (FAO) of the United Nations proclaimed 16 October 1981 the first World Food Day and has now made it an annual event. FAO's objective is to promote widespread public knowledge and concern about food and hunger problems throughout the world, and to this end the WFD Secretariat commissioned several papers which were to be published in five or six languages and sent as a kit to the dozens of national committees to aid them in their observance of World Food Day. I accepted the Secretariat's invitation to write one of these papers and revised it several times to conform as closely as possible to the needs and desires of FAO. Although I accepted changes suggested by the World Food Day staff and avoided unfavourable mention of specific countries, publication was ultimately refused. I was told off the record by the kind and somewhat embarrassed editor I'd been working with that the piece was still too polemical and political for FAO's taste.*

*The Organization honoured its contractual obligations to me and has graciously consented to publication here. The article appears in its final version (with only minor stylistic changes) as it came back from the Secretariat just before the final refusal. The reader must judge whether the latter was warranted.*

Perhaps World Food Day calls for commemoration, but surely not celebration. How could one 'celebrate' a day on which as many as 40,000 people will succumb to hunger? Moreover, barring an unforeseen, major overhaul of the world's political and economic system, there is every reason to suppose their numbers will be even greater on 16 October 1982, 1983, 1984 ...

One hopes this observation may provoke first outrage, then inquiry and, finally, action. If 16 October is to differ from any other day, it will be because widespread observance of World Food Day helps significant numbers of people throughout the world to move from indignation (without which there is no motivation) towards accurate analyses of the issues (without which there can be no effective action) and from this anger and understanding onwards to organization and practical politics.

## Relatively Small Amounts of Food Are Needed

Estimates of the number of severely malnourished people range from 450 million (FAO) to a billion (the World Bank). Experts agree that the relative and absolute numbers of hungry people have never been so high, and that they are increasing.

The 15 million children who, according to Unicef's estimate, die prematurely each year from hunger or hunger-related illness *could* be saved by an infinitesimal portion of the food harvested in the world. Simple arithmetic demonstrates how this is so:

- There are about 3,500 calories per kilo of grain, so a ton supplies an average 3,500,000 calories.

- FAO says 2,300–2,400 calories a day are usually adequate for proper *adult* nutrition.

- We shall be extra careful and assume that children should eat as much as adults.

- At 2,300 calories × 365 days, each child would thus need 839,500 calories a year, which means each ton of grain could provide for over four children (4.17, to be precise).

4

- A million tons would feed more than four million, and to provide all year long for all 15 million children who now die from hunger, we would need to count on just about 3.6 million tons of cereals altogether.

Does this sound like a lot?

It may, until you learn that world harvests in 1980 were 1,556 million tons of cereals. The share needed to save 15 million young lives is thus equal *at most* to a two-thousandth (0.002 per cent) of global crops – a figure as ludicrously small as it appears to be tragically unobtainable. Even this tiny figure exaggerates, because we have not only assumed a high daily ration, but we've also proceeded as if no other resources existed besides cereals – not even breast milk.

We could apply the same sort of arithmetic in discussing food for the 450 million people FAO classifies as severely malnourished. Let's grant a very generous ration of 2,740 calories a day, or one ton of grain per 3.5 adults per year. We would arrive at 128 million tons of cereals required to wipe out serious hunger and malnutrition – 8 per cent of the world's most recent harvest, less than the United States feeds to its livestock.

In practice, however, needs are much less, since we've assumed 100 per cent dependence on these cereals – that is, 450 million people with zero resources of their own, who have neither fish nor fowl, root crops nor oil seeds, fruits nor vegetables, milk nor meat. A World Bank economist wrote recently that a mere 2 per cent of world grain harvests would provide enough food for *over a billion* people who need it.[1]

## Victims, Resources, and Crucial Questions

Showing how little food, proportionally, would be required to rid the world of hunger may help prompt indignation; unfortunately, it contributes very little to analysis. Numbers like the ones just given have three major drawbacks:

1. They mask the fact that the needs of poor people with no purchasing power do not create what economists call 'effective demand'. The poor cannot express their needs in terms of money, the only language the market economy understands. Food *ought* to be a basic human right. However, this right cannot be exercised in a system which divides people into two categories: those who can pay (called 'consumers') and those who cannot.

2. These figures imply that the problem is 'to feed' people. If only we could manage to divert $x$ per cent of our abundance, 'we' could feed 'them' and no one would go hungry. The problem, however, is to make sure people can feed themselves. Given the opportunity, they will do just that; they will not need 'us'. Unfortunately, through no fault of their own, fewer and fewer people *can* feed themselves.

3. These numbers also concentrate on quantifying the victims (and the resources theoretically available to help them out). It's not that the victims are unimportant – but if we focus only on them, we shall lose sight of the really crucial questions:

   ● *Who controls* food and food-producing resources, especially land?

   ● *Who decides* what constitutes the agricultural 'surplus' and how it is distributed?

   ● *Who has the power* to determine that some will eat while others will not?

## A Question of Relationships

For a world so proud of its science, its technology and its management skills, eliminating hunger should be child's play. Since it still exists, one logical conclusion is that hunger is not primarily a scientific, technical or organizational problem.

Suppose we change the angle of vision? What if we consider, not the poor and hungry themselves, but their *relationships* to society, particularly to its powerful members, locally, nationally and internationally? 'Conventional wisdom' focuses on the victims of hunger and always sees them as people *lacking* something – food and money, of course, but also technology, skills, knowledge (and, in the worst cases, even intelligence). What if, on the contrary, we regarded these millions of poor people as a rich national resource who lack only *power*, the power to control their own environments and the circumstances of their lives? By up-ending it, we shall discover that the problem of hunger is not one of technology or organization but of politics; morally, the issue is not charity, but justice.

## From Development to Underdevelopment

In former times, the least powerful people seem to have been better off than they are today, relative to the situation of the most powerful.

> They have wine and spices and fair bread, and we have oat cake and straw and water to drink. They have leisure and fine houses; we have pain and labour, the rain and wind in the fields. And yet it is of us and of our toil that these men hold their state.[2]

This text, 600 years old, is taken from a sermon preached during an English peasant rebellion in 1381. Has anything much changed? Yes – today, the really poor are found in different areas, and they may not even have 'oat cake, straw and water to drink'. One area in Asia is reporting deaths from exposure for the first time. Why? Because straw, with which the very poorest people cover themselves during the cold nights, used to be free. Now it has a price, which they cannot afford. So they freeze.[3] Pure water to drink is the exception rather than the rule for poor Third World people. And how many would be glad to have oat cake or any other grain, along with labour of any kind, even in the rain and wind in the fields? While tragic famines could and did strike with awful regularity in precolonial times, historical and anthropological evidence suggests that poor people in the now 'underdeveloped' countries once had far easier access to food than they have today.[4]

Throughout history, ruling groups have tried to keep a great secret: they need the peasants – the producers of wealth – far more than the peasants need them. Patron/client relationships in most 'traditional' societies limit the exploitation to which peasants need submit and offer some security in times of hardship. Those who control land and other resources have responsibilities towards those who serve them. Self-interest opposes killing the goose that lays the golden eggs. As a result, in 'traditional' societies, the peasantry survives in all but the most dire circumstances.

Today, however, patron/client arrangements nearly everywhere have broken down and have been replaced by capitalist relationships. Land, food, and human labour alike become nothing but commodities and sources of profit.[5] As a result, hunger is increasing in both scope and severity. Deprivation on today's scale is a thoroughly modern phenomenon. Humanity has taken several thousand years to reach its present stage of underdevelopment.

## Candidates For Hunger

In many countries with serious food problems, at least a third of the rural population is totally landless. An additional third may exist on holdings of less than a hectare.[6] Both rural and urban unemployment are on the upswing, while the Third World labour force is likely to increase by nearly half a billion before the end of the century.[7]

All these people are candidates for hunger. Instead of searching for the economic and political causes and implications of this drastic situation, many 'experts' focus our attention on the victims. We are told that people – the landless and the jobless – go hungry through their own fault, that they are pushing themselves off the farms and into unemployment; they are worsening their own plight because they have too many children.

Any analysis should, however, not only ask *why* the poor have children (risk-spreading, security, etc.)[8] – but also *who decides* how many is too many. *Who determines* what constitutes 'over' population? 'Over' in relation to what? In relation, no doubt, to some ideal level where available resources, including food, 'balance' with the number of people who want to consume them.

In fact, where *does* the imbalance lie today? The rich countries (not quite 25 per cent of world population) consume between two-thirds and three-quarters of the world's production, including its food production. Their animals alone eat nearly a third of all cereal grains harvested.[9]

While huge imbalances in consumption exist between rich and poor countries, the most perceptible gaps are those between the rich and poor citizens of developing countries. To predict levels of hunger and malnutrition in any country, one need look only at the degree of land concentration, the circumstances of tenancy, and the proportion of landless labourers. The more unequal the holdings, the more insecure the tenancies, the higher the proportion of landless people, the greater the incidence of hunger will be. When fewer than 5 per cent of the landholders control 70 per cent or more of the cropland (a commonplace occurrence); when tenants must pay exorbitant rents and are vulnerable to eviction at the landlords' pleasure; when large numbers of rural dwellers have only the off-chance of selling their labour power standing between them and starvation, then one need look no further for the immediate causes of hunger. If the first priority is to maintain this status quo, it is quite true that there are 'too many' people.

## Inequality Breeds Inefficiency

Inequality also severely limits the amount of food that can be produced. A number of studies have shown that smaller holdings produce more food than large estates.[10] When farmers have secure tenure and know the benefits of their labour will accrue to them and their families – not to a landlord, a money lender, or a middleman – then they will work very hard indeed.

A more just society is a better-fed society. When the rich take the best, large numbers of peasants must make do with a tiny proportion of second-best land. 'Over' cultivation or 'over' grazing results. When development experts ascribe such sins to small peasants and herders, their vocabulary focuses on the supposed wrongdoings of the victims, deflecting attention from the meagre resources that the landholding minority allot to the poor majority.

When even 'over' cultivation fails to ensure survival (for, of course, an environment limited both in size and in quality *does* deteriorate under population pressure), the alternative is migration to an already 'over' crowded city.[11] Here the term 'over' populated describes very precisely the unliveable Third World shanty-towns inhabited by desperate, displaced ex-peasants.

## Development Games

Today, it has been officially recognized that gross inequalities contribute to hunger. Even the bland recommendations of international conferences now call upon governments to display the 'political will necessary' to eliminate them. These resolutions do not, however, explain why governments whose supporters have a deep stake in the status quo would willingly destroy their own power base.

Governments – if we assume that they are genuinely concerned for the poor and hungry – will find that some development policies are easier to carry out than others. An analogy from game theory illustrates why. In a zero-sum game, if A wins, B must lose: all the points won and lost cancel each other out. Health and education are not zero-sum development games. If A earns his first degree certificate, B need not give up his Ph.D.;

when C receives prenatal care, this does not imply that D will have a heart attack.* Indeed, when poor C risks catching a disease, then so does rich D. Dominant groups sometimes feel that environmental and health improvements are a necessity – and the poor benefit as a result. One Latin American country recently stamped out an epidemic by vaccinating 80 million people in ten months.[12]

An all-out attack on hunger is something else. Workable anti-hunger strategies strike landholding elites, and rightly so, as zero-sum games: if the landless and the small peasantry gain greater access to land, credit, and other food-producing resources this must almost always be at the expense of those who control them at present. Therefore, one finds dozens of historical and contemporary examples of the wealthy's refusal to play any game at all – until violence becomes the only recourse of the deprived. It is thus logical that as landlessness and hunger increase, repression must also increase and that a part of the arms trade – estimated at 1 to 2 billion dollars annually – is devoted to weapons designed to quell internal revolts.[13] When uprisings succeed, hunger may decrease dramatically. In the single year following the victory of the Sandinistas in Nicaragua, basic grain production went up by fully one-third, and was far more equally distributed.[14]

## Strategies to End Hunger

Steps to alleviate hunger never take place in a social vacuum. Inevitably, a power structure is already in place. Advantages of any anti-hunger project or strategy are likely to flow towards better-endowed groups (in both industrialized and developing countries), unless stringent precautions are taken to ensure that the benefits actually reach the poor. Donor agencies and

---

*This is not to say there are no problems of *budgetary* allocations between primary, secondary and higher education, or between city hospital-based and decentralized health care.

governments, however well-meaning, would thus do well to keep the following propositions in mind:

1. Development strategies benefiting the least favoured classes (or nations) will not be acceptable to the dominant classes or nations unless their interests are also substantially served.

2. Development strategies which benefit *only* poor classes or nations will be ignored, sabotaged or otherwise suppressed by the powerful in so far as possible.

3. Development strategies serving the interests of the elites, while doing positive harm to the poor, will still be put into practice and if necessary maintained by violence, so long as no basic change in the balance of political and social forces takes place.

Currently many people claim that the Brandt Commission strategy[15] – a massive transfer of resources from the industrialized to the developing countries – would end hunger and underdevelopment. They stress that this strategy is *not* a zero-sum game; that both rich and poor nations would ultimately benefit. Such reasoning is fine as far as it goes. It has the advantage of realism since it appeals to the self-interest of the rich nations – not to ethical principles. It stops short of asking how resources transferred will actually be shared with the worst-off. Three decades of failed 'trickle-down' development should have taught us some scepticism on this point. And even if equitable sharing were to take place, there is no guarantee that the Third World could achieve food self-sufficiency through resource transfer alone in the absence of major structural – even psychological – changes. Two formidable obstacles to ending hunger would remain: the 'cash-crop imperative' and the 'modernization syndrome'.

## Crops and Robbers

Many Third World countries have opted for a development strategy encouraging cash crops for export at the expense of food production. While some privileged groups may profit handsomely from prolonging such colonial production patterns or from introducing such non-traditional crops as fresh fruits, vegetables, flowers (plus livestock) for off-season delivery to northern markets, overall these countries have been swindled. For them, participating in the world market is like playing Monopoly against partners who begin the game with all the most desirable properties.

Tropical commodity prices fluctuate wildly and unforeseeably. The only predictable thing about them is that they decline constantly compared to the prices of manufactured goods poor countries must import. Of every $100 consumers spend on tropical products, in their final form, producer countries get only $15. The remaining 85 per cent lines the pockets of those in industrialized countries – mostly transnational corporations (TNCs) – which control shipping, processing, and merchandising.[16]

Cash crops also hog scarce resources like fertilizers and credit; as a result food production inexorably declines. In turn, this must be compensated for by importing increasingly expensive foods from abroad: in 1979–80, developing countries imported about 85 million tons of cereals.[17] (At the World Food Conference in 1974, FAO feared imports of 85 million tons in ... 1985.) The Third World is thus in the unenviable position of exporting greater and greater quantities of tropical agricultural products at (falling) prices it does not control in exchange for greater and greater quantities of vital foodstuffs at (rising) prices it does not control either. This is one manifestation of power relations at the international level. The victims are entire nations, particularly the poorest among them. Fairer and more stable prices for cash crops (as recommended by Brandt, UNCTAD, etc.) are necessary, though not sufficient, conditions for an effective anti-hunger strategy.

## Modernization: Remedy or Disease?

Most countries, however, can't get off the trade treadmill even when they recognize the danger, because they must repay their crushing foreign debt, now estimated at $400 billion.* Thus they continue to submit to unequal exchange in the marketplace. This is a fairly straightforward kind of exploitation. A more subtle aspect of the control that dominant countries exercise over their poor Southern neighbours can be described as the 'modernization syndrome'.

Victims of this syndrome assume that the agricultural practices of industrialized countries (especially North America) are the most 'modern', the most efficient and consequently the most desirable. These techniques are, in fact, often seen as the *only* way to improve output in countries whose agriculture is considered, by comparison, backward.

North American agriculture is of dubious 'modernity', even on its home ground, as a good many Western experts are beginning to recognize. It consumes enormous amounts of expensive, non-renewable energy, much of it in the form of manufactured inputs. It depletes and pollutes the environment through poor conservation practices, land and water 'mining', overuse and run-offs of agricultural chemicals.[18] Farmers have fallen under the control of non-producers – giant corporations that provide inputs and buy the produce, enormous banks that furnish costly financial credit. While this agriculture appears to be immensely powerful and productive, yields per hectare in the United States of all the major food grains have stabilized or fallen since the early 1970s.[19] Most important of all, the North American system grew up under unique historical conditions which included a vast frontier and relatively few people to farm it. Consequently, the whole thrust of this agriculture has always been to obtain the greatest possible yields *per person*, not *per unit of land*.

Conditions in most developing countries are exactly the opposite: they have relatively small amounts of arable land per person and vast numbers of rural people who need employment. What

*It tripled to $1,200 billion in the seven years since this paper was written.

14

could be less 'modern' – if eliminating hunger is the goal – than to model development on a system expressly designed to substitute fossil fuels and industrial products for work done by people? No wonder Third World rural unemployment is on the rise.

'Modernization' downgrades the potential contributions of peasants' practical knowledge to improving production. If Western recipes for development were abandoned, peasants, now perceived as 'obstacles' to development, could occupy their rightful place as intelligent farmers and sources of agricultural knowledge.[20]

Because 'modernization' implies extensive use of very expensive inputs, wealthier farmers benefit most. They may indeed increase their production (just as the corporations which sell such agricultural inputs increase their profits), but this increase may contribute to hunger.

That hunger will automatically diminish when food production increases is a common but naïve assumption. Higher productivity – and higher profits – actually mean more hungry people when they bring evictions, foreclosures on debts so owners can control more land, more labour-saving machinery, higher rents, higher prices for land, lower wages for growing numbers of available labourers, etc.[21] When governments neither subsidize nor protect smaller cultivators and market forces are left free play, the weak will lack access to the 'modernization package'. They will be eliminated when agriculture becomes more a way of making profits than of feeding people – as happens all too often in 'modernized' systems. The problem is not improved technology *per se*, but to whom it is available.

## Dependency is Undependable

A country cannot be independent when it depends on the goodwill of rich consumers to keep on buying its coffee or its fresh strawberries even in periods of economic crisis and spending cutbacks. Nor can it be free when it depends on TNCs for pricing, processing and marketing its agricultural products; or on the wealthy countries for vital foodstuffs, or on food aid; or on foreign funds to finance these imports. Landless labourers and poor cultivators at the bottom of the Third World ladder cannot win when they depend on the diminishing goodwill of their richer, better-endowed local neighbours who hold literal life-and-death power over them and their families.

When concerned citizens and those professionally responsible for confronting problems of hunger and underdevelopment face up to a few unpalatable truths, we may then make some headway:

1. That all governments are concerned for, and representative of, the majority of their people is patent nonsense. Plenty of governments are most concerned with enriching those who keep them in power. Human rights, including the right to food, run a poor second.

2. Very little is to be expected from most industrialized countries (except that they will encourage dependency). Food aid decreases as need increases and prices rise. Socialist industrialized countries contribute a far smaller proportion of their GNP to development aid than capitalist countries whose own record is, for the most part, dismal. The only way to get more help from such bastions of national selfishness is to convince them it is in their interest to aid poor countries (as the Brandt Commission attempts to do).

3. The present world capitalist order sanctions private ownership while taking no responsibility for those who own nothing. It has been incapable of setting upper limits for accumulation of riches by an individual, a corporation or, for that matter, a nation. By contrast, the lower limit – death by hunger – is very clearly defined. For a world economy ruled by competition and the profit motive, millions of people are utterly useless. From capital's viewpoint, they are not needed for food produc-

tion – machines and chemicals will do as well – and they are not even needed for consumption so long as enough consumers with purchasing power will reliably upgrade their diets in value (more animal products, more off-season, expensive perishables), thus ensuring continued profits. In food systems dedicated to eliminating labour, poor people are a drag on the economy, not the asset they would be if labour-intensive food systems were designed.[22] World capitalism would prefer that such 'useless' people disappear – at present, starvation is one avenue towards this end.

## Conclusion: Some Suggestions for Action

For international organizations and governments to become more effective in acting against hunger, they must receive considerable help – some of it in the form of criticism and pressure – from concerned citizens all over the world working through their own non-governmental organizations (NGOs). Here are some major goals. The first two are politically the most difficult to achieve, the others more immediately feasible.

● Wipe out Third World debt. Without relief, countries can't even make a choice between food crops and cash crops. This would, among other things, mean that rich countries would have to pay off their own banks.

● Limit development aid and projects to countries whose leaders have demonstrated their concern for their own poor through real land reform, income redistribution policies and the like. No rewards for those countries where aid reinforces the repressive capacity of an already dominant, and rapacious, class.

● Increase food aid – but only for emergency purposes. Institutionalized food aid has consistently discouraged local production and side-tracked governments from undertaking serious reforms and cereals policies.

- Insist on more socio-economic research about the effects of past, present and future development projects and strategies on the worst-off. Few agencies welcome independent evaluation of their work – an indication that such is needed.

- Continue to push for the basket of measures summed up in the 'New International Economic Order'. The NIEO wouldn't eliminate hunger, but it would at least allow governments to plan more rationally.

- Help NGOs that sponsor small projects directly beneficial to peasant communities aimed at increasing local self-reliance and greater popular control over resources.

- Support alternative agronomic and ecological research that rejects conventional 'modernization' in favour of improving local systems in the context of local environments. Treat the peasantry as a source of knowledge, not as an obstacle to progress.

- Accept new technology selectively, and only when it enhances local solutions, ultimately reducing dependency.

We should encourage whatever measures help local or regional food systems protect peasant self-sufficiency and reduce their vulnerability to outside pressures. Conversely, we should reject incorporation of local food systems into larger, more powerful ones directed by the richest countries for their own purposes. To do this, we must find available political spaces and work in them, and we must create new ones. Hunger will never be vanquished unless we can strengthen the weak and weaken the strong.

# 2
# DANGEROUS EMBRACE:
## CULTURE, ECONOMICS, POLITICS AND FOOD SYSTEMS

*In late 1979, the United Nations Economic Commission for Europe (ECE) – including both Western and Eastern Europe – held a joint seminar with the UN Environment Programme (UNEP) on 'Alternative Patterns of Development and Lifestyles' (Ljubljana, Yugoslavia, 3–8 December 1979). The seminar was attended, inter alia, by 'senior advisors to ECE governments on environmental problems' and part of the discussion was devoted to relationships between ECE countries and the Third World. The UNEP and ECE Secretariats commissioned a certain number of background papers, including this one. My editor for this contribution was (quite properly) demanding: this resulted in an unusually high proportion of endnotes to text, and it's possibly the most closely argued paper in this collection. The language is not UNese, but it is as neutral as my language ever becomes. The paper is reproduced here with the kind permission of the Secretariats of the ECE and of UNEP.*

Every food system – defined as the totality of tangible and intangible means employed by a given human community for the production, conservation, distribution and consumption of food – has profound effects on the environment. There is no such thing as a 'natural' ecosystem; each one is shaped by the cultural perceptions, economic arrangements and political confrontations of human beings in their efforts to assure themselves of this most basic human necessity. It is, furthermore, impossible to look at food systems as closed, static entities. Not only are dynamic historical processes occurring within each society to transform them (and, with them, the environment) but interactions between food systems in different parts of the globe are taking place with increasing frequency and intensity. The result is that these systems, in most parts of the world, are today wide open. As the secretariat of this seminar has noted:

> Countries of the world are closely linked through the mechanisms of international economy, political, scientific-technological and cultural relations and exchange, as well as through the environment. Events and actions by one country ... have repercussions and impacts on others, on the international community as a whole and on the biosphere.[1]

This is nowhere more true than in the realm of food, but in order to understand the full magnitude of the impact of changes in food systems today, we would do well to examine first some of the processes which have shaped our food systems and environment in the past. It is not merely physical factors but culture, economics and politics that are the prime determinants of food systems and the environment in which they exist.

## Cultural Impact on the Environment

Ecologists study patterns of plant/animal species development; some take into account the impact of human farming techniques on these patterns, but few note that the way in which people use their environment for subsistence is dictated not only by the *physical* capacity of that environment to sustain certain kinds of plants or animals but also by the view the community has of its own nature and its relationship to the rest of the universe. Diets in fact represent a cultural – even ethical – choice among the range of foods that are physically feasible in a given environment.[2]

It is impossible to account for the ecological differences between southern Spain and northern Morocco without contrasting Catholicism and Islam. The original ecosystems of these areas were virtually identical from a 'natural' point of view, and yet were utterly transformed by people who, if they were Muslims, needed large numbers of sacrificial sheep, but did not eat – and therefore hunt – wild boar any more than they drank wine. Catholics, on the other hand, terraced their hillsides with vineyards and raised a variety of animals (eating a variety of plants) and hunted the wild boar to near extinction.[3] Quite evidently flora and fauna are not the whole story.

Our physical surroundings, the aspect of our landscapes can thus be 'decoded' as incarnations of culture. But the above examples of the impact of food/cultural systems on the environment are still relatively simple because they have been confined to specific geographic areas and self-contained human communities where the pace of historical transformation and conflict was relatively slow.

## Economic and Political Pressures on Food Systems

In contrast, prolonged or intense interaction with *outside* food systems will accelerate the processes of history; changes wrought in a community's original food system may have unforeseeable consequences to the point where that community may lose control over its own environment. These changes may involve the use of superior force to oblige one group to devote its land and labour to satisfying the needs of another (agricultural tribute, colonization); or they may be introduced peacefully and yet have violent consequences.

The effects of introducing a single hitherto-unknown plant or animal species into a new environment can be immeasurable. Could Philip Miller, Curator of London's Chelsea Physic Garden in the eighteenth century, know that he would lay the foundations for a whole new mode of life (and, as has been submitted, for a Civil War) when he sent the first packet of cotton seeds to the recently founded American colony of Georgia?[4] When Christopher

Columbus took the first specimens of sugar cane to the Antilles in 1495, who would have predicted that great maritime and commercial empires would be based on the sugar trade and that Africa would be ravaged to provide slaves for Caribbean plantations? Ships carrying slaves out to provide labour for sugar or cotton economies, furthermore, brought back new plants from the Americas on the return voyage – among them groundnuts, corn, sweet potatoes and manioc – all still mainstays of African diets.[5]

In our time, the introduction of large-scale commercial soyabean cultivation in Brazil since the 1960s has, in a remarkably short period, altered land-use patterns over vast areas. This has reduced the availability and raised the prices of staple foods for the average Brazilian and had important, generally negative, consequences not only for nutrition but for small business and levels of employment. Black beans, once the staple protein source for poor Brazilians, have recently been in such short supply due to preferential land use for soya cultivation that riots have occurred at city supermarkets; municipal elections in Rio de Janeiro produced a huge write-in vote for *feijaos*.[6]

The use of superior force to alter food systems to one's own advantage is a more straightforward case, whether such force is exercised by the dominant class in a particular society or by outsiders over another country. Recurrent problems for governments everywhere are feeding the populations of the cities (if they are not fed, mobs may riot and sometimes overthrow the rulers) and, secondly, acquiring enough cash for national treasuries to maintain civil and military bureaucracies (as well as provide some luxuries for the elite that form their power base). The countryside must therefore be controlled and the peasantry kept in line lest it refuse to provide the surplus necessary to these ends. Needless to say, this 'surplus' is rarely perceived as such by peasants themselves, who are always the first to go hungry. Thus it is not surprising that food was routinely exported from pre-revolutionary France, even in times of famine, nor that agricultural exports from the Sahel actually increased during the recent severe drought and food crisis.[7] Economic, political and, where necessary, military pressures brought to bear on one class by another are thus vital determinants of food production and distribution.[8]

## Colonization: From Abundance to Scarcity

Superior force is also exercised at the international level; the most obvious case is that of colonialism. Empires throughout history have commandeered another people's food supplies (for example, the Roman use, and eventual exhaustion, of North Africa as a granary). The colonial empires of modern times ushered in a new phase, however, by using colonies to furnish the cash crops that fuelled their own industrial development; they thus became architects of radically different food systems and environmental transformers on a huge scale.

Societies that now suffer endemic food shortages were, on the whole, food-abundant societies in precolonial times. Dr Moises Behar has, for example, shown that the Mayans, prior to the Spanish Conquest, had no serious nutritional problems. They ate corn, beans, fruits, vegetables, and game meat; they cleared land, farmed it briefly, then let it revert to jungle, thus preserving the ecological balance and soil fertility.[9] With the Conquest came malnutrition – not only because the Spaniards took over the crops and sold them back to the Indians for gold, but also because they forced them to clear land for cotton, sugar and coffee.

European travellers to Africa in the sixteenth, seventeenth and eighteenth centuries often noted the prosperous agrarian life. One of them recorded the response of an Ethiopian peasant to his amazement at the food abundance: 'Honoured guest, do not be amazed . . . if it were not for the multitude of locusts and hail . . . we should not sow the half of what we sow, because so much remains that it cannot be believed . . . (Even if all these plagues came at once, there would still be food reserves) . . . We have no scarcity.'[10]

Closer to our own time, we have the word of a French colonial inspector who wrote to his government in 1932 on his mission to famine-stricken Upper Volta:

> One can only wonder how it happens that populations ... who always had on hand three harvests in reserve and to whom it was socially unacceptable to eat grain that had spent less than three years in the granary have suddenly become improvident. They managed to get through the terrible drought-induced famine of 1914 without hardship. (Although their stocks were depleted, they were soon able to reconstitute them, at least until 1926, a good year for cotton but a bad one for millet.) Since then, these people, once accustomed to food abundance, are now living from hand to mouth ... I feel morally bound to point out that the intensification of the policy giving priority to industrial products has coincided with an increase in the frequency of food shortages.[11]

The inspector has here put his finger on the causes of hunger: not drought, hail or locusts – environmental hazards which peasants took into account and had learned to cope with – but enforced cash crop production for metropolitan countries. Just as the early Spanish colonizers in search of cash crop products pushed American Indians on to soil-poor and easily eroded hillsides where their descendants still live, so was much subsequent dislocation in previously efficient food systems directly induced by commercial interests backed by national ones – the ancestors, one might say, of today's transnational corporations (TNCs). A few examples of such dislocations follow.

In the first decade of this century, the Anglo-Peruvian Amazon Company recruited hundreds of employees to 'organize the collection and portage of rubber to river stations by thousands of natives ... The means of coercion used against them included the withholding of food by driving them from their subsistence plots and thus rendering them dependent upon foodstuffs imported by the Company ... possibly thousands lost their lives from hunger and murder.'[12]

Similar events occurred in the Belgian Congo on a larger scale:

'Since the conquest, difficulties in recruiting workers hampered colonization: it was necessary ... violently to expropriate the peasants from their collective landholdings ... Mercilessly crushing the old African agrarian system, the finance companies proceeded to make gigantic expropriations, seizing millions of hectares, burning villages ... forcing [the people] to gather plantation crops at gunpoint.'[13]

French methods were sometimes more subtle but had the same destructive results for local food systems. Taxation was the chief coercive instrument employed; it gave peasants no choice but to produce groundnuts or cotton for sale to French companies. Taxes were demanded even in periods of acute famine (itself engendered by cash crops, as seen above). As the French governor of Niger said to a subordinate who had informed him that there was neither money nor food in his district in the famine year 1931: 'I wish you to be less lenient and, on the contrary, expect you to hasten the collection of taxes owed by those under your jurisdiction.'[14]

This is the framework created by the earlier interventions of industrialized countries in Third World food systems. It is the setting in which today's development efforts must take place. An analysis of the contemporary situation requires that a further dimension be added, as it is now recognized that our planet is a global system and that there is no chance of Third World food systems reverting to relative autarchy. They must try to evolve towards a new, different, yet viable, equilibrium starting from a historical situation basically unfavourable to them.

## Authentic Food Systems versus the Dominant Model

One goal of any national development policy should be to arrive at a food system which (a) is environment enhancing and ecologically sustainable, (b) provides enough foodstuffs at reasonable cost to the entire population, including the poorest strata, for a nutritionally balanced diet while remaining consonant with its cultural preferences, and (c) provides great enough quantities to ensure national food self-sufficiency, as a guarantee against outside political manipulation through food aid or exports.

Let us call such an ideal food system 'authentic', drawing etymologically on *authentés/authentikos* as Greek for 'one who does anything by his own hand'. An 'inauthentic' system would, therefore, be one directed by outside hands; usually, such a system cannot satisfactorily feed its own people (though it may be efficient at feeding outsiders). In the contemporary world, there is competition between food systems; the model of the industrialized countries is now dominant and this model is being exported as a solution to development problems in the Third World. However, food system models are in fact non-exportable: any successful development of authentic food systems will have to be based on local bioregions and local solutions, on a cultural renaissance and a scientific upgrading and enrichment of locally accumulated knowledge and techniques.

There are naturally many gradations along a continuum of authenticity/inauthenticity. One system can remain authentic while incorporating elements from another, but only when it does so on its own terms. Unfortunately, there are few historical or contemporary examples where both systems profit through mutual, beneficial incorporation. Note that the authentic food system has been defined as one serving the entire population. It is, of course, quite possible that the dominant class of a system may have something to gain from either self-reliance or inauthenticity. The physical resources of all but the smallest Third World countries (and perhaps even theirs) are sufficient for attaining authenticity. The obstacle is, rather, the permeable nature of their food systems and their vulnerability to outside pressures.

While outright imperial violence is now rarely used to alter a developing country's food system (and may tarnish the prestige of States that use it), detrimental forces are still at work. To make clear the nature of these forces, and in support of the proposition that the industrialized countries' dominant model is being exported, we must see how and why this model itself developed. The point of the exercise is to show its costs and diminish its prestige – a prestige which gives this model a psychological advantage directly influencing decisions made in the Third World. Countries though nominally independent may still be colonized both economically and intellectually. This state of affairs is often promoted by industrialized countries which have a short-term interest in keeping the Third World dependent on their agricultural methods, processes and products, and in maintaining an international division of labour in which the southern hemisphere continues to supply cheap traditional cash crops as well as, increasingly, luxury agricultural products to northern markets. The rich countries may also, consciously or unconsciously, regard their own achievements as the only viable solutions for problems posed elsewhere.

This combination of forces creates a three-fold and self-sustaining dependency. First, southern countries accept and practise an imported food system model, requiring expensive inputs, as a supposed avenue towards development. Second, this model proves incapable of solving their food problem and thus fosters increased food imports. Third, to pay for these imports, agricultural export production (using, again, costly imported techniques) must be increased, thus reducing resources devoted to the attainment of an authentic national food system. And so on, in a vicious spiral.

What, then, is the nature of the dominant model? For the sake of clarity, one can show a food system as a line composed of three segments:

| INPUTS | AGRICULTURAL PRODUCTION | POST-HARVEST ACTIVITIES |
|---|---|---|
| including physical inputs, research and financial credit | | including storage, processing and distribution |

These categories can be considerably refined; they nevertheless apply to the means employed by any human community for feeding itself. In the now developed countries, the first and last segments of the line have come entirely under the control of industry (often called 'agribusiness'). This development has made it meaningless to speak in classic economic terms of the primary (agricultural), secondary (industrial) and tertiary (services) sectors at a time when agriculture has itself become entirely dependent both on industrial products and on services (like bank credit and transport) both upstream and downstream from the farm.

## Historical Development of the Dominant Model

The historical conditions of countries where the high-technology (HT) food production and distribution system developed made it an entirely rational and effective response to the problems posed in these societies. In the United States, for instance, vast land areas coupled with limited manpower made early mechanization imperative – indeed agricultural productivity in the United States has *always* been measured in terms of output per man, not per unit of land. By the 1850s, tens of thousands of machines were already used in America. Harvesters were most popular because they insured the farmer against disaster and helped him spread his risks. With a harvester, he could reap crops on as much land as he could sow – impossible if he relied on hand cutting. An inventive explosion of agricultural technology – all of it labour saving – took place in the nineteenth century: steel-share mouldboard ploughs, drill planters, mechanical screws for land clearing, barbed wire allowing enclosure of much larger areas in a shorter time, and grain binders were a few of the items, besides harvesters, enjoying widespread use in the latter half of the century. The Civil War, which took so many men away from farming, the emancipation of slaves and the burgeoning industrial development creating a demand for factory workers all strengthened the trend towards HT agriculture.

The desired results were soon manifest: in 1800, 373 man-hours were needed to produce 100 bushels of wheat and 34 man-hours for the same amount of corn. By 1900, the figures were reduced respectively to 108 and 147. But by 1959, the necessary man-hours were only 18 and 22.[15] The first agricultural revolution in the now-industrialized countries consisted in a shift from human to animal-mechanical power. The second revolution, which has taken place especially since World War II, is based on scientific innovation and automotive power. It has reduced labour input even more drastically through the use of self-propelled machinery, genetically improved varieties and much greater amounts of fertilizers and pesticides.

The HT model is today capable of feeding 220 million Americans through the efforts of fewer than 2.5 million farmers and of producing millions of tons for export besides. There is no question that it has been successful. There is no question either that this model is generally regarded throughout the world as the most 'modern' and 'efficient' ever devised. This is true enough – but only for those countries whose specific needs are met by it. The United States was land-rich and labour-poor. Nearly all today's developing countries are land-poor and labour-rich. A production system entirely conceived to economize labour and spare workers for other tasks will have the same consequences when used in countries whose chief unresolved dilemma is to give productive employment to the great majority of the population that lives in rural areas yet which cannot find a livelihood there. Countries which adopt such a model must, therefore, expect it to contribute to labour displacement and to encourage out-migration towards already unmanageable cities where few jobs in industry or services are available. On these grounds alone, there is reason to question both the 'modernity' and the 'efficiency' of the HT model when applied to the Third World.

## Costs of the High Technology Model

There are other serious costs – economic, social, and environmental – inherent in this model also. It is so expensive to use that only the most competitive farms stay in business: just after World War II, US farmers spent half their gross incomes on production expenses; the figure is now 80 per cent and rising. Farm supplies are a $90 billion annual business and borrowing to purchase them has resulted in $120 billion agricultural credit outstanding. To sustain the cost/price squeeze, farmers must try to expand at the expense of their less fortunate neighbours. Four and a half million family farms have been eliminated since the 1930s, and today one-third of all food produce is supplied by a mere 2 per cent of farmers grossing over $200,000 yearly, while the top 20 per cent raise 80 per cent of all crops and animals.[16] Land concentration is expected to continue: one US Department of Agriculture scenario predicts that by 1985, over 60 per cent of all farmers working in 1975 will have disappeared.[17] It now costs about $400,000 to create a single job in agriculture, approximately ten times the cost of an average job in industry.

The struggle to survive imposes a goal of maximum yields today – whatever the long-term costs. Monoculture and economies of scale become the only answer: a farmer cannot afford to leave space for trees, hedges, pastures, fallow fields or 'low-value' crops. A detailed description, impossible here, of the ecological damage wrought by this system would include the increased use of fertilizers with rapidly diminishing returns; disastrous pest outbreaks (for example, the cotton boll worm) created by pesticide use which destroys natural predators, and the pollution of land, water and the rest of the food chain by these chemicals. Non-renewable energy to keep this system functioning amounts to 1,400 litres of oil per American per year. If one attempted to feed the world's 4,000 million people on an American diet using US agricultural production technologies (assuming oil were the only energy source) all known petroleum reserves would be exhausted within eleven years. Underground water reserves are being 'mined' for irrigation to the point that one reservoir, currently supplying seven States, will, at present rates, have disappeared by the year 2000. A third of US topsoil has already been irrevocably lost.[18]

Perhaps most alarming of all is the narrowing of the genetic base of North American crops. The devastating US corn blight in 1970 prompted a study by the National Academy of Sciences which concluded that North American crops are 'impressively uniform genetically and impressively vulnerable'. A mere six varieties of corn account for nearly three-quarters of all production, two varieties of peas for 96 per cent, four breadwheats for 75 per cent of all Canadian harvests, etc.[19]

When we examine the post-harvest segment of this 'modern' and 'efficient' food system, we find that it is incapable of providing a balanced diet to the entire population at a reasonable cost. The negative health aspects of the so-called 'affluent diet' are too well documented to need elaboration here.[20] What is perhaps less well known is that malnutrition and outright starvation were so prevalent in the United States in the late 1960s that a federal crash programme in food assistance was undertaken. Its cost to taxpayers is presently close to $10 billion annually, and one could argue that the United States could not long sustain a post-harvest system subservient to a highly concentrated food processing industry without subsidizing the poorest consumers. About three-quarters of all profits realized in this sector go to some fifty companies; they benefit both from the sale of highly elaborate products to the majority of consumers as well as from food assistance programmes. The latter are 'backed by the American food industry which is strengthened by a substantial boost in purchasing power'. Even so, several million hungry and malnourished Americans, especially in rural areas, do not receive the food assistance to which they are theoretically entitled.[21] A similar analysis of European food systems (themselves much imbricated in that of the United States) would yield similar conclusions.

We have, then, a food system which is neither environment enhancing nor ecologically sustainable, costly yet incapable of providing a nutritious diet for all the citizens of one of the wealthiest countries on earth. Its production system may – for the moment – be effective, but it is also scientifically crude and linear, relying on industrial techniques to yield an end-product (the system's only goal) that will fetch the best price on national and international markets. It is based on the survival of the fittest and elimination of all but the largest producers. Yet this is the system that more and more Third World countries are adopting – or attempting to adopt – because their dominant classes see it as more remunerative for themselves; or, to give them the benefit of the doubt, because they mistakenly equate 'Western' with 'productive' and 'superior'. The prestige of the HT model has grown highest in the developing countries at the very time when significant numbers of knowledgeable Americans and Europeans are questioning the economic, social and ecological relevance to national needs of their own systems; and particularly questioning the oligopolistic control agribusiness exerts over them.

## The Interaction of the High Technology Model and Third World Food Systems

We have described the HT model, for the sake of convenience, as if it were closed, but we have already seen that no food system (even, or especially, a dominant one) is self-contained. The industrialized countries' system could not function without substantial inputs from the Third World – in fact, luxury supplements to northern diets are more than ever provided by countries which themselves have a serious food problem.

Among possible objections to the above analysis are these three:

1. At the factual level, one might argue that the Third World is not adopting the dominant food system model, nor is it continuing to supply outside food systems, along colonial lines, on unfavourable terms.

2. Assuming that developing countries are adopting the dominant model, the negative consequences described have only

recently become serious. Forewarned is forearmed: these negative aspects can be foreseen, counteracted and mastered. In any
event, the only way to conquer hunger is to increase food
production, and the only way to do that is to modernize
agriculture in ways that have proven effective in the in- du-
strialized countries.

3. The role of bilateral and multilateral assistance is to help Third
   World governments attain the development objectives they
   have themselves defined, and modernization along dominant
   model lines is what they want. It is not in the province of
   donor governments or agencies to contradict them.

Concerning the first objection, I have attempted elsewhere to
show in some detail that the Third World is in fact adopting the
dominant model as well as supplying its supplementary food
needs on unequal terms.[22] Suffice it here to summarize some
major points.

### The Third World as a Market for the HT Model

The Green Revolution strategy is a text-book case of the industrial
input-intensive method of agricultural production. It should have
been clear from the outset that only the better-off Third World
farmers with access to credit would be able to adopt it and that
small producers would find themselves at an immediate competitive disadvantage. This is exactly what has happened. Competition for land has increased as agriculture has become a profitable
investment and rural dispossession has, as a result, intensified.
The outcome is that while food production has indeed increased
(although less than often claimed) fewer people proportionally are
able to buy it and millions have been deprived of the means of
producing food for themselves.[23]

Such effects were perhaps not intentional, but this commercialization of agriculture was certainly encouraged, as one US
planner noted:

> The agricultural modernization (the Green Revolution) seeds signal could be the seedbed of new market economies in the world's low income countries ... [Green Revolution farms must] make economic ties to a wide array of agribusinesses – manufacturers of agricultural equipment and chemicals, storage and warehousing operations, processing firms and distributing organizations ... Businessmen from the more developed economies and international lending agencies are all engaged in efforts to ... spread the use of the new technologies.[24]

Mechanization is not, strictly speaking, necessary to Green Revolution husbandry, but it is often perceived by larger landholders as an effective means of social control and preferable to dealing with potentially restive agricultural labourers. Many governments' policies, particularly in Latin America, have directly encouraged mechanization, with the result that, by 1972, 2.5 million jobs had been lost on that continent alone, according to a 'conservative estimate' by an FAO expert.[25]

The Green Revolution has also had the effect of reducing drastically the genetic variety of cultivated species in the Third World – thus increasing vulnerability to disease and eliminating part of the germ-plasm resources upon which all countries must rely for genetic improvements in the future.[26]

Large centralized storage and processing facilities for cereals and oilseeds on the industrialized country pattern are increasingly favoured by lending agencies (and TNCs). An FAO expert paints this picture:

> Piles of rice bran rot in a government rice mill. Groundnut mills set up as outlets for farmers' crops stand idle because of lack of supplies. A grain marketing board operating grain stocks ... finds that it must add 100 per cent to its purchasing price to cover all costs and losses incurred. Another board sends soldiers to induce farmers to sell their grain ... Further examples could be cited in the livestock, meat and dairy sectors. Most of these operations were initiated and implemented in developing countries with the assistance ... of bilateral or international expertise ... What went wrong?[27]

34

His answer is that the realities of local economies are not considered; post-harvest losses increase (in transport or through quickly spreading infestations) while the cost added to food by centralized storage and processing is at least 20 per cent. Family or village level storage and processing is far less wasteful and less costly.

But foreign food-processing firms typically gain returns on investment averaging 14 to 16 per cent in Latin America (doubtless more in Africa and Asia) as compared to 4 to 6 per cent in developed countries.[28] This gives them an obvious incentive to produce in the poorer countries where labour is cheap and generally unprotected by trade unions. They then tend to siphon off local raw materials for processing the same kinds of high-value-added products they manufacture in rich countries. The promotion of baby formulas, bringing increased infant mortality and malnutrition in their wake, is one of the best-known examples,[29] but soft drink, breakfast cereal, snack food, and other processors have all found lucrative markets in the Third World. The role of TNC advertising firms is crucial in this regard.[30] Animals are increasingly fed with grain suitable for human beings – or with feedstuffs grown on land previously devoted to food crops. Hatcheries, ranches and even beef-cattle feed-lots are now among the preferred investments of TNCs.[31]

*The Third World as Supplier of Northern Food Systems in a Context of Uncertainty*

On the supply side, developing countries are now providing industrialized country markets not only with traditional tropical cash crops but more and more with luxury goods like meat, fish, off-season fruits or vegetables, flowers, and even pet foods. Traditional Third World exports are declining in relative importance and value. Taking 1967 as a base year with an index of 100, US imports of tropical products reached all of 101 in 1977. But the US Index for 'supplementary' imports (that is, animal or vegetable products which can also be raised in temperate-zone countries) was 165 in 1977. Total US imports of supplementary products were valued at more than $6 billion in 1977, and over 50 per cent of these products came from developing countries. Poorer nations of Latin America or Asia now supply 20 per cent of US meat imports and over 70 per cent of the imported vegetable products.[32] Similar trends are apparent in Europe, for which Africa is the chief supplier of off-season luxury produce, frequently grown by peasants under contract to TNCs.[33]

Meanwhile, agribusiness TNCs are developing strategies for reducing their own dependence on tropical products from the Third World. Substitutes for jute and cotton are already widely used, while industrial use of sugar is gradually giving way to high-fructose corn syrup. It is now even possible to produce coffee and cocoa substitutes from plentiful temperate country crops like soya or barley. A shrub which gives natural latex as good as the *hévéa*'s is being grown experimentally. Higher prices for tropical crops (negotiated in fora like UNCTAD) will encourage recourse to substitutes, so that exporting countries have no guarantee they will be able to sell the same quantities as before, even if they gain concessions on prices.[34]

The Third World is more than ever a supplier of food products at prices it does not control and a purchaser of staple foods (70 million tons last year) at prices it does not control either. A bushel of US wheat which cost $3.12 in late August 1978 sold for $4.30 in September 1979. As a whole, the Third World now buys about 30 per cent of all American agricultural exports – and up to 60 per cent of that part of the US wheat crop that is sold abroad.[35] 'Comparative advantage' as a doctrine for development seems to have become bankrupt – except for the rich countries.

### Increasing Production: A Solution?

Let us take the second possible objection – that one can guard against harmful effects of the dominant food system model;

production must, in any case, be increased. The relevant question here is 'Production for whom?' In our present system, production is indeed being increased, but much of it is going to the already well-fed, because purchasing power is the magnet that draws food, both nationally and internationally. Through the dominant model, income and capital are concentrated in industrialized countries and in the hands of a Third World minority. It might be possible to guard against negative trends (although I do not believe it possible in market economies); what is evident is that such precautions have not been taken to date. Agrarian reform has made little progress, land ceiling legislation is not applied; while 'the market', i.e. competition, allocates access not only to food but to food-producing resources, including land.

Powerful commercial interests have a stake in promulgating the dominant model, either to sell agricultural products and expertise or to produce exportable agricultural goods more cheaply than they can do in rich countries. These interests are frequently aided by governments and by the UN system itself. Tied aid is one mechanism encouraging dependency on an imported model. The largest bilateral donor (the United States) ties 73 per cent of its aid, while the OECD Development Assistance Committee countries as a group tie over half of theirs.[36] American food aid is legally conditioned by the recipients' acceptance of Green Revolution-type techniques, while the European Development Fund gives over half its agricultural assistance to cash, not food crop projects.[37] The US government's Overseas Private Investment Corporation supplies loans and political risk insurance to agribusiness companies' projects in the Third World, generally producing for export or for the moneyed elites of poor countries. Until recently, over one hundred TNC agribusinesses were integrated in FAO as the 'Industry Cooperative Programme'.[38] Although the Director-General of FAO disbanded the ICP in 1978, it has regrouped and obtained consultative status with the UN Development Programme. In spite of such State or

37

international agency support, no evidence has yet been supplied that TNCs contribute to authentic food systems.

*Has the Third World Had a Real Choice of Food Systems?*

The third possible objection – 'this is what the developing countries want' – brings us back to the problems of economic and intellectual colonization and to the responsibilities of developed countries. Decades of interference and technology transfer have resulted not only in economic dependency but in a transfer of values and attitudes as well. The dominant model is what the Third World 'wants' – or may have been obliged to accept – because no one, with the exception of a few imaginative non-governmental organizations with no stake in dependent development, is offering anything else.

Northern governments and multilateral donors tend to finance the kinds of projects they understand (based, necessarily, on their own food systems) and those which will bring an immediate tangible return (in the form of traditional or luxury cash crops or purchases of inputs and expertise). This is, however, an extremely short-sighted policy on the part of donors whose own economic and political futures will be partly determined by the nature of the development process in poorer countries. The Iranian revolution was, for example, partly a violent reaction against the foreign takeover and large-scale destruction of a national food system which had resulted in the forcible displacement of several hundred thousand rural people and annual food imports costing half a billion dollars (from the United States alone) – this in a country which had once been self-sufficient.

## Is There a Realistic Development Policy Alternative for Industrialized Country Governments?

Third World governments which accommodate easily to dependency and inauthentic food systems may not be in power for ever and those who replace them will tend to have long memories concerning those outside influences which either helped or harmed their nations. Despite recent historical examples of the violent rejection of dependency, it is none the less realistic to assume that most industrialized-country governments will prefer to support Third World economic partners doubling as political allies. Real development always implies gains for some and losses for others (at least temporarily) and many northern governments would probably find the political costs of undermining some of the interests of Third World elites that presently support them too great. Rich countries also back the activities of their own corporations, consulting firms, etc., which, as we have seen, find considerable profit in interference in Third World food systems. Thus governments would have a good many difficulties in altering their development policies so that they might bring greater benefits to the majorities of poor and hungry people. It is normal that States act on considerations of political power and economic advantage; they cannot be expected to behave altruistically nor respond to moral exhortation. This being said, it is still important to be somewhat 'utopian'. Governments are not monolithic; the role that particular individuals and agencies can play in reshaping at least some aspects of policy should not be discounted. Let us indulge, then, in a 'conditional idealism' and venture on to the problematical ground of the possible, rather than confining ourselves to the pessimism of the probable. Assuming the developed countries are interested in lessening Third World dependency, how might they help southern hemisphere food systems evolve towards greater authenticity?

## A Re-examination of Industrialized Countries' Consumption Patterns

First of all, rich countries would need to carry out a self-examination, facing squarely the situation in which their own past or present practices and demands have placed the developing countries. This would involve a critical look at the way their own consumption patterns influence land use and investment in the Third World. They should particularly try to discourage the relatively recent, so less entrenched, production of luxury foods (the aforementioned off-season vegetable products, meat, fish, and pet-foods) produced on some of the Third World's best agricultural land; and which contribute marginally if at all to the well-being of developed-country citizens. This might be done by placing heavy import taxes on such items.

The New International Economic Order (NIEO), particularly as it concerns fairer and more stable prices for tropical commodities, would not of itself create authentic development, partly because incremental revenues would accrue mostly to dominant groups; partly because of the substitution phenomenon discussed above. It should, nevertheless, be supported, because it would provide the only means available for Third World governments to plan land and resource use more rationally. At present, they are devoting huge areas and heavy investments to cash crops because 'boom and bust' cycles make this structurally necessary. That is to say, when the price of commodity X rises, producing countries (which have no mechanisms for consultations among themselves) try to grow more of that crop to take advantage of this price. When these unconcerted actions result in a glut – as they eventually do – the producing countries still try to grow more so as to keep their revenues stable in the face of falling prices. The NIEO, properly applied, could have the result of diminishing the area used for cash crops which are today more a part of the problem than a part of the solution.

### Food Aid Policy

Since direct food assistance represents a high proportion of total development aid, a thorough examination of the impact of past policies should pay particular attention to it. Stepped-up food aid in the Sahel has, for example, had a number of negative consequences. It has resulted in taste-changes, prompting huge increases in wheat and maize demand ($+234$ per cent and $+207$ per cent respectively between 1965 to 1967 and 1975 to 1977) whereas local wheat production covers only 2 per cent of requirements. In a recent report to an inter-governmental conference called by the Club du Sahel and the CILSS (Permanent Inter-State Committee on Drought in the Sahel), an FAO expert spoke of the 'desire for bread' and pointed out that:

> Due to changes in feeding habits, the outlets available to traditional cereals remain limited and the incentives to increase production are small. In such a context, food assistance appears to be an easy solution, enabling urban populations – or privileged groups – to be supplied at relatively low prices, but failing by this very fact to achieve self-sufficiency in the matter of food supplies ... Whereas Sahel States have granted, since the 1960s, priority to the extension of ... groundnuts and cotton and have sometimes achieved spectacular success ... it cannot be said that any real cereals policies have been implemented so far.[39]

Much the same could be said for other major food aid recipients like Bangladesh, where donations rarely reach the people most in need, but whose sale to the better-off provides a substantial part of the national budget. Food assistance has frequently been specifically geared to increasing subsequent cash sales (this objective figures, for example, in the text of the US 'Food for Peace' law). Industrialized countries must determine whether they choose to aid themselves (by getting rid of surplus or increasing commercial food exports), political/military 'clients' (who will in turn sell the food aid to their own clientele) or, rather, populations which are truly at risk. If authentic food systems are the goal, policies stressing short-term, disaster-related food aid and direct relief for the poorest would be much more beneficial than the present long-term institutionalized programmes. Low-cost food imports should never be allowed to compete with local food production and thus destroy local incentive.[40]

## The Case for a Temporary Reduction in Development Aid Funding

The suggestion of a temporary reduction in development aid is, perhaps, the ultimate heresy, and as such would doubtless be seen by northern governments as a political liability (or an easy alibi) and by southern ones as another proof of First World selfishness. But there is ample evidence that present levels of aid are actually accelerating rural polarization, especially landlessness and loss of employment, because so much of it accrues to the higher strata of Third World societies.

Even conclusive evidence that certain development projects would cost less and have a much greater positive impact on poor local people will not prevent the adoption of their exact opposites. Comparative cost/income calculations showed in 1974, for example, that for oil palm development schemes in Nigeria, if 'based on village processing units, growers' family incomes would be approximately 50 per cent higher and over-all investment in transport and processing facilities 75 per cent lower than in a large-scale industrial scheme'.[41] The World Bank nevertheless made loans in 1975 and 1978 totalling $95 million – for large-scale, centralized industrial oil palm development in Nigeria.[42]

The cynical view of such activities is that agencies dominated by First World governments will encourage dependency by promoting projects relying on equipment procurable only from industrialized countries. A somewhat more charitable opinion would hold that lending agencies are (or at least want to be) permanent institutions and are thus obliged to spend huge sums of money, even if they worsen the position of the poor, because they must dispose of this year's budget in order to secure next year's. One would like to recommend, with little hope of being heard, a brief moratorium on aid combined with much higher spending on research (and a commitment to accept the policy implications of that research[43]).

A brief hiatus could institute much longer time-scales for project implementation. There is now much talk of 'local participation', but few agencies are willing to allocate the necessary time for detailed research and necessarily complex consultations. Real participation would even entail, in many cases, the building up of rural organizations in order that their members might speak out without fear of reprisal from powerful local interests. Despite their crucial role in food production, processing (and sometimes marketing), rural Third World women are the most forgotten group of all, possibly because most development planners are men. Schemes that do not take women's specific skills and problems into account deserve to fail. Unfortunately, they sometimes 'succeed' by making women's lives even harder.[44] Time 'lost' in obtaining popular participation, including that of the lowest social strata and women, would be made up in time gained in effective project implementation. If the rural poor are convinced they have something to gain from a project, they will act as fast as any agency could wish, but they will quite properly resist 'modernization' from which only the better-off groups (or only men) stand to benefit.

Lower cost projects, relying on a high labour content, are furthermore the only ones that stand a chance of replication throughout the country as a whole. It may be possible to create developed 'pockets' by saturating a small area with capital and personnel, but such islands have little significance for the economy of the country as a whole and merely increase inequalities because they are too costly to generalize.

*Recognizing the Relativity of Industrialized Country Food Systems*

This is a complex recommendation because it runs counter not only to entrenched interests but also to entrenched mentalities. Industrialized countries should nevertheless try to re-examine the axioms of their development policies in order to accept the cultural, economic and environmental relativity of their own food systems, as outlined above, rather than continue to think of them as panaceas for radically different societies. If this relativity could be accepted, it would amount to an intellectual revolution and could bring the goal of authentic food systems closer. If the industrialized countries could view their own systems not as universally applicable, but as local solutions to local problems and conditions, they would simultaneously have an effect on decision-makers in poorer countries – helping to rehabilitate the prestige of local solutions in these countries as well.

The introduction of the dominant food system has pushed Third World countries towards the kind of homogeneity which now prevails in industrialized countries; for example, hyper-specialized monoculture and reduced genetic variety; commercially induced food habits encouraging the consumption of identical products throughout the world (bread where no wheat is raised, soft drinks, infant formula, etc.). The structural homogeneity of the developed countries' food systems is masked by an end product exhibiting great commercial pseudo-variety (one observer recently counted eighty-five different kinds of bottled salad dressing in an American supermarket). But this variety is spurious and is controlled in reality by a very few firms using diverse labels made 'different' through advertising.

Traditional Third World food systems may, on the contrary, be characterized by relative monotony of diet (broken by festivals and feasts) but be based on wide genetic and species heterogeneity. One Philippine tribe practising shifting cultivation is able, for example, to identify and use 1,600 different plants. In one part of Tanzania, peasants cultivate twenty-four different kinds of rice; other examples of this empirical knowledge of species could be cited.[45] Traditional cultivation systems are also founded on heterogeneity – mixed cropping of trees, bushes, standing plants, and even certain 'weeds' which play a positive protective role. Such techniques are time-tested responses to risk: homogeneity is vulnerable, but diversity is resistant and risk-spreading. Systems breakdowns are far more likely under conditions of structural homogeneity (blights over large areas, as have occurred in the Philippines and Indonesia – not to mention the Irish potato famine or the US corn blight). Monoculture is linear, seeking a single product year after year and paying the price in industrial inputs. Traditional systems are circular and return to the land what has been taken from it.

44

Peasants, left to themselves and given enough physical space, are environment improvers. The first farmers did not follow Ricardo's principles by using the best land first (it was beyond the physical capacity of the farming group, mostly women, to clear it) but the more easily worked terrain. As Professor Michel Cépède notes, 'Fertility is progressively built up on naturally poor land.'[46] Even today, in poorer countries, small plots worked by peasants have proved up to thirteen times as productive as large mechanized holdings,[47] although this is no longer possible when the resources available to them are drastically reduced. Then they are accused of 'overcultivating' and 'overgrazing' the little that has been left them – as indeed they must if they hope to ensure immediate survival.

Even if we take a country like Tanzania, generally regarded as striving for autonomous development, we find peasant knowledge neglected and significant inroads made by the dominant model. 'Maize plantations as monocultures are considered a symbol of progress. In reality they present a great danger to soil fertility.'[48] No one is studying the agricultural practices of the Tanzanian peasants, who cultivate twenty-four varieties of rice, although grants can be obtained for work on imported rice hybrids. Limestone powder from the major cement works is thrown away, whereas it could make excellent fertilizer – and chemical fertilizers are imported. As a Heidelberg University team working on improved agricultural methods reports on Tanzania:

> Until now, there has been nothing available except the strategy of high-yield varieties, fertilizers, pesticides and mechanization ... A country like Tanzania which has decided to obtain independence even with economic disadvantages should be interested in [alternative 'ecofarming'] methods. This is not yet the case; the influence of foreign advisors supporting the ideas of the Green Revolution, considering only the interests of industrial countries, is still too strong.[49]

What, then, must the influence of the 'advisors' be in countries

45

far more open to neocolonial influences than Tanzania? Local practices in some areas have been all but blotted out and absorbed by colonial or postcolonial cash crop production. In such areas, their resurrection would demand a veritable archaeology of rural traditions. Elsewhere, there are better possibilities to collect, collate and codify local knowledge, but few local or outside agencies and institutions take an interest in such activities.

Let us make quite clear that we are not advocating a 'Garden of Eden' approach; suggesting a return, pure and simple, to ancestral methods, nor an artificial polarization with peasant practices at one extreme and industrialized country methods at the other. Peasant practices represent very real knowledge – not always easily accessible to outsiders – which has ensured food supplies for generations. But they are not perfect: they should be regarded as perfectible. Inputs from other food systems can be beneficially incorporated in these practices, but it should be the community itself which decides how and when. Mechanization, for example, can cause unemployment, but in a different social context it can also increase employment when used (as in China) to raise the number of possible yearly plantings, clear new land, etc. Whether outside elements are beneficial or harmful will greatly depend on the balance of social forces – and thus ultimately on the structures of power.

Isolated, generally ill-funded scientific work is being undertaken on the best 'mixes' of peasant empirical knowledge and Western scientific techniques, but the creation of a new body of knowledge combining the two is still in its infancy. As one researcher has said: 'Agricultural research in developing nations has been conditioned by cropping systems of the more developed countries [so] little attention has been paid to indigenous cropping systems ... It is the lack of knowledge of the principles underlying mixed cropping that has prevented the application of improved technology to these farmers.' One can, however, now show scientifically that indigenous cropping systems use labour more efficiently, give more stable yields from year to year and are 'intrinsically

46

higher yielding' than monoculture. 'The subsistence farmer has developed a highly sophisticated system ... based on good economic sense.'[50]

Such systems, because they are based on high labour input, are the only ones that could employ the many willing hands now idle in the Third World, as they are the only ones that could serve as a basis for authentic food systems at the national level because they are less costly, replicable, and maintain ecological balance. Unfortunately – and this is a crucial drawback – they contribute very little to anyone's immediate profits – except for the local communities that employ them.

## The Real Interests of Industrialized Country Governments

It is obviously not enough to point out the harmful effects of present policies, nor to propose more ecologically and socially rational ones so long as donor governments do not see their own interests served by a change. Ultimately, such governments have something to gain, even commercially, from more progressive policies, less subservient to short-term economic interests. Mahbub ul Haq of the World Bank explained this vividly:

> The [New International Economic Order] is not a one-way street of benefit only to the developing countries. Any new deal, whether it is negotiated nationally or internationally, ultimately must insure the viability of the entire society ... My own favourite parallel is the comparison with the New Deal in the United States in the 1930s. What it did was to elevate the working classes from their status of dependency and uncertainty to a status of greater partnership in management by arranging a more equitable sharing of profits ... I am sure that at the time, the people who ran corporations in the United States thought that President Roosevelt was a raving maniac and that the New Deal spelt the demise of capitalism. But with hindsight, one can see that it was an act of unparalleled leadership which saved the American system from its inner contradictions.[51]

47

Such arguments apply as well to the help the industrialized countries could give Third World governments in progressing towards authentic food systems. Improving rural prosperity for all – not just privileged groups – would increase demand for all kinds of goods. A distinguished American economist has shown, for example, that more stable prices for Third World commodities instituted ten years ago would have resulted in economic gains for the United States of $15 billion over the decade in prevented unemployment and GNP loss.[52]

Northern governments could also promote mutually beneficial trade by concentrating on writing off Third World public debt. In some cases, up to a third of export revenues immediately returns northwards as annual debt-service. Debt reduction could be an alternative to direct funding of projects.

If developed country governments took the lead in necessary economic restructuring, if they were the first to point out the intrinsic value of local food systems, Third World governments might begin to take a renewed pride in their own cultural inheritance. If donor countries trained their own aid cadres and scientists to start from and build upon the local situation, rather than to alter it along industrialized-country lines, local cadres and scientists might begin to see their own peasantries as an indispensable and precious resource rather than as an obstacle to development, as is so often the case today.

There will be formidable pressures against First World cooperation in the development of authentic Third World food systems. Some pressures will come from within – from the interests that have a financial or ideological stake in dependency. Some will come from without – from elements among Third World elites desirous of maintaining systems that cater to their needs or whims at the expense of their poorer compatriots. Yet a politics of vision should look towards a farther horizon; towards that diversity and authenticity – cultural and agricultural – upon which depends our common prosperity and survival.

# 3
# FOOD, FAMINE AND SERVICE DELIVERY IN TIMES OF EMERGENCY

*The International Council of Voluntary Agencies (ICVA) held its triennial General Conference in Dakar, Senegal, in May 1985. Both the venue and the audience attracted me. The former turned out to be a hotel-conference complex on the sea, gorgeous but far removed from Senegalese life, of which I learned only a little; the second was made up of about 150 voluntary agency representatives from around the world, including a lot of Africans. The general keynote speech was delivered by Cardinal Paulo Evaristo Arns of São Paulo, a hero of mine if not of the Pope's; and there were three other 'theme' keynotes including this one. The title of the speech isn't mine, but it's marginally snappier than the one ICVA initially asked me to deliver, which was 'The strengthening of voluntary agency cooperation and partnership on a global basis'. Professor Amartya Sen was supposed to deal with 'Food, famine and service delivery in times of emergency' but unfortunately he couldn't come. Some shuffling took place and I got his topic, one on which I was, and am, singularly unqualified to speak. I have never worked in, nor indeed even visited, a 'famine camp'. So I tried to imagine the impossible demands made on the courageous people who devote their lives, or part of them, to relieving acute distress and to explain the context of famines.*

*What's really needed to make emergency aid forever unnecessary is action before outright famine occurs. Biologists know that if you put a frog in boiling water it will jump out. But if you put the frog in cold water and heat it gradually to boiling point, it will stay there and be*

49

*boiled alive. The frog has not been equipped by nature to re-spond to incremental increases in temperature. Human beings do not have the frog's excuse: all the signs of impending famine have been identified; they are among the easiest of social phenomena to predict. Governments are not always, however, terribly interested in devoting resources to saving the lives of poor people, which is why they will require the services of ICVA's member agencies for a long time to come.*

Here is a short programme for agency personnel and field staff which will help them in future to avoid the criticism that is so frequently and so generously bestowed on them, especially in emergency situations.

First, they must take graduate degrees in social anthropology, geography, economics, a dozen or so difficult and unrelated languages, medicine and business administration.

Second, at a slightly more practical level they must demonstrate competence in agronomy, hydrology, practical nursing, accounting, psychology, automotive mechanics and civil engineering.

In addition, they must learn to give a credible imitation of saintliness, and it would be well if they could learn sleight-of-hand as well, since they will often be called upon to perform feats of magic.

After the successful completion of this programme, they will take on jobs that don't pay much, but in exchange they will be allowed to work long hours, often under material conditions of extreme deprivation.

Such a programme just barely exaggerates the qualifications and outlook that seem to be expected, explicitly or implicitly, of agency staffs. It's amazing so many still want to work for them; to devote their lives, or a part of them, to alleviating human suffering wherever it may occur. And it's clear that no single person – not even a group of people – could possibly bring together all the knowledge and skills needed for perfect food crisis management.

Without, however, obtaining a basketful of Ph.D.s, it's still possible to keep in mind a few helpful general principles and to avoid the worst traps. Where relief efforts fail or become entrenched without apparent prospect of ending, usually, as one scholar has put it, *the heart of the problem is that no consensus exists about the origins of famine nor on the underlying question of the root causes of Third World underdevelopment.*[1]

What are some of the things we now know about famine which could and should inform the response of those attempting to cope with it? We can usefully break down this general question into subsets. What do we know about the way famines build up and how can we learn to read the warning signs? Will we ever be able to capture public and government attention and direct them to famine prevention, or will they always prefer the fireman's approach and the full-blown disaster? How does the phenomenon of famine affect the victims – both individuals and societies? And how do their reactions bear on the response of relief agencies? Finally, what is, or should be, the political role – in the broadest sense – of agencies on behalf of famine victims?

Though there may still be more questions than answers, these are some of the themes I hope we can explore during our time here together. For now, I shall make only the briefest attempt at an outline.

Far too large a segment of public opinion – and even some governments – still look on famine as a consequence of drought, full stop. Nevertheless, among people who devote serious thought to the question, the consensus is that famines are definitely not *natural* phenomena. They are not caused by drought, floods or other acts of God, even though such acts may prove to be triggering events. Although such people do not discount the role of population pressures and ecological stress, many would also say succinctly that there are no environmental problems – what do exist are the social and political problems that invariably underlie and cause ecological strain.

As long ago as 1926, the Italian economist and statistician

Corrado Gini pointed out that famines are economic disasters and represent for poor countries what full-scale economic depressions and crises represent for rich, industrialized ones.[2] Though still occasionally resisted, this conceptual approach has been confirmed again and again by the facts: famine represents the breakdown of a whole society, a reshuffling of the economic and political cards. After a famine, the situation will never return to the status quo ante – a whole new social structure will have taken its place.

Paradoxically, famines take place in the countryside – where people do produce, or could produce, food. Though towns may experience shortages and rationing, they are generally exempt from outright famine, as Amartya Sen has shown.[3] Because city people are concentrated and therefore potentially dangerous, they are taken care of by the State, which is anxious to prevent upheavals and to preserve its own power. This situation may, of course, change as more and more rapid urbanization takes place and governments become less and less able to cope. But in our time, famine is a predominantly rural event.

Poor people in the countryside are vulnerable, they lack buffers, and the smallest change in their fragile equilibrium can spell the difference between life and death. When people live close to the brink of survival even in 'normal' times, events that might seem insignificant to us – a tiny increase in the price of some necessity, especially food, the death of an animal, reduced wages or a sudden dismissal – can sink the vulnerable because they have no fallback position. If these incremental changes strike enough people at once, the result will be widespread hunger and, if nothing is done, outright famine. Climate alone is clearly not to blame. Here are some of the traits vulnerable people usually have in common:

- They have no cash reserves. In times of poor harvest and food shortages, prices rise. Poor farmers have already sold their crop just after harvest when prices are lowest, in order to pay off their debts. They will have to buy back later in the year when prices have doubled or quadrupled. Speculators make fortunes. The poor often have to borrow just to keep on eating. With famine comes greater indebtedness.

- They have no food reserves. When dire shortages strike, they eat their seeds, slaughter or sell their animals, and mortgage or realize assets like tools, jewellery or, in the worst cases, land itself. These transactions will of course reduce the next year's yield. With famine comes greater land concentration and greater polarization of the society between rich and poor.

- They have no job opportunities. As food grows scarcer, the number of people seeking work goes up. Competition for jobs drives down wages – just when food prices are shooting up. With famine comes higher unemployment.

- They have nowhere to go. They look for jobs over a wider and wider area. Finally migration to the nearby or faraway city may seem the only option – at least they may find a soup kitchen there. With famine come swelling urban populations made up of the masses of ex-peasants.

This is a simple scenario. It grows more complex when civil war or great power struggles are added to the plot, but essentially provides a basis for understanding how shortages build towards social crisis and sometimes society's collapse.

These observable trends can also serve to predict – and ideally to prevent – food crises. Some agencies and governments are now trying to foresee food shortages and famines, using complex meteorological models and satellite photography. Apparently they believe that the fancier the technology the more accurate the results. This is not necessarily the case. Again, social and economic indicators are likely to engender far more precise information. Experienced agency field staff are especially well placed to notice small changes which, read together, can become the most efficient of early warning systems.

The most obvious warning signs are rising food prices, unusually high sales of animals at steadily declining prices, longer queues of people looking for work, more married men seeking seasonal employment elsewhere, more women gathering typical 'famine foods', more trees being cut down for sale, more beggars going from house to house, higher than average sales of implements, jewellery or land and the like. Any seasoned observer with a sensitivity to local conditions could draw up a list of danger signals in five minutes. Anyone who is accustomed to talking with and listening to the local people will know sooner than the authorities when distress is felt. The problem may not be so much to discover that a serious food shortage or famine is looming, but to get that information passed upwards and taken seriously.

Agencies that are not already doing so should encourage this kind of informal monitoring, and might even decide to formalize it, where staff numbers and time allow. The British developed a monitoring system that was instituted in India from 1913 onwards – one could do worse than to adapt to local conditions the series of questions they expected to be answered weekly, fortnightly or monthly by their District Officers.[4]

People who will be expected to cope with food crises should be trained to recognize potential breakdowns in both physical and social systems. There are different ways to help them. Some scholars suggest drawing *critical event trees* that show how various events interact and may lead to crises. The branches of the tree can be labelled in different ways, depending on the situation one wants to keep track of, but for analysing a food system the tree should certainly include branches labelled Political Events, Production, Distribution, Employment, Storage, Credit, Consumption, Relief. A critical event on one branch may not have much impact on the food situation all by itself – for example, an outbreak of border fighting on the political branch alone might have no effect on people 100 miles away. If, however, the fighting provokes an influx of refugees or if the military decide to hoard food stocks as a result and if, further, there is a critical event on the production branch like a pest attack – then the society may find itself well on the way towards serious shortage and perhaps famine. Crisis managers should learn to chart, read and expect such interactions.[5]

Another aspect of Third World food situations which has received far too little attention is the quite obvious fact that agriculture is a 'seasonal' activity. On the whole, we Westerners have forgotten how great an impact seasons have on rural people's lives. Here again, agency staff and managers should learn to map events on a monthly basis – and, in time of impending crisis, even a weekly one. Certain times of the year are particularly hard on poor people – especially the lean season just before the harvest or the rainy season. These two may coincide. Food prices always tend to rise as the agricultural year wears on, while employment may be available to some labourers only at sowing and harvest time. Even pregnancies and births may be lumped together at the worst possible time of the year when there is the least food or the most work for women. This may happen for the simple reason that conceptions occur most frequently after harvest when people are happier and better fed.[6]

Let me suggest a basic training exercise for agency people of my own concoction. I can see a set of overlapping, transparent seasonal calendars – one for each of the important activities in a given rural community. Naturally, we need a production calendar that charts sowing, weeding, harvesting and the like, because this will tell us both when the most physical work is required and about times of greater and lesser food availability. It would be better to have one calendar apiece for women and for men, because stresses on each sex may come at different times of the year – or be unfairly shouldered by women throughout the year, as so often happens in Africa.

Then we will need a financial calendar for income and outlays. When can people expect to sell harvests for cash or to earn wages, and when must they pay taxes? What other activities may bring in cash (like beer-brewing for the women, or artisanal work, or seasonal outmigration for the men)?

Do school fees and expenses come due just when people have the least money, and could this be one reason so many children are left out? Do other essential commodities besides food fluctuate with the market – like kerosene or soap? What about contracting and repayment of debts – these too will very likely show peaks and valleys.

A third calendar for health will reveal the worst periods of illness and mortality, as well as concentrations of births and weanings. Often women must wean babies abruptly because their work schedule demands it. Superimposing the health and production calendars should tell agencies at a glance when extra nutritional and health services would be most needed.

These are some of the ways we can learn to interpret danger signals, but they do not tell us much about how individuals and communities actually experience a food disaster. An anthropologist who made an extensive survey of the literature on famine world wide looked for the responses of individuals and societies and found a consistent three-stage pattern emerging.

First comes the *alarm reaction*. People redouble their efforts to seek food and outside employment and/or relief. At this stage, social cooperation and sharing of resources generally prevail.

Second, if people have found neither food, employment nor relief, they enter the *stage of resistance*. Except for the efforts needed to find food or other necessisties, people conserve their energy. Families stick together but withdraw from the community, and social ties start to weaken. Sharing and cooperation cease.

Thirdly, and finally, if no food arrives, individuals reach the *stage of exhaustion*. At this stage, society becomes completely atomized as even family ties break down and individuals make desperate attempts to survive. Total social chaos ensues.[7]

Naturally, any agency would rather intervene during stage one when cooperation, sharing behaviour and social dynamism can only enhance its efforts. However, as we all know and deplore, it is very difficult to alert public opinion and donor governments to the gathering danger until stage two – or, worse still, stage three – has overtaken the hapless victims.

Stages two and especially three are those of camps – which I've heard more than one relief worker describe as *cancers*. Like famine, cancer builds up slowly, but when it has metastasized the doctor may have to make some very quick decisions if the patient is to be saved. Real stage-three famine situations require equally speedy decision-making, for which many agencies are simply not equipped.

Last month, a young relief worker just back from Sudan told me how 5,000 Ethiopians were arriving daily at his camp. This means, he said, the time scale for decisions has to be hours, not days or weeks. You may need to buy or lease motor tankers, or get pumps or other equipment urgently. The UN system is structured to demand three tenders for every purchase, and the contracts all have to go back to Geneva. He spoke of the people on the terrain as very good, completely dedicated and totally frustrated by the administrative procedures they're expected to follow.

We concluded that if agencies are supposed to be dealing with emergencies, they have to be structured to do so. I can only hope that telling this story is superfluous, and that it is not applicable to anyone present. In any case, the best advice an outsider can give to an agency is that it hire the best people possible, then give them substantial autonomy and the financial means to sustain it. Better they should have orders to be flexible rather than work to rule.

Let me conclude this outline with some remarks about politics. I'm aware that the very word politics is anathema to many voluntary agencies. It seems to me, however, that there is no avoiding the subject, in the broadest sense, because all action ultimately has a political impact. Agencies and their people are actors in history, whether they like it or not.

There is currently a huge controversy about what is called, unkindly I think, the *band-aid* approach versus the long-term development assistance approach. Those who are providing emergency relief in the camps of Ethiopia or the Sudan today would probably think it black humour even to speak of long-term development just now. It is still scandalous that the United States government specifically refuses in certain cases to provide development assistance and limits itself to emergency relief. If this attitude were universally shared, agencies would become nothing but cadres of firemen racing to put out one blaze after another.

There are, of course, less extreme cases. In *stage one* or *stage two* food shortages, many agencies try to contribute to development assistance through food-for-work projects. These have lately come under heavy fire.[8] The point the critics are making is a valid one and it is a political point. Who, they ask, are going to be the real beneficiaries of food for work? Only too often, work accomplished by the poorest and most vulnerable adds to the assets of those who are already the wealthiest and most powerful in the society. Since these additional assets will increase the repressive capacity of the local elite, food-for-work projects may, in some cases, actually be asking the poor to contribute to their own future oppression!

At the very least, agencies must ask serious questions about the impact of their projects on local hierarchies and they must try to weigh this in the balance against the local social and political structures that set the stage for disaster in the first place. The more inequitable the society, the more likely are disaster situations, including famine. More and more private voluntary organizations (PVOs) recognize now that their role is to help the most vulnerable to gain more control over the circumstances of their own lives, and that this may mean acting consciously against the interests of the elites, whatever the pressure.

This leads to the delicate, even terrible, moral questions agencies must so often face when they choose to work with certain governments. How relieved I am that I need not personally come to grips with this issue! I honestly do not know if saving some lives can morally justify working with a government whose avowed aim is to use famine as one instrument that will contribute to subduing seditious provinces. All I know is that no man – and no agency – is an island. We cannot be neutral. We must bear witness.

This means that agencies must choose to inform their own constituencies in the developed countries on the real issues. More development education today in the rich countries would lead to a more effective approach tomorrow. Agency people could stop being firemen and become masons, carpenters and architects. Public opinion would begin to understand that to erase the images of starving children from our television screens for ever, longer-term work is needed. People would further understand that this work will require changes – political changes – in both the North and the South. I hereby make a proposal for a levy of at least 10 per cent on agency budgets for development education at home, even and especially when their principal mission is to alleviate suffering abroad. Emergency aid is by definition aid that arrives too late.

One final note of caution. I really must share my fears with you. Have you noticed how popular you've become lately? Haven't you been flattered to be courted by so many rich, handsome and, let's face it, unlikely suitors? Today, everybody loves the NGOs. The monster agencies like the World Bank, the tentacular inter-governmental organizations like the OECD have set up their own special units to liaise with the private agencies; the most reactionary governments cajole and coax them to cooperate. There are probably two major motives for this behaviour, one only slightly more cynical than the other.

The first is that the large, wealthy official agencies know they've failed. They've had over thirty years to promote something called development and they've totally blown it. This is not the time or place to discuss the reasons, only to note the fact. Consequently they are casting about for solutions, and they think the NGOs may have some of the answers. Hence their interest. Beware the agency that has so much money that you – and the people you want to help – could easily drown in it.

The other motive, this one mainly of governments, is avarice. Certain governments, which shall be nameless, have an obvious desire to worm their way out of commitments to public, inter-governmental agencies while displaying an uncanny interest in private ones. Their ultimate aim is doubtless to spend infinitely less on overseas aid than they did before, but to get enormous public credit by giving whatever tiny sums remain to the NGOs.

I call upon the agencies here present to turn a flinty eye and a deaf ear to these blandishments. I implore you to guard your independence as you would the proverbial crown jewels and the honour of your family escutcheon. Just remember, if somebody still dislikes you, you must be doing something right.

In conclusion, I would like to put forward two general principles and two personal prejudices:

- *First general principle*: No progress is possible without con-centration on, and cooperation with, small farmers. Food security and anti-famine strategies must be based on them.

*To Implement Such a Strategy*

1. The North must stop trying to *modernize* other people's farming systems: modernization along Western lines leads to land con-centration, loss of employment, outmigration to cities, and other harmful consequences. The purpose of any agricultural strategy should be to keep people in the rural areas, by improv-ing their chances of a decent livelihood there and improving the quality of life. Real modernization would involve much more research on actual peasant practices, which are based on biological complexity.

2. The South must devote the aid it receives to these same goals. Of $7.5 billion worth of aid sent to the Sahelian countries from 1975 to 1982 (amounting to about $44 per capita per year)

only 4.5 per cent was spent on improving rain-fed agriculture
(and another 4.5 per cent on animal herding). Yet virtually
the entire peasantry of these countries (80+ per cent of the
overall population) depends on rainfed agriculture.

NB: Especially in Africa, a great proportion of food producers are women. The UN has forgotten this: according to the
World Food Council, of all UN system aid going to Food and
Agriculture over the past decade, only one-tenth of one per
cent (.001 per cent) has gone to programmes for women.

● *Second general principle*: The debt crisis is undermining development efforts by official agencies and NGOs alike.
We need a concerted strategy/campaign on alleviating debt
which amounted to $895 billion at the beginning of 1985
and will probably reach $1 trillion by the end of this year.

In Africa (according to figures used by J. Nyerere) debt is $150
billion, which means about $15 billion in yearly interest payments
alone. We have now reached a situation of overall transfer from
poor countries to rich ones ($21 billion in 1983 = reimbursements
minus new loans).

Possible solutions must not further deprive the poor nor provide rewards for profligate and non-representative governments.
An immediate cap on interest rates is one feasible step – one
expert calculated that every time the interest rate goes up a
point, the land equivalent of two Nicaraguas goes under cash
crops. Governments may have to bail out private commercial
banks that hold 50–60 per cent of Third World debt (especially
in Latin America) but this should be accompanied by transfer
of ownership and decision-making power. Governments should
continue to pay back interest, but in local currency and into a
revolving development fund which could be managed by local
development organizations, perhaps in cooperation with the UN.
IMF conditionality should hit military and other non-essential

budgets first, rather than eliminating poor people's meagre safety-nets.

*First personal prejudice:* Tigré. Many agencies now fear that they cannot work in Tigré without incurring the displeasure of the Ethiopian government. This is not borne out by the experience of some agencies which are already working with both the Derg and the Relief Society of Tigré. Without increased NGO involvement, there are going to be hundreds of thousands of deaths in Tigré – the government seems more determined than ever to use the famine to bring the rebellious province under control.

*Second personal prejudice:* Nicaragua. Here we are witnessing the strangulation of a successful experiment (as a recent OXFAM publication's title puts it, *The Threat of a Good Example*). The present UNDP Nicaragua Resident Representative with twenty-five years' field experience says this is the first country he has ever served in where the government was making real and heroic efforts to supply basic needs to the whole population, urban and rural. The French have a legal concept called *non-assistance à personne en danger* which means that those who witness a crime or who see a person in danger and do not give assistance can be prosecuted exactly like the criminal. We need a concept of *non-assistance à peuples en danger*. Small countries should have the right not to become a part of great power struggles; this goes for Afghanistan as well as for Nicaragua.

The recent report for the Independent Commission on International Humanitarian Issues (*Famine: A Man-Made Disaster?*, London, Pan Books, 1985) says, 'In Africa, liberation movements have been an acceptable channel through which to pass international refugee assistance, whatever the government concerned might say. Where there is major disaster, humanitarian considerations must override sovereign prerogatives. Bluntly, the UN should be prepared to trespass on State's rights when these are in conflict with the rights of disaster victims.' ICVA members could usefully make this recommendation their own, and fight for it.

# 4
# FOOD STRATEGIES
# FOR TOMORROW

*'Food Strategies for Tomorrow' first appeared in* The European Community's Development Policy: The Strategies Ahead, *edited by C. Cosgrove and J. Jamar, a collection of contributions to the College of Europe's annual symposium, held at Bruges, Belgium, 4–6 July 1985. It was subsequently reproduced in booklet form by The Hunger Project as No. 6 of* The Hunger Project Papers *series (December 1987) and distributed in over 20,000 copies. It is thus one of the few papers collected here to have reached a sizeable audience already. Directed, mostly, at policy makers, it is written in the sober style one assumes such people prefer.*

Allow me first to set the context for my remarks: food strategies and indeed the question of the European Economic Community's development policy can be usefully discussed, in my view, only in a broader geopolitical framework. I should therefore first like to suggest why it is important for Europe to establish a different and original relationship with the Third World(s),[1] of which alternative food strategies could be a cornerstone.

## I. The Community's Development Policy: an Assessment

Until relatively recently, European history was full of fratricidal wars, stained by colonialism and marked by brutal class relations. But at the same time, Europe had a *project* (in French, *'projet'*, encompassing the notions of 'undertaking' and 'grand design' – not fully translatable by 'project'). She had a *projet* of culture, of civilization, as well as of the State: the Enlightenment was one expression of this; revolutionary and national unity struggles were another. These manifestations were accompanied by an outburst of creativity in arts and letters, science and technology.

Today Europe – like the rest of the world – is undergoing a crisis. None the less, in the 1980s a war between Western European nations is as unthinkable as one between the US and Canada. The stain of colonialism has been wiped out, however painfully, by national liberation struggles. The material and political gains of workers, farmers and women over the past hundred-odd years have made life in Europe a lot more bearable for the least well-off, however much may remain to be done. In sum, Europe is now rid of the major blights and blots on her past. But in the process, she seems to have lost her civilizational *projet* as well.

Can a renewed European *projet* be born in the shadow of the superpowers and the transnational corporations (TNCs) that now make many of the decisions affecting the continent? The answer to this question will decide the future of Europe. Yet on the face of things, the odds are against a positive reply. The systems that dominate the world are increasingly global, and the degree of European control over them is not encouraging. Consider, for example:

● *The food system.* Though now self-sufficient in the major cereals thanks to the Common Agricultural Policy (CAP),[2] Europe is still heavily dependent on protein inputs from the US; the European Economic Community (EEC) is still the United States' major agricultural customer ($7.4 billion worth of imports in 1983, or 20 per cent of total US agricultural export receipts). Meanwhile, the CAP is under assault from within (unrealistically high costs, dissension on price levels) and from without

65

(the US offensive). Many agricultural input, manufacturing and food-processing activities are also dominated by the US.

- *The energy system.* European countries depend for much of their energy supply on decisions made by others (for example, oil transnationals, the Organization of the Petroleum Exporting Countries [OPEC]) and must adjust their diplomacy in consequence. Little has been done with regard to serious energy conservation or development of new sources (except nuclear power – against the will of a growing number of citizens).

- *The monetary/financial system.* The European Currency Unit (ECU) was a definite step forward, but the world financial system is still dominated by the dollar and institutions wholly or largely controlled by the US (the Federal Reserve, the International Monetary Fund [IMF]). Interest rates in the US have a seriously debilitating effect on Europe's economic health and growth (capital flight, financing the US deficit), and the value of the dollar determines the price of oil and other vital commodities.

- *The military system.* The system is determined by the superpowers. 'Defence' of Europe under the US nuclear shield is regarded by greater and greater numbers of EEC citizens as a sinister farce. Even so, in most quarters, the idea of developing alternatives to the Nato/Warsaw Pact dichotomy seems the ultimate heresy.*

- *The information system.* Information dissemination is dominated by the US both in terms of satellites and computerized networks and in terms of 'cultural products'. Public opinion is conditioned by television and by advertising, both increasingly globalized (which is to say, Americanized).

*I am correcting proofs in late December 1989 in the wake of the Romanian revolution and a year which has changed this perspective radically.

● *Scientific, technical and manufacturing systems.* These systems are again largely dominated by the superpowers (for military technology) and on the civilian side by the US and Japan. Data bases and scientific publishing are overwhelmingly located in the US – and in English. Of the top 200 transnational corporations, 80 are American, 35 Japanese and 60 European. US and Japanese corporations account for over 64 per cent of total revenues accruing to these 200 TNCs; European TNCs account for 27 per cent.[3]

All these systems are by nature integrating and, for those who do not control them, dependency-creating. Naturally, Europe has more to say about some than about others, but on the whole must accept many decisions made elsewhere.

These remarks may seem a rather long way round to a discussion of Europe's relationship with the Third World and particularly its cooperation in food strategies. I hope to show, however, that this apparent detour is in reality one of the most direct routes towards a new civilizational project for Europe. Overcoming present dependency will require conscious policies of unity, renewal and non-alignment, in which relations with the Third World could become a vital component. With enough political – and moral – courage, Europe could provide an alternative to the less and less attractive models offered by both superpowers.

The once-prestigious United States model is losing ground in the Third World. The Vietnam war badly tarnished America's image; the current Central American crisis is completing the job, especially in Latin America. President Reagan's visible contempt for any semblance of 'North–South dialogue', the adamant stance of US commercial banks and the US government on Third World debt, the assault on international development agencies like Unesco and tragedies like Bhopal do not help to project the image of a nation that cares for anything beyond its own power and profits.

The Soviet model, which for a time attracted the sympathetic adherence of some newly independent Third World nations, is also discredited both economically and politically.[4] Centralized planning in agriculture (as in other areas) has been demonstrated not to work – even hard-line governments like Mozambique's are backing off. Repression in Poland and the war of attrition in Afghanistan have further served to make the USSR model a repulsive one.

In this moral and political vacuum lies a historic opportunity for Europe. General de Gaulle once said, 'States do not have friends, only interests.' While this is doubtless true as well for the group of States that make up the European Community, the pursuit of its interests in the Third World should not be interpreted narrowly as an opportunity to impose its own technologies, corporations and values on poor countries. Europe could, however, try to break the present US/USSR strategic deadlock, which reduces all North–South problems to East–West confrontations. If it succeeded, the EEC would assert its political independence and enhance its prestige in the process. By espousing the cause of three-quarters of humanity, Europe would also, in the fullness of time, reap the more traditional commercial and financial benefits.

Assuming Europe recognizes the political importance of proposing and nurturing an alternative development model, then surely devising food strategies capable of alleviating hunger should be the cornerstone of such a policy. The chronic hunger of hundreds of millions is not just morally indefensible; it is one of the most politically destabilizing forces in the world today. Several Third World countries have recently experienced food riots. Up to now, these riots have been brutally put down; there are, however, no guarantees that repression will save these governments for ever.[5]

Furthermore, even the most casual observers – including those in the poor countries – can now see that hunger is unnecessary. Ten years ago, some national leaders and international bureaucrats still took the Malthusian line and claimed absolute world food scarcity; their fears were echoed in the calling of the World Food Conference in 1974. Such arguments were never adequate and are clearly implausible today in a context of price-depressing grain surpluses in the US and Europe and another global bumper harvest of some 1.63 billion tons of cereals expected for 1985.[6] EEC surplus commodities in storage are valued at $4 billion;[7] the sums rich countries now spend on storing food surpluses are far greater than those they devote to development aid.

In other words, the injustices of hunger are becoming daily more visible – and more dangerous. If Europe is to help eliminate them, she will need to make difficult political decisions. For the purposes of this report, I shall not try to determine the feasibility of various political strategies – this is up to the politicians themselves. My own limited usefulness here, as I see it, is to suggest strategies that would contribute to eradicating hunger. These may be considered utopian: so were proposals to overthrow the French monarchy or to eliminate slavery in centuries before our own.

Strategies reflect analysis, and food strategies are no exception. The ways in which one explains the causes of hunger will determine the ways by which one seeks to do away with it. Until recently, most official actors on the hunger and development scene have not called into question their own performance over the past thirty years or so. They seem, implicitly at least, to believe that without the decades of the development projects and food aid policies they designed, the present hunger crisis would be even worse. If this view is correct, then there is no reason to alter present food and development strategies – one must simply spend a lot more money on them. This is basically the position of the Brandt Commission (which calls for 'massive transfers' from North to South, in a face-lifted version of the worn-out 'trickle-down' theory) and of the Group of 77, which wants more of everything, including more aid.[8]

This position is not entirely indefensible. Basic economic injustices obviously exist between North and South, and the Lomé Convention is one European effort to remedy this, however marginally.[9] On a global scale, however, rigor mortis has overtaken

69

the New International Economic Order. The Group of 77 is too disorganized and dispersed; so long as it does not choose to use the political instruments theoretically at its disposal (for example, a united front on the debt issue) the North as a whole is under no pressure to make concessions.

Traditional food and development strategies have a fatal flaw: their assumption that the world is a harmonious place. Countries are encouraged to trade according to the principles of 'comparative advantage', which supposedly will result in a fair deal for all. Third World elites, whose wealth and power are invariably increased by aid programmes, are assumed ready to share these benefits with their less privileged compatriots. Accumulated failures show that these assumptions are untenable. Harmony does not yet seem to reign, either at the international or at the national level.

One obstacle to reaching the poor and hungry is the ability of elites to corner most of the benefits of aid. Another is that the people most at risk live in the countryside. According to the World Bank, the overwhelming majority (90 per cent) of the 'absolute poor' are rural. This proportion may change as Third World countries undergo rapid urbanization, but, for the moment, food strategies, to be effective, must somehow bypass both the rich and the city dwellers. This is no simple task, given that most Third World governments are kept in power by just those groups. Resources devoted to the peasantry are notoriously meagre, whereas this peasantry generally supplies much of the country's wealth. It is the most numerous group that has the least influence.

One goal of any donor whose objective is to reduce hunger should be to help increase the bargaining power of this poor and politically marginalized peasantry. This is admittedly difficult when donors must deal with governments whose priorities do not include strengthening the poor rural majority.

There are, however, ways to help the worst-off and thus to improve food security for the population as a whole. The first is the judicious use of food aid. Since two sessions of Working Group II deal with this question,[10] I shall merely note the points most worth bearing in mind.

In recent years, no aspect of aid to the Third World has come under more fire than food aid. Its damaging effects in a wide variety of situations and countries have been so amply documented that all statements on aid now seem to contain a compulsory self-exculpating sentence or two. Donors declare that while food aid *can* indeed discourage or ruin local production, increase dependency, alter food habits, encourage corruption and not reach the people who need it, none of this *need* happen under proper surveillance. The new watchword seems to be that food aid, when used for development purposes, will have none of the former drawbacks.

Unfortunately, awareness of such problems does not necessarily guarantee their avoidance. Individual European donor countries and the Community as a whole, under pressure from their farmers, live with the permanent temptation to equate food aid with surplus-dumping – a temptation to which they often succumb. The leader of the most powerful agricultural federation in France says, for example: 'Food aid can be increased, it's a question of political will; a European Marshall Plan for the Third World could be set up which would ultimately be an investment and which would allow disposal of surplus production.'[11]

These temptations for the EEC can only increase as the US steps up its subsidized grain-export war against the Community. Europe will retaliate, and the chief losers in this war will be unsubsidized Third World smallholders who cannot possibly compete with wildly underpriced cereals from abroad. In contrast, direct farm subsidies in 1984 totalled $19 billion in the US and $17 billion in Europe.[12]

Nevertheless, the EEC should be congratulated for commissioning and publishing critical reports on its food aid practices and for being the only important donor in the world to carry out a real institutional debate on the subject.[13] Many of the strategies one would like to see the Community follow have already been mooted in this debate.

First comes the obvious need to reduce the number of decisions required for each allocation of aid (up to 18) and exorbitant time-lags between initial requests and final delivery (an average 377 days for cereals and 535 for dairy products in the early 1980s). Even 'emergency' aid takes about six months to arrive.[14] An audit of 31 December 1984 speaks of delays of up to 419 days for cereals and 578 for butter oil; but these figures, says Director General of Development Dieter Frisch, are 'absurd', because the Court assumes 1 January as the effective arrival date for the whole year, whereas supplies are programmed to arrive throughout the year.[15] It is therefore impossible for an outsider to give an accurate assessment of true delays; but, to say the least, this problem does not appear to have been eliminated.

Reducing these delays would also allow the Community to better tailor food aid to real needs and actual harvests in the recipient countries, which is rarely the case today. 'In practice,' a team of specialists reports, 'European food aid policy works on a kind of "subscription" basis both for cereals and for dairy products. Once a country has received food aid, it generally renews its request and is practically assured of a favourable reply . . .'[16]

Untimely delivery may trigger some of the most harmful consequences of food aid. When foreign cereals appear suddenly and massively on relatively limited Third World markets, and when their appearance coincides with the country's own harvest, many local producers will be ruined. (This happened, for example, in the late 1970s when US food aid to Bangladesh drove producer prices down to a quarter of their normal levels.) If the EEC cannot fine-tune its grain arrivals to coincide with the 'hungry season', it would do better to wait even longer before delivering, rather than wipe out local farmers. Every ruined peasant who migrates to a city makes one less producer and one more consumer (not counting family members), thus perpetuating the need for future food aid.

Even the severest critics of food aid do not deny the need for intervention in cases of natural or man-made disasters, provided it is of short duration. If food aid were not automatically renewed regardless of need, the EEC might find it easier to devote greater attention (and greater quantities) to real emergencies. It is relatively difficult to estimate what proportion of total aid currently serves emergency purposes. The World Food Program's figure of 20 per cent (for 1983) is almost surely inflated, whereas the critics' estimate of 7 per cent may be too low.[17] Ten per cent may be closest to the truth; but whatever figure one adopts, too little aid goes to emergency situations, and the little that is allocated takes far too long to arrive.

Aside from helping to palliate the worst effects of *some* disasters,[18] food aid could make a tremendous contribution to development in the rare cases where countries make genuine efforts to transfer power and resources to the poorer bottom half of the population. Take the case of Chile in 1972: redistribution of income resulted in a 12 per cent jump in food demand in the space of a single year – proving that malnourished people spend incremental income first on food. Chile's own agriculture was unable to respond to the challenge, food-price inflation ensued, and the Allende government made desperate attempts to import wheat. The United States (and its commercial banks) meanwhile cut off all financial credits, without which commercial wheat purchases were impossible. These actions contributed in no small measure to the economic destabilization and eventual overthrow of the socialist government and to the bloody dictatorship that still holds sway over Chile. Timely food aid for a transitional period might have helped avoid both. Nicaragua is in similar straits today. But in order to help such national experiments encouraging greater social justice, Europe would have to risk the displeasure of the US and underwrite a truly non-aligned foreign policy.

However much one might like to see all other kinds of food aid abolished (aside from emergency and transitional help as described above), this is not at present a realistic proposition. Structural, institutionalized, 'subscription' food aid will be with us for a while, and we must make the best of it. Since about two-thirds of all food aid is sold locally, for local currency, 'making the best' means making the best possible use of counterpart funds. An additional 15 to 16 per cent of food aid is devoted to Food for Work projects, so we must also see how these could be made to serve the whole society.

US Public Law 480 (the 'Food for Peace' law) makes elaborate provisions for the uses of counterpart funds – all of them destined to serve American interests in one way or another.[19] Europeans have taken the line up to now that the recipient country should be allowed to use counterpart funds generated by the sale of food aid as it sees fit. At the same time, the EEC (during Edgard Pisani's term as development commissioner) has lately tried to use food aid to enhance food security and self-sufficiency in Third World countries. Unfortunately, the EEC's concern for national sovereignty on the one hand and for rural development on the other are not necessarily compatible, since recipient governments may not, as noted above, put their own peasantries high on their list of priorities.

A debate has thus arisen on how use of counterpart funds might become subject to negotiation, to a kind of 'conditionality' and to quasi-contractual arrangements. Because European (as opposed to American) food aid did not begin on this basis, partner countries have sometimes been quick to see 'interventionist' or 'neocolonialist' designs in any suggestions for consultation. In the case of Mali, however, agreement has been reached on how counterpart funds could better contribute to development (by improving producer prices, for example). It is too early to evaluate such innovations.[20]

Food for Work projects should theoretically contribute to development. All too often, they contribute far more to the capacity of elites to repress the poor, as Tony Jackson's research has shown.[21] Furthermore, it is often the people who need food most who are least able to work – the very young and old, the ill, pregnant and nursing mothers. Other project food aid (school lunch, mother–child health programmes and the like) may simply bypass the groups most at risk (the child fed at school may get less at home; preschoolers may get nothing).

European food donations devoted to Food for Work or other 'project' aid should be subject to the kind of critical checklist Jackson's work suggests: *Who* will ultimately benefit from the projects? Do they increase the material assets of the privileged minority (for example, wells or canals dug on their lands)? Do they promote social cohesion or dislocation? Are the really malnourished being reached by the programmes? Those who have found Jackson unduly abrasive ('his solution is like suggesting to someone who has a toothache that he cut off his head'[22]) should recognize that the best refutation would be to remove the grounds for criticism he has so ruthlessly uncovered.

Some small and highly successful experiments with *triangular food aid* have been carried out with the cooperation of European non-governmental organizations (NGOs). The basic idea is to purchase grain in a Third World surplus area and transfer it to a deficit area. Sales revenues are committed to a revolving fund to supply rural credit or to support other development projects (improved storage and transportation, for example). These operations have none of the drawbacks of foreign food aid: they involve locally grown products, so they do not induce new and dependency-creating food habits; they encourage peasant production; they generate cash for development purposes; and they can be managed by local NGOs.

The official aid programmes both of individual European countries (France, Belgium, Holland) and of the EEC itself now recognize the value of these triangular operations. The European Parliament and the Commission have established excellent working relations with the European NGO collective called 'For the Right of Peoples to Feed Themselves'; the latter has proposed specific amendments that have met with varying fates. NGOs, concerned Members of the European Parliament (MEPs) and their supporters must continue to call for more flexible aid provisions in subsequent Community budgets.

In particular, the EEC must not penalize countries which are making a genuine effort to implement their own food strategies to increase self-sufficiency. In practice, this means that cash aid for development projects (or simply for balance of payments support) should replace the value of food aid as the latter is phased out. If the Commission continues to refuse substitution measures, then we will have to recognize that its food aid *is* after all only about surplus-dumping and all the rest is mere window-dressing. Furthermore, if food and financial aid are not made interchangeable – at least during a transitional period – the most improvident recipient governments will reap the greatest rewards!

One final remark on food aid: dairy aid should be eliminated as rapidly as possible (this should become easier as milk surpluses are curbed). It is not adapted to most Third World circumstances or dietary habits and skim milk powder can rarely be reconstituted hygienically. Even the EEC's showcase project Operation Flood (long criticized by Indian scholars and development experts), with the possible exception of Gujarat, is not an unqualified success. 'The often advanced suggestion that Operation Flood is making important inroads in the struggle against rural poverty does not appear to be well founded and has certainly not yet been proven. At best it does provide *some* extra earning opportunities to *some* rural poor,' say two conscientious Dutch evaluators whose conclusions have now been substantiated in several studies.[23]

## II. The Possible Strategies

Food aid represents about a third of the Community's total cooperation budget. Let us now look at more general strategies that the EEC could pursue in order to help alleviate hunger. Though far from perfect, the Community's aid package still has a number of praiseworthy characteristics. For example, it features an exceptionally high percentage of grants – 80 per cent of total disbursements – as opposed to only 33 per cent of disbursed funds in grants from other multilateral sources.[24] Furthermore, European aid to the agricultural sector in the Third World has grown from just 16 per cent in the first European Development Fund (EDF) in 1958 to about 40 per cent today. The share devoted to cash crops, though still too high in an age of food crises, has fallen from 45 per cent to 30 per cent.[25]

The Lomé III Convention, signed at long last in December 1984 after fourteen months of negotiations, will doubtless never become the exceptional instrument for promoting development in the African, Caribbean and Pacific countries (ACPs) that many hoped for in 1975 when its ancestor Lomé I first came into being. It still contains many useful features that can be built upon, and the satisfactory renegotiation of this convention in an era of general Western retrenchment from Third World problems may be seen as an achievement in itself.[26]

These are encouraging trends. So is the general and widespread debate in the EEC on development issues, and particularly on food strategies, launched by the so-called Pisani Memorandum of October 1982. Though it is difficult for an outsider to determine how pertinent this memorandum remains today, several elements should certainly be retained in any future EEC development cooperation strategy. One such change evident both in Lomé and in the Memorandum is that agriculture is now recognized as *the* priority (and high time too!).

In spite of these signs of progress, all is not well with EEC development cooperation. A major contradiction and danger of the Lomé Convention, with its Stabex system,[27] is that it may entrench a 'cash crop mentality' in partner countries that produce woefully inadequate quantities of basic foodstuffs. A similar contradiction in the Pisani Memorandum is the absence of any effort to relate the concerns of DG VIII – the Development Directorate[28] – to those dealing with EEC internal policy. For example, heavily subsidized Community sugar production directly reduces the amount of sugar that small and highly dependent tropical countries can sell. ACP countries obviously have a far smaller range of export choices than the diversified economies of Europe.[29]

In a similar vein, the Community's Mediterranean policy is ill-defined, contradictory and likely to become more so with the entry of Spain and Portugal into the EEC. Over the past ten years, southern Mediterranean countries have come to count more and more on exports of fruits, vegetables, oils and the like – and they have furthermore concentrated their export strategy on Europe. Now, with the advent of Spain and Portugal (in addition to Italy, Greece and southern France), the EEC will become self-sufficient in these commodities, just as it did for cereals, sugar, or dairy products earlier in its history. The loss in revenues for several Third World Mediterranean countries will be sizeable, particularly in relation to their inability to diversify their exports rapidly. The EEC-12 have yet to recognize in concrete terms the consequences of Community enlargement on smaller, weaker nations.[30]

One could cite other contradictions that impede definition and implementation of workable food strategies with Third World partners. For example, European-based transnational corporations are often actively engaged in underpaying for Third World agricultural raw materials. Since countries must earn a minimum of hard currency, they will tend to produce greater amounts of cash crops – which will hog productive resources – just to keep their incomes stable. Food crops will obviously suffer. In the same way, excessive debt, often accompanied by IMF 'adjustment' or 'austerity' programmes, forces countries to export, come what may and regardless of their internal food situation. Aid given with one hand is thus taken away with the other. In 1983, the net financial transfer from the poor countries to the rich (reimbursements minus new loans) amounted to $21 billion. EEC governments, along with the United States, make sure their own commercial banks are paid back; they also help to set day-to-day policy at the IMF.[31]

These remarks are meant to show that the definition of development policy in general and of food strategies in particular cannot be left to the DG VIII alone if it does not have the active cooperation of the other Directorates. Third World cooperation and development strategies must be seen not as some sort of appendage, but as an integral part of overall European policy – financial, commercial and agricultural.

If the EEC takes development seriously, it must make sure that DG VIII has the resources to carry out its mission. Currently, DG VIII's disbursement per official is about the highest in Europe. 'For example, DG VIII's budget is about the same as the British bilateral aid programme, yet the British programme has nearly three times more personnel.'[32] While this may show commendable efficiency in the DG VIII, there are limits – particularly since Lomé III now commits this Directorate to enter into 'development dialogues' with ACP states. Even worse, the EEC reportedly employs only 'one man and a secretary to supervise the evaluation of all EEC-funded (development) projects. The evaluation unit is too small to spend its budget.'[33]

The EEC is not the most important donor for most of the ACP countries and, in some cases, is a very minor one. The Community accounts on average for about 10 per cent of the aid received by the ACP group in any one year. The impact of its aid must, then, necessarily be based on *quality* and *innovative ideas*, not on financial clout. The EEC has already established partnership relations with four African countries (Mali, Kenya, Zambia, Rwanda) around the idea of the food strategy. Thus it would be useful to examine some of the general conditions food strategies must observe in order to be successful.

The food crisis, particularly in Africa, has at least served to create a consensus that *nothing is possible without the participation of the small peasantry*. African countries, and the 65 ACP countries as a whole, cannot count on trade to solve their problems; in spite of Lomé, their exports to Europe have actually declined, from 25 per cent of all Third World exports to Europe in

1975 to 18 per cent in 1982. To solve their food problem, they must become more inward-looking and not count on export crops to provide revenues to purchase food from abroad. The first principle of a food strategy is that it must increase incentives to producers while protecting the lowest-income consumers.

Lomé III finally mentions the critical role of women in food production. In 1979, the International Labour Organization (ILO) carried out a study of agricultural tasks in Africa. Of seventeen identified tasks, it found that women were responsible for fourteen. If women's special needs are not made a cornerstone of food strategies, they will fail. Placing the accent on poor peasants, and, among them, on women, will require radical changes in present African policies; the EEC should be prepared to make these easier, but also to make its aid conditional upon such changes.

In defence of this proposition, here are two items: of the $7.5 billion worth of aid mobilized by the Club du Sahel between 1975 and 1982, only 4.5 per cent was devoted to rain-fed agriculture (and a further 4.5 per cent to animal raising) on which virtually all poor Sahelian peasants depend. A report of the World Food Council on UN-system aid to food and agriculture informs us that over the past decade programmes specifically designed for women received a contemptible one-tenth of one per cent! (Doubtless even this tiny sum was spent on 'home economics' type programmes!) Clearly, without some judiciously applied pressure, all African governments cannot be presently counted on to direct the money where it is most needed.

The phrase 'policy dialogue' during the Lomé negotiations became a kind of bugbear for the ACP representatives, who often saw it as a code word for neocolonialist intervention. Nevertheless, if the EEC is serious about alleviating hunger and about food strategies, it must, by its own behaviour, make this dialogue credible and prove to the recipient countries that it is in their best interests to pursue it. This will mean, among other things, long-term commitments on the part of the Community and the possibility for the recipients to draw upon budgets according to need, not according to an artificial annual schedule.

Human rights was another sensitive issue during the negotiations – prompted by a situation that arose in the course of Lomé II, when the EEC was legally bound by Stabex to transfer funds to the Idi Amin Dada regime in Uganda. Some European governments proposed that Lomé III allow them to cut off funds to ACP governments guilty of 'serious and continued violations of fundamental human rights'.[34]

The ACP countries were able to counter that EEC governments maintained relations with South Africa – the major violator of human rights on the African continent – and that this effectively disqualified them from making any judgements on ACP countries. *Touché!* A clause was subsequently introduced in the Convention committing the EEC and the ACP to 'work effectively for the eradication of apartheid'. Again, in the interests of its own credibility, the EEC and its member governments must implement this clause in their economic and commercial dealings. The link between human rights and eventual aid cutoffs does not figure officially in the Convention, but the EEC will be in a better position to insist upon it when it has put its own house in order.

In short, food strategies must be based on the small peasantry, especially women; be designed in cooperation with the recipient government ('policy dialogue'); and include a strong and credible human rights focus. Part of this focus will mean helping and trusting peasant communities themselves to carry out the strategies. If these are nothing but a product of national governments' planners, without the initial and continuing cooperation of those most concerned, they will become simply another example of 'top-down' development plans, which have notoriously failed. If rural development is to become 'bottom-up', then the peasants must be consulted, and they must be helped to form – or to strengthen – their own representative associations. If a recipient government cannot agree to this basic condition, which will necessarily alter the internal balance of power, then it would be better for Europe to abstain.

Although there has been some effort to make food aid a part of food strategies, as noted above, unless I am mistaken no similar effort has been undertaken to integrate EEC small-scale project funds into such strategies. Lomé I allocated 'as an experiment' 20 million ECUs to small projects to be cofinanced with the host government and sometimes local financial input. The success of this initiative resulted in Lomé II's allocation of a further 45 million ECUs through to the end of 1983. The European Development Fund (EDF) financed 45 per cent of total costs for the more than 4,200 projects set in motion during this period. This figure testifies to the demand for small project assistance, and Lomé III reflects this reality. One innovation with regard to the first two conventions is that an ACP State need no longer make a financial contribution to a given project. This means in effect that the Community could in some cases work directly with a grassroots ACP community.[35]

Small projects have a proven record of success. Perhaps not all Third World problems can be solved at the local level, but we have surely not yet reached the outer limits of those that can. For this kind of participatory development to occur, however, some overhaul of EEC and ACP machinery will also be needed. One expert, a former Commission official, makes several cogent recommendations:

- 'Local communities need much greater help to organize themselves and identify projects. Training and backing local animators is a good way of doing this.'

- 'ACP administrations should provide more support for local initiatives. The bureaucratic processing of applications should be streamlined. Local communities who have local authority approval should be allowed to approach the EEC delegation directly.'

- 'EEC delegations should have access to, and local decision-making capacity for, a small annual budget for micro-projects [block grants].'

- 'The Development Directorate ... should set up an inter-service "Small Projects Advisory Group."'

- 'European NGOs should recognize the complementarity of their work with that of official bodies ... They should increase their efforts to provide information to and technical back-up for local communities ...'[36]

These recommendations are quoted at length because they pinpoint the present obstacles, which the EEC should eliminate, to a higher level of self-reliant development. These obstacles are more organizational than substantive in nature, but their removal could have far-reaching effects in partner countries. The more local initiative, the more democracy internally; the more people are allowed to accomplish through their own efforts, the more they can achieve in the future. Each successful project builds expertise and self-confidence. Neighbouring villages see progress and seek to imitate it. Replication of small projects is infinitely easier than that of large, capital-intensive schemes which may create islands of development but few benefits for the country as a whole. European NGOs are already on the spot in the ACP countries and can help, when needed, to identify and train local groups. They could also contribute to processing of applications and to evaluation.

Unfortunately, present EEC structures do not lend themselves to this extremely effective kind of cooperation. The DG VIII unit that dealt with micro-projects has been disbanded and responsibility spread among the geographical desks, where overworked officers have little time to devote to such small undertakings relative to their total caseload. Who can blame the official who would rather process one large request than ten small ones?

Such officials would also have to rely far more on the expertise of local and European NGOs than on classic feasibility studies or outside experts.

Assuming the Community is prepared, as it should be, to devote greater bureaucratic and financial resources to small, locally initiated projects, here are a few criteria for ensuring their success:

- Projects should be designed so that they contribute to the country's overall food strategy, but this does not mean that people must not be consulted as to their *own* priorities. Women should be consulted separately; otherwise, their voices may not be heard, and men's perceived needs are not necessarily the same as theirs. Local officials should be charged with helping the Community design its project so that it is also compatible with national policy.

- Projects must be based on the local ecological and social context; that is, people must work within the constraints of their own environments. This is a basic rule because every project must eventually become self-sufficient and self-managed with no further infusions of foreign funds after an agreed time-limit.

- Europeans helping to design projects should remember that the nature of *time* is different in Europe and in, for example, Africa. It takes time for people to discuss matters and to decide for themselves what they can do. Their present situation has been shaped by 100 years of colonialism, twenty-six years of 'development' that left rural people out, and ten years of drought thrown in for good measure. It cannot be altered in two weeks.[37]

Because of the name chosen, we may tend to forget that a 'food' strategy must go far beyond the mere production of food. Personally, I would have preferred 'food system strategy'. Though

84

less catchy, this phrase would help to make clear that production is only a part of the food problem – sometimes not the most important part.[38] In order to produce, farmers must have physical inputs and credit, and they must have them at the right times of the year. To keep the food they have produced, they need adequate storage and/or processing; and if they depend on their crops for an income as well as for feeding their own families, they need a decent marketing service and a fair price for their efforts.

*The hunger problem is furthermore as much about work as about growing food.* 'Employment', though much favoured by Western economists, is the wrong term, because much if not most of the productive work in the Third World is not wage-remunerated. As Robert Chambers explains in a brilliant analysis:

> For many of the rural poor ... their concern ... [is] less with employment than with livelihood – levels of wealth and of stocks and flows of food and cash which provide for physical and social well-being and security against impoverishment. Most families of small and marginal farmers and of the landless are concerned not with a job or a workplace, but with sustaining and improving a repertoire of activities which will provide them with an adequate and secure level of living around the year. These may include cultivation, keeping livestock; collecting or catching, and consuming or processing and selling; common property resources (firewood, charcoal, fish, grass, medicinal plants, wild animals, bamboos, reeds, tree fodders, etc.); casual labour; hawking; seasonal public relief works; seasonal migration; work as artisans (pottery, basket- and mat-making, earthenwork, blacksmithing, weaving, thatching and the like); and many other activities.[39]

Chambers's catalogue, as he is the first to point out, is not complete but it goes a good way towards demonstrating that food strategies, to be effective for the poorest and hungriest people, must consider a whole complex range of activities – not just farming or paid labour. A major objective of any food strategy is almost too obvious to be stated: it should keep people in the countryside by multiplying the opportunities for productive work there and by making the quality of life in rural areas competitive with advantages to be found in cities. Promotion of small industries and of environment-enhancing activities (tree-planting, erosion control, water-catchment and the like) that contribute to food production and food processing is one way. In some countries, a coercive policy towards professionals would help – for example, doctors, teachers, administrators and others who have received their education thanks to public funds should spend a specified time using their knowledge in the villages.

Two further aspects that should be part of any food strategy usually do not receive the attention they deserve: the highly seasonal nature of hunger and malnutrition and ensuring early warning of scarcity or famine.

Because we in the industrialized countries tend to deal in annual statistics and in averages – and because most of us live in cities – we have stopped noticing the obvious fact that rural people's lives follow the rhythms of the seasons. So, to a large degree, does hunger. With few exceptions, and except in cases of the most dire, entrenched famines, even poor people have enough to eat in the weeks or months that follow the harvest.

It is when their food supplies start to run out that timely intervention can make the difference between keeping their liveli-hood and becoming landless, between staying in the countryside and migrating to the city – even between life and death. Especially during the difficult time before the new crops can be harvested, there is competition both for food and for work – food prices go up just as wages (in cash or in kind) go down. This is also the period when people, in order to eat or to buy seed, contract debts that may dog them for years to come. Naturally, illness also strikes most readily when people are hungry. Food strategies (and food aid) should be attuned to seasonal needs. Less costly and more effective, well-timed short-term help also allows the poorest people to keep something as important to them as food – their dignity.

Early warning systems can usefully complete seasonal analysis as indicators of the need for food aid or other exceptional interventions. The Food and Agriculture Organization (FAO) has on the whole promoted technological systems (satellite photography, plus Meteosat and Agrhymet weather and rainfall data). Such technology can show, rather crudely, the areas likely to be affected by shortfalls in food production, but tells us nothing about the number of people who may be affected, when they will need help or can be expected to migrate. A less costly system, which can be managed by the people themselves (perhaps with NGO help to begin with), would rely on socio-economic indicators – for example, rising grain and falling livestock prices; sales of jewellery, implements, draught animals (or, worse still, land); unusual numbers of people emigrating in search of work and the like.[40]

Early warning systems are vital because, properly conceived and implemented, they could prevent disasters on the Ethiopian scale. Victims of food crises could be reached in *their own villages* before they had to resort to feeding camps. Famines, as opposed to seasonal shortfalls, build up over long periods and display common features which can be 'read' – like the signs listed above. It would cost the EEC far less to set up a network of early warning systems, with the cooperation of partner ACP countries and NGOs, than to intervene with massive famine relief when full-blown disaster strikes.

Finally, cooperation in agricultural research for and with the poor peasantry could make enormous contributions to food security. Not nearly enough research has been devoted to the day-to-day problems of peasants, although this is one of the chief keys to improving their productivity. Since this is an enormous and complex subject, the reader (and, with luck, the policy-maker) is referred to the insightful and exceptionally readable book by Robert Chambers, *Rural Development: Putting the Last First*.[41]

We began this exercise by claiming that Europe has much to gain from cooperation with the Third World in developing food strategies that work. In the moral, but also in the political sense, what could be a greater achievement than to prove we can put an end to the age-old scourge of hunger? The difference in the late twentieth century is that hunger is no longer a scourge – it is a scandal. But it is not intractable: the causes are known, the remedies exist. The superpowers are too involved in their own rivalries to care about the plight of the billion or so people who suffer from malnutrition, chronic hunger or outright famine – including those within their own borders.[42] If Europe has the vision and the courage, it can take its place as superpower of the human spirit.

# PART II
# SCIENCE AND TECHNOLOGY

# 5

## CAVEAT EMPTOR:
## THE 'TRANSFER' OF TECHNOLOGY

*Dr Zafrullah Chowdhury is an exceptional man – the product of an upper-class Bengali family who trained as an MD in Dacca and London and returned to his country during the liberation struggle against Pakistan to care for wounded combatants. He soon after realized that the kind of medicine he had been taught had very little to do with the health problems of the poor rural Bangladeshi majority.*

*After the war, instead of going into a lucrative urban practice, Chowdhury set up the Gonoshasthaya Kendra – People's Health Centre – in the countryside north of Dacca at Savar; armed with near-zero funds and a boundless faith in the need for decentralized health care serving the real needs of people living in poverty. The Centre is now a full-fledged, self-sufficient community reaching out to several tens of thousands of Bangladeshis. It grows its own produce on land previously considered untillable, maintains a school for local children, and has set up an agricultural credit bank and workshops for carpentry, textiles, metal and leatherworking that provide employment primarily for rural women. A small hospital has been built on the premises, but more important are the paramedics (largely women) who have been trained to cope with most of the health problems encountered in rural Bangladesh, as well as to provide basic obstetrical and family-planning care. They range far and wide in the countryside around Savar, and several subcentres have been established in other parts of the country, staffed in the same way. Chowdhury's latest achievement is a pharmaceuticals factory (largely financed by a Dutch development aid agency and modern in every respect) that will be able to provide basic drugs at a far lower cost than those now sold in Bangladesh by American and British transnational corporations.*

*None of this has been easy. One can perhaps put up with the austerity of living conditions (Chowdhury's daughter is called Bishti, which means 'rain' in Bengali, because the hut he and his German-born wife Suzanne lived in when the baby was born was awash during the rainy season). The outright hostility of many better-off Bengalis who feel threatened by the GK Centre is something else. One of the paramedics was murdered in 1976 by assassins who have been identified but never brought to justice. While I was in Savar, absentee landlords from Dacca and their hired thugs physically attacked GK workers and tried to bulldoze temporary structures on land the government has promised Chowdhury for an extension of the Centre. The landlords have simply noted that the land is worth something after all – and violence is a standard means for gratifying greed in Bangladesh. Chowdhury's next project is to build a teaching hospital where the curriculum will stress not only people-oriented health care but the sociopolitical conditions that breed poverty and disease.*

*The following text is the keynote speech Chowdhury asked me to give for the 'Transfer of Technology' conference he organized at the GK Centre in January 1982. Most of the participants were foreign or Bengali health care professionals; several had important responsibilities in government ministries.*

When Dr Zafrullah Chowdhury invited me to give the keynote speech for the opening of this seminar, I accepted immediately, not only from gratitude for the honour, but especially because it gives me the opportunity, on behalf of all the foreign participants, to salute the remarkable work being done here at Savar by Dr Chowdhury and all his colleagues. Examples of grass-roots, integrated, autonomous and authentic development are all too rare in Third World countries, and while I've often cited Savar as just such an example, I'm enormously pleased at last to see it in operation and also to note that its work is receiving greater and greater support and is being actively encouraged by the people and the authorities of Bangladesh itself.

The greater part of the work of our seminar will be devoted to problems posed by transfers of technology in the fields of health, medicine and pharmaceuticals. This is as it should be, given the long-term orientation of the Savar Centre and its most recent achievement – the resplendent new pharmaceuticals factory. Many other participants will address these topics with great professional competence in the coming days. My task, as defined by Zafrullah Chowdhury, is to try to place the problems of technology transfer in a more general perspective.

Speakers should adhere to one simple, cardinal rule: talk about what they know. My direct experience of the Third World is limited and this is my first, although I hope not my last, visit to Bangladesh, so I have no pretensions to speaking about the effects of technology transfer in this country. What I hope I know a little more about, as a citizen of one rich, industrialized country and a resident of another, are the nature of Western technology and the plans the ruling elites of the rich countries have for the poor countries as we move towards the end of the twentieth century.

No one here needs to be told that the present world system is in crisis. Poor countries are hit particularly hard – more expensive imported food and energy, crushing debts, dwindling prospects for their own exports and so forth. What I'm concerned with here, however, is how the *rich* nations, and especially their transnational corporations (or TNCs), are reacting to the crisis. Their reactions, as I hope to show, are crucial for the future of the Third World.

In a world of rising costs and diminishing profits, it becomes more important than ever for the industrialized countries and the TNCs to maintain and to reinforce their hegemony over the global economy. They *must*, from their point of view, increase their control over world production, and world markets. People who believe that the interventions of TNCs in Third World countries are primarily for the good of those countries; those who believe that these companies have any object besides the enhancement of their own profits are making a serious mistake. The uses – and the abuses – of technology are among the instruments they employ in orchestrating global control.

Let's begin by taking a critical look at our vocabulary itself. Technology is not 'transferred' – that is a nice, sanitary, aseptic word. Technology is bought and sold, full stop. The word 'transfer' also implies that 'recipient' nations gain real control over a technology deposited in their laps and which then becomes wholly theirs. This, too, is a mistake. Another popular misconception is that 'technology' is merely some sort of machinery or apparatus. In reality, technology is never just a *product*. It is also a *process*, and those who buy technology from the West are usually getting a lot more than they bargained for. Let me explore this notion of technology as a process a little more fully.

Present Western technology should not be looked at as a 'given' which just happens to be there. A more accurate way to see it is as the *result of several centuries of the history of Western capitalism*. The technology we now use in the West – the same technology that is sold in a stage of greater or lesser obsolescence to the Third World – is by no means determined by pure considerations of efficiency and it is even less determined by the needs of society as a whole. The technology the West uses is the outcome of a social and political process and of social and political struggles. It embodies relationships between social classes in a particular kind of social organization and has been developed to serve the needs of those who have come to dominate society.

Unfortunately for the masses of people in the West, the outcome of this centuries-long social and political process has been much less satisfactory – that is, for the vast majority of workers or farmers or service industry employees. During the nineteenth century, the large, centralized factory entirely replaced the small, decentralized (even individual) production units which had previously been the rule. This change took place not so much because the factory system was necessarily more efficient: its outstanding advantage was that it allowed a far greater measure of social control over the workforce.

Who can believe that Western workers would choose of their own free will the 'Taylor' system of the assembly line with its speed-ups, its repetitious, meaningless gestures and ruthless supervision, dehumanizing and alienating the workforce from the final product of its own labour? Has a later generation of workers 'chosen' the technology of industrial robots which is now rapidly eliminating their jobs in the automotive and textile industries, with electronics and others to come? Have farmworkers 'chosen' the mechanical lettuce- and tomato-harvesters developed in direct response to the strikes led by Cesar Chavez? These harvesters are replacing thousands of them in the United States – and will soon do so elsewhere. Have US farmers 'chosen' an agricultural technology so expensive that they can no longer meet its costs, so that an average of 800 of them go out of business every week? Have office employees and clerks 'chosen' the technology of office automation which will replace up to 40 per cent of their numbers before the year 2000, according to recent studies?

Anyone who buys Western technology should understand that he is not just buying a product, but rather a distinct set of social relationships which have now become so embedded in the technology that they are nearly invisible. Along with the technology comes a hierarchical, authoritarian way of organizing production itself – and one which will dispense with human labour whenever feasible. Furthermore, purchasers of technology are buying the end result of our inability in the West to create the desirable society, in spite of all our wealth. I will go even further and say that they are, in effect, buying a kind of *crystallized failure* – the failure of struggles of working people in the West to create full employment, a humane production process, consumption based on socially useful goods and an unpolluted, sustainable environment in which all could live harmoniously. They are also buying, conversely, the crystallized success of our ruling elites in imposing productivity and profit as the only goals of human existence. Put another way, the technology we use and are selling to others in the 1980s is certainly not the *only* technology we could devise – just these products, just these processes and no others – inevitable and somehow foreordained by disembodied, pure reason. The technology we have devised represents a series of *choices* among a whole range of possibilities, and these choices were dictated by a minority whose goal was, is and always will be its own greater power and profits.

I'm fully aware that this way of looking at present Western technology may surprise you, and that your first reaction may be that millions of people in Bangladesh would consider the lot of a Western worker, small farmer, or employee – even an unemployed one – sheer paradise. Fair enough. But consider for a moment what we *might* have done with our wealth – much of that wealth acquired by exploiting Third World countries.

We could have had more labour-intensive technologies ensuring full employment. Instead, we have at least 30 million unemployed in the OECD countries (Europe and North America).

We could have provided an abundant, varied and healthy diet for everyone, regardless of social status. Instead we have chemical additives because they contribute to long product life and thus to the profits of the food industry. We have increased our consumption of highly processed junk foods with little or no nutritional value while consumption of fresh produce has declined. There are millions of malnourished people in the United States and Great Britain (especially among old people and minorities) although you might not always recognize this malnutrition because it often shows up as obesity.

We could have had technologies safe to work with. Instead, to give only two examples, there were five deaths and over 500 serious injuries of workers in a single California shipyard in a single recent year. *Business Week* has just reported 'a sudden rise in miners' deaths'. Occupational health and safety technologies are readily available, but they are also more expensive for companies than sloppy and dangerous methods. Thus thousands more workers in close daily contact with dangerous chemicals or radio-active materials are being slowly poisoned.

We could have had fast, cheap, efficient public transportation. Instead we've given priority to the costly, energy-devouring private automobile. And in Western countries without an adequate national health care system, like the United States, millions of people live in fear of illness, because hospital care – and our hospitals are full of beautiful shiny technology – will eat up their life's savings. Our technologies are not even clean, so we must eat, drink and breathe the pollutants they leave in the environment.

I could go on giving examples, but my point is that our Western technology – so much admired, it seems, in Third World countries – is far from perfect and serves chiefly those whose incomes put them at the top of the ladder. Obviously I do not wish to do without my telephone or the machine that served to type this speech – but I hope I'm also aware of the harassing working conditions of telephone operators, and that few people who need an electric typewriter as much as I do can afford one.

The phrase *caveat emptor* – 'let the buyer beware' – has never been truer than for the case of Third World purchases of Western technology – especially if the buyer does not realize the whole social and cultural history that lies behind the products and processes he is getting. As the Indian scholar A. K. N. Reddy has put it perfectly, technology is a carrier of the genetic code of the society that produced it. Once given, genetic codes are invariable. Those who purchase Western technology had best be prepared to adapt to it, because Western technology is not going to adapt to them.

An overwhelming share of technological research and development (R&D) is done in the industrialized countries – only about 2 to 3 per cent of the world's total R&D capacity is located in the Third World. So it's not surprising that technology transfers are one-way streets, that Third World nations have little influence on the types of technology developed and that their specific needs are not served by this technology.

One can cite such obvious cases as the huge sums expended on military R&D which, in 1979, amounted to $35 billion, with more than half a million scientists and engineers devoting their full time to the destruction machine. This represents about a quarter of the world's entire outlay for R&D.

There are non-military dangers as well. When pollution-control laws are passed in the rich countries, we transplant our dirtiest industries to countries where legislation is weak or non-existent. We even use Third World people as guinea-pigs for our potentially harmful products – for example, oral contraceptives were tested on Third World women before being marketed in the industrialized countries. Even research that can be classed as oriented to life rather than death is usually irrelevant to Third World needs. Thus the United States spends about nine times as much on cancer and heart disease R&D as the entire world budget for tropical medicine research.

But let's examine the kinds of technology that *are* useful – or at least are *used* in the Third World. Remember that this technology is almost exclusively transferred by TNCs directly or by aid programmes that call upon these same corporations. In my workroom at home, I have pasted up a small cutting from a corporate advertisement in *Business Week*, because it sums up admirably what TNCs are all about. There are only five words in the ad: 'Objective: Maximize Return. Minimize Risk.' How do Third World countries fit into this succinct programme?

First, they are not allowed to interfere with maximizing return. As the Group of 77 pointed out at the 1979 UN Conference on Science and Technology, 90 per cent of the patents granted, supposedly, to Third World countries are, in reality, granted to foreigners – which is to say, to subsidiaries of TNCs. Even worse, only about 10 per cent of the patents granted are actually used – but so long as they are in force, no one else can use them. The function of the patent system is to *prevent* the generalization of technology developed in the non-industrialized world.

India's experience with TNC technology transfer is instructive, not least because India has a highly sophisticated technological capacity of its own. A recent report by S. K. Goyal of the Indian Institute of Public Administration comes up with the following results: in many industries, including pharmaceuticals, the impact of supposed 'technology transfer' is nil, because local affiliates act only as 'bottlers' – they simply repack in small containers bulk drugs imported from the parent firm. Routine assembly of components manufactured elsewhere is the rule in electronics, business machines and other high-technology product lines – even though India boasts plenty of skilled workers able to manufacture these components.

Whatever advanced technology does come into India tends to stay within the four walls of the TNC subsidiary where Indians work only as labourers and junior technicians. Parent companies take substantial precautions to prevent their equipment and processes from benefiting the country as a whole. The real crunch comes when the parent transfers – so to speak – an item to its subsidiary, because the subsidiary must then make payment for that item out of India's foreign currency reserves at whatever price the company sets. For Imperial Chemical Industries' Indian affiliate, the technical collaboration agreement on polyester fibres involved the affiliate's commitment of £2 million for engineering and design charges made by ICI. This payment does not include a 3.5 per cent royalty charge on the value of any and all polyester fibres produced in India in the future. This drain on the country's foreign currency reserves is a recurrent and standard aspect attached to TNC technology transfer. Goyal's team showed that the 189 Indian TNC affiliates that made up the sample not only earned *no* foreign exchange but actually *cost* the country a minimum of $25 million in 1976 alone.

Transfer pricing is a well-developed art for TNCs – they overvalue what they import from the parent firm and undervalue what they export back to it. Thus Goyal concludes: 'The practice of exporting goods to parent companies at a loss is obviously an indirect method of transferring resources from India, and the motivation for accelerating such exports is to defeat the spirit of foreign exchange regulations, *not* to promote Indian national interests.' This is all part of 'maximizing return'.

TNCs are not interested in integrating with the rest of a country's economy. They are much more apt to import their raw materials – again paying with precious local foreign exchange – than to encourage raw material production from the local market. But their most negative impact is doubtless on employment.

The number one problem in the Third World today is job creation. Number one – because with millions more jobs, other huge problems like hunger could be virtually eliminated. The International Labour Organization estimates that at least 300 million Third World people are totally unemployed. The figure swells yearly: in India, for instance, an estimated 100,000 people are added to the potential workforce every *week*. Probably 35–40 million Third World people join this huge army every year.

It is simply not possible, using Western technology, to create anywhere near the billion jobs the Third World will need by the year 2000, for the excellent reason that each industrial job created in the West requires a *minimum* investment of $20,000. A single job made available in US agriculture costs a staggering $400,000 in capital investment. TNCs claim that they create employment – and this may be true in a few small enclave countries like Singapore or Hong Kong. But TNCs neglect to tell us how many jobs they *destroy*. A recent ILO study has shown, for example, that in Brazil, from 1970 to 1975, 200 smaller food-processing companies went out of business as a direct result of competition from foreign agro-industrial firms. Overall, TNCs create far less employment than is generally supposed and account for only one-half of one per cent of total Third World jobs, again according to ILO. No one has fully measured their negative influence on employment.

Here is an example from another continent, taken from Stephen Langdon's work on the soap industry in Kenya. Before the advent of TNCs, soap-making in Kenya was a highly labour-intensive industry. All stages of production – mixing, moulding, drying, cutting, wrapping, warehousing and distributing – were carried out mostly by hand with the aid of simple equipment. Then the TNCs, including Unilever, arrived with their modern technology, imported, at a price, from the home countries. As the local manager of the Kenyan affiliate of one of these companies explained:

> We have a long history throughout the international firm of being very, very aggressive about the numbers of people we employ ... It's a corporate objective we have to follow. Labour costs are insignificant here, [less than] one per cent of variable costs. And on that basis, we spend an inordinate amount of time searching around for labour reductions. This is a thing we are expected to do. And if I don't do it in my job, then I'm not doing my job right as far as [the parent company] is concerned. So, basically, it's an objective which is in conflict with what this country needs.

This manager did indeed eliminate 19 per cent of his labour force in five years, in spite of huge increases in sales.

This company, like most others, imports its raw materials instead of using readily available local palm oil, so it gives no incentive to agricultural production.

Any TNC which really wants to make a place for itself in a Third World country has options no local company can possibly match. The relatively small market provided by each individual country is only a tiny part of the firm's overall operation. The TNC can thus afford to practise what is called 'deep-pocket financing' – meaning it can undersell local firms, and even sell under its own costs when necessary – until it has captured the market and conveniently eliminated the local competition. When this has occurred, the TNC will naturally put its prices back up to more realistic, not to say monopolistic, levels. There are many hidden costs that come with apparently superior technology. Perhaps the most surprising of these is the fact that Third World countries are themselves financing the expansion of TNCs. In country after country, one discovers that these firms bring relatively little cash with them, and instead finance their operations from local savings. Third World banks consider TNCs more reliable customers than local firms – so the international companies get first go at bank loans at the best credit rates. They thereby indirectly prevent the creation or expansion of national firms which are short of working capital.

In my own work, I've been particularly preoccupied with the harmful effects of the transfer of Western agricultural technology to the Third World. Here I shall limit myself to a single remark. Expensive technology produces expensive food. Someone will have to pay for purchased seeds, chemical fertilizers and pesticides, irrigation equipment, mechanization and the like – and that 'someone' is the final consumer as well as the State. A new area known as post-harvest technology – meaning storage and handling – is now very much in fashion. I believe this vogue is partly due to the fact that this part of the food system has been, up to now, only marginally penetrated by foreign agribusiness, and that companies see this as a potentially profitable activity; as a way of gaining more control over food systems as a whole. In this sense, post-harvest technology investment opportunities could be to the 1980s what the Green Revolution was to the '60s and '70s. Be that as it may, we can be sure that centralized storage, using costly silos and warehousing as opposed to family, village or regional level storage, adds at least 20 per cent to the final cost of the stored food, according to an FAO expert. This kind of cost increase is enough to price the poorest consumers out of the market – the very people who are already suffering from malnutrition.

Whether we're talking about food, health or any other vital area, Western technology has these two characteristics: it favours centralization – meaning cities – and it caters to demand expressed in purchasing power rather than to human needs. The handsomely equipped Third World hospital, rivalling anything in the United States or France, but eating up so much of the State health budget that little is left over for the majority in the countryside, is an excellent example of the centralization syndrome. The introduction of profitable processed foods or cola drinks only a minority can afford (and which are, in any event, an expensive way of consuming empty calories) puts technological expertise to work for socially useless ends. From capital's viewpoint, however, human beings are divided into two groups: those who can pay and those who cannot. The first group is called consumers. The needs of the second are not even noticed. This is how one 'maximizes return'.

The second part of my *Business Week* ad says 'minimize risk'. TNCs have no intention of giving up real control over the production process, nor of sacrificing any profits to be made, so host countries that welcome their technology should understand that they will be unable to challenge the way the corporations have decided to organize production. An illustration is the electronics industry in Asia. I've seen these operations in Malaysia's Free Trade Zones and it's obvious the companies have very little fixed investment; they could pull out tomorrow with no loss if it became more profitable to produce elsewhere. Meanwhile, they employ young women from about the age of 16 to 25 – after that, the women's eyesight becomes too feeble to continue working all day through a microscope. Then a fresh younger group takes over. A recent study by the Max Planck Institute in Germany indicates that the German work-year in electronics is 1,800 hours, whereas in South Korea it comes to 2,800 hours for equal or superior productivity and, naturally, at far lower wages. This is just common exploitation. But TNC insistence on a docile, risk-free workforce also carries a cost for the whole society. As the Max Planck study points out: 'It is not surprising that the list of those countries in which free production zones and world market factories are in operation . . . is to a great extent similar to a list of those countries in which labour unions are either prohibited or greatly hindered and in which strikes are largely suppressed.' Denial of labour rights – even human rights – and TNC investment tend to go together.

Even when countries are willing to create what the companies blandly call a 'favourable climate for investment', or, more baldly stated, to carry out repression, the host country may find little residual benefit in the way the TNC has decided to organize production. The firms' strategies are, as their name indicates, *trans*national. Some of the more powerful TNCs with a great many subsidiaries have invented a new technological twist. The Ford Motor Company calls it 'complementation'. This strategy consists of producing only one element of the final product in each national subsidiary – say the gearbox or chassis – and assembling these elements subsequently in a third country. Ford is moving towards the 'global car' and when this strategy has reached maturity there will be at least two countries manufacturing each vital component. This not only creates a strike-proof industry: it means that if a country should decide to nationalize the factory, it will not get an automobile plant. It will get nothing but a gearbox or chassis plant of absolutely no interest to anyone but Ford. Following a trip to nine Asian countries, Henry Ford announced, 'Complementation holds far more promise for the region than adherence to old-style purchasing, assembly and manufacturing methods.' From his point of view of risk-minimization, I'm sure that's true.

To sum up, technology transfer is much more often than not labour-displacing and dependency-creating – just the traps Third World countries should most avoid. Many countries believe they are buying independence when they buy technology packages. But because the firms keep control over the *way* this technology is used, independence is not what they get. Rather, as the German scholar Dieter Ernst has said, 'A strategy which seeks to strengthen national political and economic autonomy through aggressive acquisition of high technology may, paradoxically, lead not to greater technological autonomy but to greater dependence at a qualitatively higher level.'

There is a final point I do not wish to gloss over. Just as we must understand the ruling elites of rich countries whose choices determine technology types for both rich and poor, so we must confront the problem of ruling elites in the Third World. There is no doubt that many of their members may find an interest – either financial or in terms of career – in cooperating with the purveyors of unadapted and unadaptable technology. There is also no doubt that these elites generally insist that priority be given to luxury goods and to the cities where most of them live. They may give little or no thought to the needs of their poorer compatriots. We can all recite tales of corruption, bribery, or just plain deals in which TNCs and local authorities and businessmen work hand in glove for mutual interest and profit.

I still believe, however, that many members of these elites are true nationalists and are working for the betterment of their countries under extremely difficult conditions. It is to such people that I should like to direct my closing remarks.

By the very fact that rich countries are rich, their technology carries with it an aura of invincibility and of perfection. It *must* be good since it has, apparently, brought wealth to the nations which produced it. This is a myth, but a very powerful one. The existence of this myth proves that rich countries do not merely dominate our economy. They also dominate our concepts and ideas – and we are all to some extent the victims of this dominant ideology. The power of this ideology also testifies to the poverty of developed country scholarship. As scholars, we haven't demystified our own societies and our own technology. It is with this belief that I devote much of my own time to a critique of the dominant agribusiness technologies in hopes that such work may in some small way help to clear the air and prepare the ground for scientific and technological renewal in the Third World.

You may have found my remarks excessively negative, but they, too, have been aimed at air-clearing and ground-preparing. I do not wish to make a plea here for so-called 'appropriate' or 'alternative' technology in the classic way this debate has been presented. Third World countries are right to be wary of 'appropriate' technology when this term actually means 'second-rate'. 'Appropriate' technology can be a way of allowing the same old TNCs – or their younger sisters – to introduce technology which may be smaller-scale but which is just as dependency-creating. Some countries can't afford the biggest and brightest, but they can still contribute to corporate profits at their own level. And this technology does not even necessarily benefit the poorest people in society, as the recent development of biogas plants in India has demonstrated.

What I *do* hope is, first, that Third World decision-makers will take a far more critical look at what they assume to be advanced technology and will recognize all the hidden costs – including the social and cultural costs – that the purchase of this technology entails.

Second, I hope they will foster and encourage on every possible occasion local solutions to local problems. The pharmaceuticals factory at Savar is one excellent example, and because it is already effective and can become even more effective, we may be absolutely certain that the TNC drug firms in Bangladesh will fight back. I look forward to learning that this fight has been won by Savar and Savar's supporters.

Third, those of us who would like to see authentic and autonomous development in the Third World – the kind of development which cannot be accomplished under the present regime of dependency – do not say Small is Beautiful or Big is Beautiful but that Choice is Beautiful. Every technological decision should be aimed at giving the country the maximum number of options. In my view, the most direct road to greater flexibility and to the creation of wealth and a decent livelihood for all is through the choice of decentralized, labour-intensive technologies. But 'decentralized' and 'labour-intensive' do not necessarily mean 'simple'. Some of these choices may, indeed, be far more sophisticated than anything the West is in a position to offer. This would be the case, for example, with agricultural technologies based on polyculture, crop interactions, and environment-enhancing crop protection techniques. By comparison, Western agricultural methods are extremely crude.

Advocates of autonomous development further believe that there are enormous reservoirs of hidden creativity in the Third World which are at present stifled or going to waste. Allowing this creativity to surface means taking the knowledge of peasants and workers into account and building upon it to improve existing techniques. Such an approach demands a great deal of political courage, because it conflicts with so many established interests at home and abroad.

If I may make one last recommendation to technological decision-makers it is this: The next time someone calls you a technocrat, be proud of the title. Remember that it comes from the Greek *kratia* or *kratos* meaning 'power' or 'strength'. This power and strength can serve the cause of outsiders and place your country under the yoke of dependency. But with the help of your people, it can also make you free.

# 6
# BIOBUSINESS:
# LIFE FOR SALE

*In June 1984, my friend and colleague John Cavanagh organized a conference at the Institute for Policy Studies (TNI's sister Institute in Washington, DC) on the theme 'Meeting the Corporate Challenge'. It turned out to be an interesting and successful mix of economists and academic specialists on several industries, trade unionists and community organizers, mostly Americans. John needed someone to write about the biotechnology industry, at that time quite new but growing fast. He picked me, knowing I had recently helped on a (UK) Central Television-Channel Four film called 'The Gene Business', directed by Alan Bell. As the on-screen presenter and narrator of the film, I'd given myself a cram course in biotechnology but was far from being an expert in the field. Happily, the television researchers had pulled together part of the documentation, so I did not have to start from scratch.*

*The context of the IPS conference explains why this piece is principally US-oriented and concentrates on the 'corporate challenge' there. John hadn't left me much time to prepare my conference communication, so, true to George Bernard Shaw's Law ('I have written you a long letter because I did not have time to write you a short one'), the original version was too detailed. I've cut it by about a quarter for publication here and made some stylistic alterations, but, just as with other pieces in this collection, have left my actual views untouched, warts and all.*

*In particular, I should have paid attention, and did not, to the possible consequences of mass release of genetically engineered organisms into the environment. On this subject, see Paul Hatchwell, 'Opening Pandora's Box: The risks of releasing genetically engineered organisms', in* The Ecologist, *Vol. 19 no. 4 (July – August 1989).*

'Why trouble to make compounds yourself when a bug will do it for you?'
Biologist J. B. S. Haldane, 1929 (when asked his views on chemists)

I

If you believe, as I do, that there is no such animal as 'pure science'; that all scientific activity takes place in a political and economic context which influences the choices and directions of research; that in advanced capitalist societies this context will favour science which contributes both to enhanced profits and to increased social control; then you will find a perfect case-study in the burgeoning biotechnology industry.

'Biotechnology' in the strict sense has existed for millennia – ever since people have practised beer-brewing, cheese-making, or bread-baking with yeast, all of which put micro-organisms to work in order to achieve a desired culinary result. People who recycle garbage into compost for their gardens are also using biotechnology to their advantage.

The term as it is understood today in the corporate culture of the 1980s is, however, new enough not to appear in the 1976 *Concise Oxford Dictionary.* Let us begin, therefore, with some home-made definitions.

Back to basics: the Greek *bios* = life; *tekhné* = art; *tekhnologia* = systematic treatment. So biotechnology = systematic application of human art (and artifice) to use, control or modify life-processes.

A more modern definition, indicating a healthy regard for economic facts of life, is this one: 'Biotechnology may be defined as the utilization of microbial, plant or animal cells, or their constituents, to provide goods and services.'[1]

But to return to the scientific context, let us recall one of the events which precipitated the so-called economic crisis of the early 1970s. This was the sudden emergence, in 1973, of OPEC on the international scene. The 'oil-price shock' was subsequently blamed for all the ills of the West. Even though authoritative bodies like the OECD announced that increased oil prices did not account for more than 1–2 per cent of Western inflation, the common perception of businessmen and ordinary people alike was that Third World upstarts were successfully racketeering Western industry.

What, exactly, was it that the OPEC countries largely controlled? Not just supplies of petrol and heating fuel, but the natural resource upon which a multitude of major industries, from fertilizers to plastics to synthetic fabrics, were based. In dictating the prices of petroleum, they affected not just a source of energy but one of the world's most important raw materials; they held a controlling interest in the geospheric resource base.

In the advanced capitalist countries, OPEC's emergence as an important piece on the international chessboard presented a specific challenge to science. Over the past ten years, science in these countries has been quietly providing a means of transition from the geosphere to the biosphere as a source of non-appropriable raw materials for industrial production. A major goal of biotechnology is, then, to use biological raw materials in order to do everything that could formerly be done with petroleum, and to create many wholly new products besides.[2]

In less than ten years, biotechnology has moved from the gleam-in-the-eye stage, to the feverish competition of rival corporate labs sprouting faster than cultures in agar jelly, to full-scale industrial manufacture and distribution of at least a few biotech products. Compared with this accelerated pace of development, the railroad, the automobile and the computer were economic snails.

The upheavals this new industry will create are, I believe, more profound than those that steam power, the internal combustion engine or information processing brought about in other times. The media have cried 'Revolution' so often that we do not leap to attention when another is predicted. This time, though, the 'bio-revolution' touted by journalists with startling originality is probably for real.

Those who are anticipating or dreading the moment when the economic crisis grows severe enough for capitalism-as-we-know-it to disappear can stop rejoicing or worrying, as the case may be. Another industrial shining knight has appeared on the horizon: though he may not be the definitive answer to free-enterprise prayers, he does bring remarkable new investment opportunities and a host of potential products that aren't simply replacements for old ones, but truly new items that will expand markets. Just behind him follow dozens of ancillary activities, from making enzyme amylase processing equipment to publishing literature servicing the biotechnicians to training the avant-garde lawyers who will thread their way through the thickets of life-process law. All this will provide gainful employment for some – mostly the highly educated – and remarkable profits for a favoured few.

## II

Citizens and consumers should understand that even before they may purchase present or potential biotech products, they will have already paid for them. This they have done indirectly through their contributions to the profits that built the great private family foundations; or directly through funding public research with their taxes. Although the biotechnology industry is a product of the last decade alone, the scientific activity which allowed its existence has a much longer history.

The processes which lead to setting certain scientific goals rather than others; the debates, the in-fighting, the struggles for funding which accompany these processes are all part of the economic and political context which determines how people will be affected by any industry that emerges from them. Thus a brief history of the underpinnings of this industry and a succinct description of earlier scientific achievements are relevant here.

The United States has not always looked upon an organized science policy as a function of government. Not until the onset of World War II was coordination of scientific endeavours recognized as necessary for national survival. Earlier in the century, especially during the 1930s, science policy formulation fell chiefly to major private foundations, with the Rockefeller Foundation in the forefront. Indeed, the terms 'molecular biology' and 'sub-cellular biology' were first coined in this Foundation's *Annual Report* in 1938.

The growth and development of molecular biology were consciously fostered by the Foundation's then Director, Warren Weaver, who speculatively compared the breakthroughs that could be achieved in biology with those that had already taken place in particle physics. His analogical argument held that, if the atom could be split with far-reaching scientific and social consequences, then so could the living cell. Weaver wanted the credit for creating this new scientific discipline. He pointed out in particular that the Rockefeller Foundation, under his leadership, had contributed $90 million to molecular biology between 1932 and 1957 and he obtained written testimonials from numerous scientists to that effect.[3]

Edward Yoxen believes that in creating the new discipline of molecular biology, Weaver and Rockefeller knew exactly what they were doing:

> What Weaver did was to develop a system of patronage and direction of research, i.e. to bring modern management to science ... [Throughout the '30s he] channelled extremely valuable support ... to a number of scientists whose work coalesced in the post-war discipline of molecular biology. But the significance of the programme lies not only in its having accelerated a selected number of linked lines of technical and theoretical activity. Weaver's refinement of

bureaucratic techniques and his development and application of a new mode of control over science illustrated ... that research could be selectively supported and officially managed.[4]

The 'horse's mouth' on matters pertaining to molecular biology is doubtless J. D. Watson who, with Francis Crick, cracked the riddle of DNA's structure, about which more in a moment. At the 1983 Thirtieth Anniversary Conference celebrating the publication of Watson and Crick's historic paper in *Nature*, Nobel laureate Watson remarked,

> I guess people like me have lots of debts to acknowledge ... there were two unique patrons – people who protect you if you're trying to do something different. One was the Rockefeller Foundation. It really started the thing ... it gave money (to several projects and institutions with which Watson was associated) ... the Rockefeller Foundation did this because of one man, Warren Weaver ... Weaver provided a spirit in which younger people could think.[5]

The wartime and post-war social context of science was a quite different one from that of the 1930s. In 1944, the Public Health Service Act provided legislative authority for the government to grant research funds to universities – an authority which continues to this day. The National Institutes of Health and the National Science Foundation were similarly established by Congress after the war. From the initial $3 million in public funds allocated for basic biomedical research in 1948, the annual figure has now climbed to over $3 billion. For the past forty years, as an MIT Professor of biology points out, 'American taxpayers [have] financed the training of biomedical researchers, the equipping of their laboratories, the salaries of support staff and the purchase of supplies and material [as well as] the organization of open scientific meetings, travel to those meetings, the publishing of scientific journals and the fiscal support for publishing papers.'[6]

Let us now note an interesting phenomenon (or, rather, its absence). Whereas major American corporations have for decades made heavy research investments in chemistry (e.g. DuPont), physics (e.g. General Electric), or cybernetics and information theory (e.g. Bell Telephone, IBM); whereas their scientists have often made outstanding advances in these fields; one would seek in vain a single company devoting comparable time and money to basic biomedical research.

The likeliest candidates would be large pharmaceuticals firms. Their research, however, was and is of a different nature, focusing almost exclusively on remedies, not on causes of disease. Research on causes might soon obviate the need for remedies, and thus for many corporate drugs, some of which must be absorbed by captive-purchaser patients for years if they are to maintain their health.

Curative strategies undertaken against major diseases like cancer, as Lewis Thomas has explained in his superb book, *The Lives of a Cell*, are hugely expensive and represent:

> ... halfway technology in the sense that these measures are directed against the existence of already established cancer cells, but not at the mechanisms by which cells become neoplastic ... This kind of technology costs an enormous amount of money ... The only thing that can move medicine away from this level of technology is new information, and the only imaginable source of this information is research ... The real high technology of medicine ... comes as the result of a genuine understanding of disease mechanisms, and when it becomes available it is relatively inexpensive and relatively easy to deliver.[7]

The last things the drug or the hospital-based health-care industries want, since they play by normal corporate rules, are measures which are 'relatively inexpensive and relatively easy to deliver'.

This brief discussion of biotech's background is meant to tell us something about science and society in advanced capitalist countries, particularly the USA. On a related subject (the so-called 'Green Revolution') I have tried to show elsewhere that private foundations based on vast family fortunes have a vital interest in maintaining the status quo.[8] Paradoxically, this means initiating change – orderly change which will be of ultimate benefit to the dominant free-market system. Such change should, ideally, also reinforce this system's ideological and economic control over the millions of people who cannot be permitted any genuine participation in decision-making, since they might then decide to upset the corporate apple-cart and demand that those who pay the costs receive their share of the benefits.

The promotion of orderly change – which keeps the system resilient and lessens its vulnerability to pressure – is not a task which corporations as such can undertake. Business's time-horizons are too short; it must concentrate on immediate profits. Foundations, on the other hand, have no balance-sheets to worry about and are accountable to no one, except to a hand-picked board. They can wait as long as need be for returns on investment: twenty years before witnessing the initial effects of the Green Revolution; even longer in the case of molecular biology and bio-technology.

Furthermore, in our century one measure of successful national policy is the capacity to fund research programmes which cannot be expected to yield immediate commercial advantages, but whose long-term payoff will ensure the continued power (sometimes even hegemony) of the State and of the global corporations headquartered within its borders. Some might argue, wrongly in my view, that business is simply too dumb to recognize what efforts will lead to profits several years down the road. On the contrary, business is shrewd enough to wait for governments to make the investments, take the risks, eliminate the less viable and more costly prospects and, in the fullness of time, deposit the lucrative results on the doorsteps of the private sector.

Today's biotechnology came from the work of thousands of people who patiently dug the foundations, built the walls and raised the roofbeams of an enormous edifice. These prodigious labours now accomplished, corporations new and old are crowding and jostling one another on the building site to put the final slates on the roof and call the whole place their own. The case of insulin, cited by Professor Jonathan King of MIT, is 'a clear example; most of the research on the biochemistry of the insulin molecule, the growth of cells in culture, the control of gene expression, the development of recombinant DNA technology was publicly developed; yet a few corporations will glean the profit off of the product'.[9] It is thus not surprising that human insulin was indeed the first fully fledged biotech product to be mass marketed (by Genentech).

## III

The existence of this new science-based industry has, naturally, provoked debate; in fact several debates. These can be classed by subject, which we will treat with unequal thoroughness. They concern (1) *safety* (will uncontrollable man-made organisms escape from labs and provoke untreatable epidemics?); (2) *ethics* (what limits, if any, should be set on human capacity to interfere with life processes and/or to create new life-forms?); (3) *legal-judicial issues* (what is patentable? who owns biotech products and processes?); and (4) *the relationship between the university and business* (what compatibility or mutual exclusion exists between free circulation of knowledge and corporate competition and secrecy; between social benefits of research and commercial applications?).

A more fundamental debate, of which the above would be subcategories, ought to be taking place, but there are few signs of it: who will (should) control biotechnology; what will (should) be its effects upon relationships between various social groups within the industrialized countries and, more broadly, between the rich and poor nations and peoples of the world?

Before trying to cope with the vast implications of all this, I shall first attempt a succinct description of the scientific principles involved (fascinating, but beyond the scope of this paper except as they bear on patenting and ownership questions); then provide a laundry list of biotech products, present and future; and, finally, recount some deals cut between academia and corporate sponsors and their likely consequences – negative, in my view – for the freedom and future of scientific inquiry.

## The Genetic Breakthrough

Several readable accounts exist on the earlier history of DNA discoveries.[10] Despite the huge body of practical and theoretical scientific work establishing the nature and structure of DNA (whose strands are the material support or substratum for any organism's genes), until the early 1970s it was methodologically and technically impossible to isolate these genes and thus to manipulate them. Problems of scale and the disproportion between the length of a gene and that of all of a given specie's DNA made genetic manipulation a technical impossibility. For example, a single gene represents about one one-millionth of the human DNA ribbon: how could one select such a minute segment for analysis and, even then, how could one obtain sufficient quantities in sufficiently pure form?

One successful strategy was the use of 'restriction enzymes' which are able not only to prise open lengths of genetic material at specifically chosen points but also leave sticky ends so that a gene from a completely different organism can be spliced in. Thus DNA from different organisms is 'recombined' and the function and behaviour of each gene introduced can then be determined by examining the new, different hereditary behaviour of the 'host' DNA, which will replicate the introduced genetic characteristic. Specific restriction enzymes always cut at exactly the same place, and the bacterium (*E. coli*) into which the new gene is introduced will reproduce itself every twenty minutes – thereby solving the problems of accurate segmentation and sufficient pure quantities.[11]

*Present and Potential Products of Recombinant DNA*

The special character of recombinant DNA (rDNA) is its capacity to create entirely new organisms which would never – not even with millions more years of evolution – occur in nature. As Haldane, quoted in the epigraph to this chapter, predicted 55 years ago, one can now 'get a bug to produce compounds'. My examples are limited here to the productions of 'bugs'; classic techniques of plant or animal breeding (a slower and more empirical method of obtaining desirable genetic characteristics) and biological (though not genetic) manipulations such as 'test-tube babies' are not included.

*Business Week* and similar publications wax lyrical on the subject of recombinant DNA products. In a sense, it's easy to share their excitement. Genetic engineering could be the key to preventing and curing major diseases in human beings and animals, to cleaning up the environment, to higher productivity in farming. I shall first describe the achievements of the biotech industry neutrally, reserving the socio-political implications for later.

As of July 1982, researchers at Cornell's Rural Sociology Center counted 350 biotech firms.[12] A year and a half later, *Business Week* spoke of 'an incredible $2.5 billion ... invested in more than 100 companies dedicated to pioneering new products from biotechnology'.[13] Perhaps both figures are correct and we've already witnessed a shake-out of 200 or so companies in the initial running. Surely there will be many more losers before we're done, and any list of products, or of companies, is guaranteed to be out of date within days of its reaching the reader.

The winners, however, will be the IBMs of the twenty-first century. The US Congress Office of Technology Assessment has predicted sales of gene-spliced products amounting to at least $15 billion within fifteen years. Some commercial sources are more optimistic still. Pharmaceuticals were first to be affected by biotech in a big way, an industry subdivided into three: curative or defensive substances; diagnostic aids; preventive substances (vaccines).

Traditionally, drug company research meant tedious testing of compound after chemical compound to see what worked. Biological techniques allow instead the identification of the body's own defences against disease. These factors can then be reproduced in the lab and, eventually, marketed. The first drug to pass muster with the FDA was human insulin. Growth hormones were next; several different sorts of interferons (which may be effective against some cancers) will follow. Other substances will prevent or encourage blood-clotting for heart patients and haemophiliacs.

In the diagnostics field, monoclonal antibodies are the stars. Paine Webber predicted in 1983 a market of nearly $4 billion for diagnostic products by 1988, with monoclonals bringing 25 per cent. The *Financial Times* notes that in the *Directory of Biologicals*, published by *Nature*, 'monoclonal antibodies, previously hardly mentioned, have proliferated to 83 different categories'. *Nature* itself comments, 'breeding like rabbits, monoclonals will no doubt overwhelm next year's *Directory*'.[14] Feverish work is proceeding in hopes of producing a herpes vaccine; one against hepatitis B seems well advanced.

A related field is animal health care. Lots of smart money is invested here – for example, in molecular genetics, which is 'trying to develop a solid financial base quickly by concentrating on animal health care products, which the government typically approves faster than it does drugs for humans'.[15] The first product marketed cures a disease afflicting calves, called scours. The President of Genetic Engineering, Inc., says, 'We are entering the era of embryo engineering' (in animal breeding). Another corporate executive reports, 'Changes that took a hundred years are now happening in two months.' Direct manipulation of the genes of cows could, according to a University of Minnesota scientist, produce an animal giving 45,000 lb of milk yearly (as compared to 15,000 lb maximum today). That is, if one isn't afraid to milk it – it would be as big as an elephant. Disease resistance and other qualities may also in future be spliced into target genes in a fertilized animal egg, or a clone.[16]

What gains does biotechnology promise for plants and for agribusiness? Two private think tanks claim that agricultural products issuing from gene-splicing techniques 'might be as large as $50–100 billion a year by the end of the century', whereas, according to them, medical and pharmaceutical applications would not ring up sales of more than $10 billion. This particular prediction may be taken with a grain, if not a bucketful, of salt: the two firms making it are selling their 457-page report entitled 'An Assessment of the Global Potential of Genetic Engineering in the Agribusiness Sector' for $1,250 a copy.[17]

A more conservative view is taken by the President of one of the major US seed corporations, Thomas N. Urban of Pioneer Hi-Bred International. He does not see genetic engineering replacing traditional plant-breeding techniques because it 'cannot simultaneously work with large numbers of genes, which is a prerequisite for most hybrid and variety improvement. Plants have some 10,000 genes, and very few of their characteristics are controlled by a single gene.' Recombinant DNA methods can nevertheless speed up present techniques. Urban also puts a damper on media hype surrounding the search for a corn plant able to fix its own nitrogen out of the atmosphere, thus eliminating the need for fertilizer. '[This] just won't happen. A nitrogen-fixing corn plant would have a 30 per cent lower yield' (because the plant would expend too much energy in fixing its nitrogen).[18]

Other companies are betting on genetically engineered corn as a middle-term prospect, but are most interested in improving its protein content or in making it resistant to herbicides. Herbicide resistance is an understandably hot research field. Now that nearly all seed producers have been purchased by chemical corporations, the possibilities for linking product sales are enormous: 'Only *our* seed will resist *our* herbicide'. It should soon be possible as well to splice genes that will 'express' themselves only in that part of the plant one chooses to modify – the roots, leaves, grain, etc.[19]

Corporations like Heinz and Campbells are interested in genetic engineering of tomatoes with less water, which could cut their processing costs and 'get more cans of soup per dollar'. As the Chairman of Agrigenetics, which is working on the problem, says, 'Tomato processors would like a wooden tomato' if they could breed one.[20]

Biotechnology is already an important factor in the food-processing industry. Future food will increasingly be fabricated food, made up not of plant or animal raw materials *per se* but of their constitutive elements, combined to make new products. For example, industry is not interested so much in 'milk' as in casein, lactose, etc. A report commissioned by the OECD notes that it will soon be more accurate to speak of a 'food extraction' industry, coupled with a 'food recomposition' industry. The first would separate the proteins, starches, sugars, flavours, etc.; the second put them back together, biologically modified, purified and stabilized into new foods I would rather call edible objects.[21]

The most potentially beneficial aspect of plant biotechnology will be its capacity to extend the number of natural environments able to sustain agriculture. Plants that prefer saline soils already exist in the lab; others could be engineered to grow in drought conditions or to resist low temperatures, thus allowing extension of farmland and earlier planting. This could lead to double or even triple cropping.

Outside agriculture and agribusiness, other applications of biotechnology are in the laboratory stage and may rapidly be scaled up to full production. 'Bugs' can be taught to latch on to certain minerals or chemicals and separate them from others. They thus hold promise for recovering valuable elements from waste material, squeezing the last drops of oil from nearly dry holes, or rendering toxic substances harmless.

## Who's Involved? Corporate–University Bed-Fellowship

I am concerned that the flow of new corporate money into the [biotech] field is having a negative impact on universities. There's not a molecular biologist worth his salt who isn't a consultant to private industry, and this will cut down the amount of basic research to be done on the public level. Free enterprise is a wonderful thing, but 'hot stocks' probably do not benefit the world of serious basic research.[22]

This not an academic spoilsport speaking but the chairman of one of America's leading seed corporations. Whatever his misgivings, university–corporate relationships have a long history in the US. The arrangements made since the advent of biotech do, however, represent a qualitative leap. When the first stirrings of the microchip revolution occurred, academics who knew computers and wanted a piece of the financial action left their institutions for good and went to Silicon Valley. Not so molecular biologists. Silicon Valley, so to speak, has come to them.

There are three sorts of actors involved in biotech:

1. The major, established, usually transnational corporation that does not want to be left out of a burgeoning field and has the money to branch out. Most of these are chemical and pharmaceutical firms. They are beefing up their in-house research capacity and also calling on the next two categories.

2. The 'research boutique', usually founded by a couple of people with a couple of patentable ideas, good enough to attract venture capital. These are the upstart firms that attracted much media hype in the early '80s. A few of these knowledge-intensive companies will acquire the critical mass needed to become manufacturers and distributors while retaining their strong and indispensable R&D base (Genentech is the most obvious candidate); others will survive as specialized science shops as the industry diversifies and the division of labour becomes more rigorous. Most will disappear.

3. Entire university departments – of biology, medicine, plant

genetics, etc., or individual members of these departments making a variety of contractual arrangements with corporations large and small, always with the encouragement and the endorsement of university governing bodies.

All activity in biotech today is the result of some permutation of these three variables: conventional marriages between a large and a small corporation or a university, or more complex *ménages à trois*. Corporations are sources of money for hard-pressed universities; even the most prestigious have gone to the altar. In return, the companies are receiving unprecedented rewards, including, sometimes, the right to demand that basic research results not be published. These arrangements are so recent and there have been so few holdouts within academia that the case seems already to have been closed before any debate has taken place.

The events now taking place around biotechnology reinforce the view that science is becoming more and more a commodity and a tool for controlling the national and the world economy. As such, it will be fought over, for enormous power and profits are at stake. Real political struggles concerning access to science will necessarily occur more frequently, and power relationships will often be expressed through control over basic science as they have been expressed over the control of technology (for example, nuclear or satellite technology). Such struggles are likely to be won by corporate entities (often transnational in scope) with assistance from the State. Whoever wins, we know that science has become far too important to leave to scientists.

*The Corporate Campus: How Business is Buying Biology*

Some academics are deeply concerned by business involvement in fundamental research. One is Leon Wofsy, professor of immunology at the University of California, Berkeley, who decided to speak out because colleagues he respected tended to see the question of scientific collaboration with business exclusively in terms of 'personal ethics'.

Wofsy situates the debate quite differently:

> The business of business is to make money, to beat the competition, and the mode is secrecy, a proprietary control of information and the fruits of research. The motive force of the University is the pursuit of knowledge, and the mode is open exchange of ideas and unrestricted publication of the results of research.[23]

Both these missions, says Wofsy, may be perfectly valid, but they ought to be kept separate.

As competition heats up to secure the services of individual biologists, so does competition between universities themselves. Thus, Wofsy points out, 'If MIT makes a deal in excess of a hundred million dollars with the Whitehead family, other universities must scramble for comparable coups − at stake is the ability to compete, claims to status and ranking, the familiar game of "Who's Number One?".'

The answer to the last question is, for the moment, MIT. Harvard Medical School trails well behind with $6 million received from DuPont for a new genetics department. The agreement specifies that Harvard will hold the patents resulting from discoveries financed by this grant, while DuPont will receive exclusive rights to make use of such patents through licensing arrangements. While $6 million may be real money for Harvard Med, it is peanuts for DuPont, whose total research budget was $571 million in 1981, the year it made the Harvard deal. Company spokespersons say that DuPont will not attempt to set the research agenda but is, rather, 'interested in contributing to basic research in the molecular genetics field, with the opportunity to draw on the results'.[24]

Another corporate contract involves Harvard's teaching hospital (Massachusetts General) which is bound to the West German pharmaceuticals giant, Hoechst. Mass General will get $70 million over ten years to establish a new department of molecular biology; it will allow the company to obtain the research findings before anyone else does and to take out exclusive licences on 'related commercial procedures'. Both granter and grantee have refused to release full details of their contract; even Congress is worried that a foreign corporation may reap the benefits of research at least partly acquired through US public funding.[25]

Other deals include Montsanto and Rockefeller University ... Montsanto and Washington University, Saint Louis ... Celanese and Yale ... MIT and Exxon. One amazing transformation is that of the Stanford University Department of Medicine. Under the terms of its contract with Syntex, each of the eighty members of this department must spend up to eight days a year consulting for this biotech firm. Since this could be judged to be beyond the university pale, the department undergoes metamorphosis as it enters into contract with Syntex and becomes the 'Institute of Biological Investigation'. Wofsy characterizes this deal as one of the 'more open, less sleazy' ones.

These contracts, however, are dwarfed by what has been termed the 'merger' of MIT and the 'Whitehead Institute for Biomedical Research', a wholly private entity. The WIBR, adjoining the MIT campus, will devote itself to molecular genetic research and developmental biology. So far so good. What makes it a new breed of cat is its 'joint faculty' with MIT (salaries paid by Whitehead), its ownership of all patents resulting from research carried out by this joint faculty, and its unprecedented right to initiate the appointments of up to fifteen faculty members.[26]

Some influential figures have been troubled by the blurring of corporate–university frontiers. President Donald Kennedy of Stanford declared to a Congressional committee in 1981 that too many university biologists with stockholdings in biotech companies are 'abandoning informal and formal communication' because of the profit-seeking that is 'contaminating' free and open scientific inquiry. 'At least three or four times in the past year', biologists giving papers at scientific meetings 'refused to divulge

some technique because it was now proprietary', Kennedy testi-
fied.[27]

Some months later, Kennedy, apparently less troubled,
convened the Pajaro Dunes Conference on 'Commercialism and
University Research'. Co-hosts were the Presidents of Harvard,
MIT, Cal Tech and the University of California. Who, then,
were the guests? The presidents and chief executive officers of
eleven biotech corporations, the lot funded by a $50,000 grant
from the Henry J. Kaiser Foundation. The meeting was organized
without the participation of the university community – much
less that of the public – and was closed to the press. One journalist
noted:

> If Pajaro Dunes was supposed to reassure the public that the integrity
> of its research dollar was unsullied by intermingling with corporate
> funds, the image it projected – a kind of Yalta of the mind, dividing up
> the future of public health research behind closed doors – achieved
> the opposite.[28]

## How Long is the Arm of the Law?

'If I had a child headed into a career now, I'd want him to be a
patent lawyer – preferably a biotechnology patent lawyer,' said
the president of a Massachusetts biotech firm in 1984. New
products and processes, new corporate–university relationships
require regulatory mechanisms and orderly procedures which
only the law can provide. Corporations hate unpredictability and
must know what the rules are, if only to get round them.

Alas, predictability is elusive. Here are some of the elements
adding to the confusion. Biotechnology is not a very precise
concept. It certainly is an industry, but one with fuzzy edges, not
based on a single product like, say, the microchip. While discussion here is limited to the implications of rDNA technology,
which presents formidable legal problems of its own, there are
lots of other biological products and processes the law must also
deal with: conventional seed and plant breeding, cloning, cell

fusion, fermentation technology, manipulation of human or animal embryos *in vitro*, etc.

Some law deals with products, some with processes. In the ambiguous brave new world now taking shape in the lab, various kinds of conventional law may – or may not – apply: patent law, licensing law, professional and trade secrets law, copyright law, etc. Further muddle is assured because legal systems, precedents and applications differ in Europe, the United States and Japan, the principal markets for biotech products. Here are the legal decisions we have to go on:

In 1972, Ananda Chakrabarty, a General Electrics scientist, applied for a patent on a lab-created micro-organism which might be used to 'eat' oil slicks at sea. When the US Patent Office refused, the matter was litigated and eventually reached the Supreme Court. Although Chakrabarty's bacterium wasn't created using recombinant DNA techniques, the Court's opinion has been considered the legal basis for rDNA products as well. It reads:

> The laws of nature, physical phenomena and abstract ideas have been held not to be patentable. Thus a new mineral discovered in the earth or a new plant found in the wild is not patentable subject matter. Likewise, Einstein could not patent his celebrated law that $E = mc^2$ ... Such discoveries are 'manifestations of nature, free to all men and reserved exclusively to none'. Judged in this light, respondent's micro-organism plainly qualifies as patentable subject matter. [It] is not a hitherto unknown natural phenomenon, but a non-naturally occurring manufacture or composition of matter – a product of human ingenuity 'having a distinctive name, character and use' ... His discovery is not nature's handiwork, but his own.[29]

The second legal consideration concerns the actual process of recombining DNA. Paul Berg of Stanford was the first person to combine genetic material from two different organisms and received the Nobel Prize in 1980 for his work. It did not occur to him to take out a patent on a scientific discovery, but Berg is an old-school type.

His method was pathbreaking but laborious; not what scientists would call especially 'elegant'. Simultaneously, biochemists Stanley Cohen (Stanford) and Herbert Boyer (UC-San Francisco) were developing a universal gene-splicing method. A small ring of genetic material called a plasmid is removed from an *E. coli* bacterium and opened up with a restriction enzyme; a gene is snipped from a different organism using the same enzyme; the gene is spliced into the plasmid, which goes back into a bacterium; the bacterium divides every twenty minutes or so, replicating all its genes, including the new one. The new organism can thus be called upon to produce human insulin, bovine growth hormone, interferon, etc.

The Cohen–Boyer discovery was to methodology what the Crick–Watson breakthrough was to description of structure – with the added advantage that the method had numerous immediate practical applications. The way *Time Magazine* told it,

> At first, Cohen and Boyer balked at seeking a patent for their work. But Stanford's licensing director ... changed their minds by citing the case of Alexander Fleming who had refused to take out a patent, thinking that this would ensure penicillin's widespread availability. Instead, since no company would take the financial risk of making it without patent protection, the wonder drug did not go into production until World War II, some 14 years after Fleming had identified it.[30]

So Cohen and Boyer filed and were awarded a patent on their process; the Supreme Court decision was held to apply to method as well as to life-forms themselves. Herb Boyer is a rich man, but that is because of his involvement with Genentech, not because of the patent, whose royalties go to Stanford.

The rule of thumb for biologists has since become 'patent first, publish later' (if at all). Genentech's legal counsel, Tom Kiley, explains that the smaller, weaker biotech companies will use patents to 'squeeze more royalty payments' to try to stay in business. This 'portends a litigious shake-out period' whose end result, Kiley believes, will be 'an industry characterized not by monopoly but by oligopoly, with relatively friendly competition and restrained use of litigation'.[31] In other words, biotechnology will come to resemble any other 'mature' US industry, where competitive price-cuts advantageous to consumers are scarcely the norm.

One legal expert, Professor Irving Kayton, argues that patent law is not the best vehicle for regulating biotechnology and calls for the application of copyright law for lab-created organisms, considered as condensed information. He says that copyright law would solve the dilemma of the corporate or university scientist whose institutions now more and more restrict the right to publish. 'Universities recognize that gold mines as well as test-tubes ... are scattered around their microbiological laboratories and that the gold is recoverable only by perfecting their property rights.' Business–academic arrangements centre on such protection. However, says Kayton, 'immediate publication and copyright protection are completely compatible. Since the creation of a genetically engineered work itself generates the protection provided by copyright, publication of research findings on the day they are made will in no way impair copyright protection of those results.'[32]

His argument has yet to be tested in court. It might, however, be the only legal way to preserve academic freedom of inquiry in the sciences. If copyright law were applied to biotech products, it would be no more shocking to reward a microbiologist who hits the research jackpot than a professor of history or literature who writes a bestseller.

### Safety and the State

During the early '70s, news started circulating in the scientific community that certain rDNA experiments planned, including one in Paul Berg's lab, might have unforeseen consequences for health and safety. In a move unprecedented in the history of science, a group of scientists led by Berg called for a moratorium on rDNA research.[33] The self-imposed moratorium was soon followed thereafter by a conference at Asilomar, California (February 1975). There, 140 participating scientists elaborated guidelines for physical and biological containment, that is, different levels of lab security and isolation according to the type of experiment; or the use of enfeebled strains of bacteria unable to survive outside the protective lab environment.

Despite Asilomar, the safety debate continued for several years. The forces inside the scientific community calling for self-regulation were the stronger: although there is a Recombinant DNA Advisory Committee at the National Institutes of Health, it is just that – advisory. Meanwhile, alarm about accidents in the lab has subsided: the mayor of Cambridge, Mass., will not find green monsters crawling out of the sewers as he feared, and scientists making remarks like some heard on the eve of Asilomar ('We are on the threshold of a biological Hiroshima') would today be laughed out of the room.

However, this doesn't mean that there should not be a safety debate on rDNA – it means simply that it should be scaled up from the lab level to that of the manufacturing facility. In Britain, the head of a team of microbiologists in the Health and Safety Executive (a counterpart to OSHA in the US) has said, 'even in microbially low-risk processes, like the processes carried out so far, which do not involve infectious or toxic hazards, allergenic risks arising from workers' exposure to foreign proteins or polypeptides have to be considered'. Companies that do not design their plants properly could expose employees to allergies and to far more serious auto-immune diseases. Correct design can be expensive: G. D. Searle spent £15 million on a genetic engineering pilot plant near London. 'A lot of money should be spent on redesigning filters and continuous monitoring of airborne contamination and the health of workers is essential,' says a professor at the British Centre for Applied Microbiology Research.[34]

So long as biotech companies remain 'research boutiques' they will probably not pose major health and safety hazards. More and more of them, however, will try to make the jump towards manufacturing in order to cash in on their research investment. They will also try to avoid government regulation (for example by the Environmental Protection Agency) and will challenge it in court. This will make the legal jungle that much thicker, and meanwhile companies may be producing biotech products unsafely. The 'biological Hiroshima', if it strikes, will be a white-collar, not a white-coat, crime.[35]

## Playing God?

At first the ethical debate on genetic engineering was grafted on to the safety debate; today it has tended to become the province of not particularly well-briefed clerics. The manifesto authored and organized by Jeremy Rifkin (and signed by everyone from the presiding bishop of the Episcopal Church to the Rev Jerry Falwell of the Moral Majority) is, in my view, unfortunate because it is wide of the mark and likely to co-opt subsequent debate on the real issues, moral and otherwise. The resolution calls for prohibition of all human gene engineering, including that which might prevent, treat or eradicate diabetes, cancer, sickle-cell anaemia, etc.[36]*Rifkin

---

* My severity here with doubtless well-meaning clergy was probably due to their signing a manifesto written by Jeremy Rifkin, whose book *Algeny* (Penguin Books, alas, 1984) is one of the shoddiest, most unscientific tracts ever published. Having thrown it across the room in 1984, I was pleased as a non-scientist to find my critical judgement confirmed in a review in *Science 85* (William J. Benetta, 'Where does this stuff come from?', July–August 1985). Some samples: '[Rifkin] shows no understanding of the biology that underlies and constrains genetic manipulations . . . To bolster [his] contentions Rifkin distorts the history, content and vocabulary of evolutionary biology, deals in sophisms only a creationist could love and borrows freely from creationist luminaries such as Duane Gish [who] . . . believes that life on earth is only a few thousand years old . . .' Given all this, and much, much more, the reviewer got in touch with the hardback publishers [Viking] to find out how this stuff saw print. 'Wasn't it vetted by somebody who understood, say, evolution or genetic engineering?' he asked. No, it wasn't, because it was considered a 'trade' book, not a textbook. 'With trade books, we just ask whether the material is consistent with itself and whether the author has said what he

says if such diseases can be cured through genetic intervention, then why not proceed to other 'disorders' which would – one gets the feeling – be defined by bodies with Hitlerian overtones. Aside from the fact that direct modification of the human genome (as opposed to diagnosis and treatment of illness caused by defective genes) is far down the road, I can only agree with David Baltimore (Director of the MIT–Whitehead joint venture) with whom I would agree on little else. He says, '[The signers of the resolution] seem happy to subject future children to torture, deformity and idiocy. What is a group of clergy doing taking that position? I can't believe they have taken into account the suffering of these people.'[37]

A real discussion of the moral issues involved (assuming direct prenatal genetic intervention becomes possible) would surely include the social pressures to 'engineer' one's children (first-class, blue-eyed, WASP genes if you have money; if not, no). Such a debate should also deal once and for all with the imbecile but ever-recurring theme, welcomed and refurbished by the right wing in every succeeding generation, of 'genetic (or biological) destiny' as a justification for all sorts of political and social inequalities.[38]

## IV

With the foregoing in mind, we will now make an attempt to assess the likely effects of biotechnology on relations between States, particularly between northern industrial countries and the

wanted to say in as clear a way as possible.' Stephen Jay Gould, a particular hero of mine, is also quoted in the review. Gould had stated, in a review of his own, 'I regard *Algeny* as a cleverly constructed tract of anti-intellectual propaganda masquerading as scholarship.' When the *Science 85* reviewer rang Gould to ask why he had taken the time to 'swat Rifkin', Gould replied, 'My attitude toward something like *Algeny* is that you should ignore it if you can. But Rifkin has gained a lot of attention and I can't hope any longer that this thing will dissolve in its own absurdities and contradictions.' I'm sticking this extra note into my own 'trade' book just in case anyone is still reading Rifkin's rubbish – even if we do have the same publisher!

Third World, and on various social groups in the industrialized countries, especially the US.

The biotech industry is likely to exacerbate competition and conflict between the industrialized countries, while simultaneously promoting the 'transnationalization of capital'. The US is ahead of the game for the moment, but other nations have recognized the value of biotech as an industry which will give a new lease on life to market economies. The US advantage rests partly on the willingness of venture capitalists to take long financial shots on fledgling companies. Major banks are also setting up specific units to invest in high-tech R&D; Morgan Stanley hired two Genentech executives to manage its unit.[39]

Britain, France, Germany and Japan rely more on State funding than on private capital, though the latter is not absent. In Britain, for example, the Government Chemist, Dr Ronald Coleman, has established an 'Action Group' made up of industrial researchers to monitor what Britain is and isn't doing in biotech. The group identifies priority research areas, promotes links between industry and academia and publishes a directory of biotech firms and venture capital firms willing to invest in them.[40]

Japan is, not surprisingly, closing the gap that temporarily separates it from the top. Between 1977 and 1981, 60 per cent of all bio-industry (not just rDNA) patents were awarded to Japanese companies. Most of the 200-odd Japanese companies now active in biotech are established firms moving out of more traditional areas like food processing or chemicals. Private investment in biotech rose 45 per cent between 1980 and 1982, according to the Ministry of Trade and Industry. MITI also started its own biotech research programme in 1981 and will divide $128 million between 113 companies over a ten-year period.[41]

Biotech corporations are already outdistancing attempts by governments to keep them 'national'. Genentech and Mitsubishi have agreed, for example, to develop jointly (and eventually to market) human serum albumin which could become immensely rewarding, since the world consumes 100 million tons of it per year. State intervention cannot really stop the transnationalization process, particularly since no international legal machinery exists on which to base it.

States may, however, refuse to take corporate activity lying down. As an Under-Secretary of State in the Carter administration put it, 'We have entered an era in which the interactions between science and technology and foreign affairs are increasingly recognized as continuous and central to many of the important foreign policy problems with which we are dealing.' The OECD has likewise acknowledged the vital role of control over science in the continuing predominance of the developed countries: 'Intellectual capital – scientific resources and the aptitude for technological innovation – constitutes the major asset of industrialized nations in the new modes of international competition and interdependence.'[42] Corporations are still likely to win the day, with the result that governments will be even more dependent upon, and subservient to, their interests than they are today.

Where does all this leave the poor nations of the Third World? Clearly, corporate control over biotech products and markets will preclude much research on 'poor people's problems' unless it is specifically funded by public benefactors. This point was graphically underlined by a stockbroker specializing in biotech companies:

> One could produce, with today's technology, a vaccine against malaria. Here, though, the question is ... the economic question ... not for the scientist to determine but a question for the businessman and for people like the World Health Organization and the medical establishment, as to what we want to do and how we are going to pay for it.[43]

The stockbroker is correct. So long as most victims of a disease cannot pay for its prevention or its cure, corporations will take no interest in them, whatever their number. Indeed, New York University researchers, with the help of USAID and WHO funding, have already developed the necessary biological knowledge and skills for creating a malaria vaccine. Scaling up these techniques to the production stage would require corporate cooperation, so Genentech was approached. After two years of negotiations, the company finally backed out because WHO would not give it exclusive licensing rights to the vaccine, i.e. the right to collect a royalty on every dose administered.[44]

The nations and people of the Third World will also be profoundly affected by the developments of biotechnology. Trading patterns, particularly in basic raw materials, will undergo extreme shifts. Substitutions for Third World products are nothing new, of course, but they are likely to accelerate. The consequences of the biorevolution may be most serious of all for the Third World peasantry, if we are to believe the persuasive arguments of a team of rural sociologists at Cornell who are examining its probable impact. The Cornell team points out that the social effects of the Green Revolution, however harmful to Third World peasants, were still confined to relatively limited geographical areas. The research that led to the Green Revolution technology 'package' was, furthermore, 'conceived and implemented within an institutional structure comprised mainly of *public and quasi public organisations*' – the network of international research institutes (funded by governments, the World Bank, and private US foundations like Ford and Rockefeller). These authors believe that 'the dislocations stimulated by the inequitable deployment of Green Revolution technologies could have been considerably worse had [these international institutions] not been committed to a mission-oriented ideology of "public interest"'.

Naturally, transnational corporations made money on GR technology – but this time round, with biotechnology, international organizations are likely to be totally short-circuited since 'private capital is willing to act as the principal agent of technological transfer and development' for the 'biorevolution'. Biotechnology can provide products allowing improved cultivation in all types of soil – not just in the better-endowed areas favoured by the GR.

For instance, 'in Southeast Asia alone there are 86.5 million hectares of poor soils unsuitable for traditionally bred [Green Revolution] High Yielding Varieties because of adverse soil conditions'. In other words, as biotech penetrates further and further into the Third World countryside, we can expect increased polarization of farmers, between those who can afford the biotechnology package and those who can't. Marginalization of the majority, already living on poorer land, will occur, just as happened with the GR, unless governments adopt counter-measures.[45]

In a narrow sense, it is clear that biotechnology, properly used and distributed, holds the promise of a brighter future for poor countries. It could add value to their raw materials (for example, changing seaweed into glucose); reduce their dependency on imported oil; provide the means to make marginal soils productive and thus grow more food, while making room for many more cultivators; produce tree-shoots in huge quantities (through cell-cloning) and solve the firewood crisis; prevent or cure the major viral or parasitical diseases, etc. One does not, therefore, want to be overly pessimistic in an assessment of the prospects for Third World countries as participants in the biorevolution.

It is, however, realistic to point out the very real obstacles they face. First is the extremely sophisticated level of the science and technology involved and the rapid division of labour they are undergoing. Most of the poorer countries have nowhere near the number of scientists needed to provide a research base; even if they had the lab support, they do not have the industrial plant to actually manufacture rDNA products. 'Simple' things – like a steady supply of electrical power – and a high level of industrial design capacity are prerequisites for success in biotech.

Second is the thorough capitalist penetration of the field. Exchanges between university colleagues and State transfers of technology under aid programmes (however limited these may have been in the past) will vanish as corporations monopolize biotech and regulate it themselves through the international legal system of patents, licensing agreements and the like. Up to now, such legal devices have always been used to prevent Third World countries from becoming technologically independent. Unless there is a unified and extremely well-financed effort on the part of LDCs (unlikely at this juncture), the promises of biotechnology will fade, and the 'revolution' will bring an increasing gap between rich and poor.

The impact biotechnology will have on the lives of industrialized countries' citizens requires only a concluding summary here. We have already covered the main points: private interests well placed to prevail over public ones and the alarming incorporation of universities into commercial ventures.

Biotech will create many new jobs – almost exclusively for the highly educated. The division of labour in science itself will be modified and further hierarchized. The most prestigious microbiologists will also be entrepreneurs and consultants; those not quite so brilliant will become run-of-the-mill, assembly-line scientists, even if they do have Ph.D.s, as most of them will. Such people will have little or no control over research goals, nor over the products engendered by their labour. In this they will be exactly like other industrial workers. Conversely, biotech will destroy industrial jobs in the traditional chemical or food- processing industries.

In the industrialized countries, recombinant DNA products have the potential to reduce private and public health costs, to improve agriculture, to reduce the costs of raw materials in nearly everything one buys, etc. It is, however, unlikely that consumers will benefit much, because this potential will remain unrealized. Corporations do not pass on savings when they reduce their costs. The present period – full of mergers, acquisitions and the general swapping of partners – will not last long as industrial time-scales go. Biotech will become oligopolistic – in the usual 'American way'. The benefit one derives from any biotechnological 'fix' will depend largely on one's income.

People on the receiving end of this new industry must first understand that they cannot count on any of the traditional forces to buffer the biotech shock; neither private foundations nor universities nor government – much less corporations – will help them out. The biotech 'debate' has opened and closed so fast that one is at a loss to know what to recommend: certainly the kind of clerical appeal described above can only be ineffectual, silly and miss the point entirely.

If it *is* possible, through public awareness, to reopen the debate, it should concern who is to control the directions and the products of biotechnology. One could not find a better point of departure than the eighteenth-century economist (who considered himself a 'moral philosopher'), Adam Smith, in *The Wealth of Nations* (1776):

> The interest of the dealers, however, in any particular branch of trade or manufactures, is always in some respects different from, and even opposite to, that of the public. To widen the market and to narrow the competition, is always the interest of the dealers ... to narrow the competition must always be against [the public] and can serve only to enable the dealers ... to levy, for their own benefit, an absurd tax upon the rest of their fellow-citizens. The proposal of any new law or regulation of commerce which comes from this order ought always to be listened to with great precaution, and ought never to be adopted till after having been long and carefully examined, not only with the most scrupulous but with the most suspicious attention. It comes from an order of men whose interest is never exactly the same with that of the public, who have generally an interest to deceive and even to oppress the public, and who accordingly have upon many occasions, both deceived and oppressed it.

# PART III

# RESEARCH, IDEOLOGY
# AND CULTURE

# 7
# DECOLONIZING RESEARCH

*This report for the United Nations University (UNU) is the result of a group effort, for which I acted as rapporteur and did the writing. In 1979, Dr Johan Galtung, who was then directing an ambitious and wide-ranging research project for the UNU called 'Goals, Processes and Indicators of Development', convened a 'Food Study Group' in the framework of the GPID project. The Group first met (5–7 February 1979) to produce a paper for a joint seminar of two UNU programmes – the World Hunger Programme and the Human and Social Development Programme (GPID was part of the latter). After this seminar, held at MIT in March, the Group reconvened with a number of new people to extend and deepen its initial considerations on research (8–10 July 1979).*

*The following paper summarizes the FSG's work on these various occasions. Some twenty people were involved in one or both of the Group's working sessions, so it's impossible to indicate here who contributed which elements.*

*The Group's full membership was: Claude Alvares, Russel Anderson, George Aseniero, Sartaj Aziz, Brita Brandtzaeg, Joseph Collins, Taghi Farvar, Ernest Feder, Louis-François Fléri, Johan Galtung, Susan George, Lim Teck Ghee, Cuautemoc Gonzales P., Papa Kane, Gretchen Klotz, Adolfo Mascarenhas, D. D. Narula, David Pitt, Rahmat Qureshi, Pierre Spitz, Filomina Steady and Ponna Wignaraja; plus two observers from the UN Research Institute for Social Development, Alemayehu Bessabih and Laurence Wilhelm. The final report is reproduced here (with a few paragraphs from the first paper for the MIT seminar added) and with the kind permission of the United Nations University.*

## Dimensions and Rationale of the Food Problem

The food problem has many dimensions, but in the context of an economy of consumption it can be visualized as a sliding scale with clinically defined overconsumption at the top and physiological starvation at the bottom, with varying degrees of qualitative and quantitative adequacy and inadequacy beween them. Such gradations correspond roughly to socio-economic categories and especially to income levels. The only *serious* food problem in today's world is, however, that of the hunger of millions of people who do not get enough to eat to satisfy their minimum needs.[1]

Hunger exists not only because of the maldistribution of food itself but also because of highly skewed income distribution which precludes the purchase of adequate amounts of food. Maldistribution of income is, in turn, a function of maldistribution of wealth and of a private ownership system which imposes no upper limit on individual or corporate control of the means of production – including those of food production – nor on the amount of wealth which can be accumulated. In contrast, the lower limit, that of zero ownership or even sub-zero ownership (e.g. in the case of chronic indebtedness), is only too clearly defined.

Hunger is also a function of the misappropriation of human and physical resources. Capitalist entrepreneurs are not in the business of providing employment nor of satisfying the needs of society as a whole, but are guided by the profit motive. In capitalist economies, income distribution determines not only consumption but *consumption patterns*. In other words, the system's priorities will encourage the production of foodstuffs and other goods which yield the highest profits and which are therefore geared to satisfying the needs (or the whims) of those who can pay. Such priorities will also, obviously, determine the *use-patterns* of human and physical resources. A perverse resource/use-pattern will correspond to a perverse income/consumption pattern in which market, i.e., monetary, demand will direct the flows of raw materials, including foods, and finished goods.

It is therefore altogether logical that countries in which a high percentage of the population suffers from hunger and malnutrition should often be the same ones that supply traditional or perishable cash crops to affluent purchasers, generally in the northern hemisphere but also to Third World elites. People without purchasing power are placed, *ipso facto*, outside the market and exert no influence whatever over what it will provide.

Arguments stressing the existence of enough food in the world to furnish each of the planet's inhabitants with a daily diet of over 3,000 calories are striking but may tend to obscure the fact that no country on earth, including the richest, has yet reached the outer limits of what its population (given sufficient income) can consume in terms of *value*, not numerical calories. Wealthy consumers often enjoy regimens of 8,000 to 10,000 calories per day if the large proportion of animal-based products in their diets is calculated in grain-equivalent terms.

It remains to be seen whether a system entirely based on profits and purchasing power will continue to provide some food for the indigent in order to forestall major upheavals which could endanger its overall hegemony. Food aid plays a vital role here, as do free, or subsidized, food-distribution schemes. The palliative aspects of food distribution under capitalist conditions will depend on the balance of forces within each particular national community and upon the rank and importance of particular nations in the international system (e.g. the major beneficiaries of food aid). Whatever the level of aid to the destitute, it constitutes neither a permanent nor a structural solution to the persistence of hunger.

## Classic Development Strategies and Control over Food Systems

In the past quarter-century, huge transfers of capital and technology have led to the extension of perverse resource-use and resource-enjoyment patterns in the Third World, where the present and probable future food situation must be examined in the context of expanding capitalist control. The tendency of Western development planners and of Third World nationals trained in their methods has been to take a piecemeal approach towards hunger alleviation. Thus, instead of seeing the food problem as a function of a chain or *system* which begins with inputs (physical as well as intangible, e.g. research and credit), proceeds through food production *per se*, and continues through the storage, processing and distribution phases before reaching the final consumer, planners have tended to focus on one or another isolated aspect of the system. The 'Green Revolution' was a strategy concentrating on inputs, the current vogue is for 'Post-harvest Technology'; both exhibit a narrow and technocratic approach.

Strategies for particular countries are, furthermore, generally viewed as operating behind closed frontiers, without reference to international market forces or to interventions by agents representing food systems external to the one of the country concerned. To hope that such strategies will succeed – whether they focus on inputs, on increased production, reduction of post-harvest losses, provision of specific nutrients, or on any other segment of the food system chain – is utopian in so far as the central issue of the whole food system has not been confronted: the issue of control.

The question 'Who is in control?' may be answered with examples chosen at random from any point along the food system chain; one might begin at the beginning with seeds. Seeds can be selected for maximum yield (given suitable and costly inputs) or for maximum reliability under stringent climatic conditions. They may lend themselves to easy self-reproduction or may deteriorate from year to year (e.g. hybrid corn); they may be geared to plants containing maximum nutritional value or, as in some developed countries, to the needs of mechanical harvesters. If *peasants* controlled current research and reproduction of seeds, it is likely that they would ask for, and get, such characteristics as reliability rather than maximum yield, reproducibility rather than deterioration, and high energy/nutritional value. Because seed research and reproduction have been largely under the control of industrialized countries, such characteristics have not generally been sought.

Control over one aspect of the food system implies its extension to others: again, the choice of seeds determines not only the inputs required but also 'appropriate' storage and processing techniques.

One highly significant aspect of this issue of control is that exercised by rural oligarchies over poorer peasants: in village after village, a tiny local power elite holds sway over credit, marketing, access to water and other essential services, and employment (including that of family members), not to mention the use of the land itself under a variety of more or less extortionate tenancy and sharecropping arrangements. Such power has now been widely recognized; even governments which have done little or nothing to redress the balance pay lip-service to the concept of greater equality and realize that top-heavy power structures act as a 'political constraint' on food production.

## The Role of Industrialized Countries' Food Systems in the Hunger Problématique

A less widely acknowledged aspect is the increasing degree of control that developed-country food systems exert over those of the Third World. The expansion of markets for Green Revolution inputs and other equipment or processes is only a part of the picture. The orientation of Third World agriculture is itself increasingly determined by outsiders who can provide cash markets for various kinds of produce. Many crops formerly produced in the temperate zones for temperate-zone customers are now grown more cheaply in tropical countries. Traditional cash crops have been joined by exports of luxury foods – many of them perishables – and animal foodstuffs.

The penetration of indigenous Third World food systems is largely, though by no means exclusively, carried out by transnational agribusiness corporations. These companies generally no longer wish to exercise direct control over Third World *land*, but gain a stronger hold over *activities*. Operations entailing risk, like farming itself, are left to the LDCs and their peasantries, while more profitable operations such as processing, marketing and the provision of inputs, credit, or management skills are carried out by foreign corporate interests. The latter have also recently shown a strong interest in providing storage facilities, an area hitherto largely under the control of families, villages or local authorities.

## The Transfer of a Dominant Model

When industrialized countries intervene in the food systems of Third World nations, they are not merely providing separate items and techniques, nor even a 'package' of techniques. With the help of their foundations, their universities, their corporations and their banks, they are transferring a *dominant model*, which, over time, will tend to become unique as it blots out and absorbs the rich variety of peasant practices.

This model originated in the West, particularly in the United States, where prevailing conditions included plentiful land and relatively little labour for food production. It was therefore economically (although no longer ecologically) a rational response to the constraints of a well-defined geographical and social situation. The goal of this model is to obtain the maximum output *per person*, not per unit of land. The conditions which gave rise to this model are wholly untypical of the LDCs, where, on the contrary, the provision of productive employment to large masses of rural people remains a major unmet priority. Because the dominant model contributes to the breakdown of traditional agriculture and to the dispossession of hundreds of thousands of peasants, it can only compound unemployment while contributing very little, if anything, to increased food production. In any event, incremental production will be even more unfairly distributed by the very fact of unemployment and consequent lack of purchasing power.

Although the promotion of the dominant model can frequently be directly traced to interventions on the part of particular Western governments, international organizations have also played a crucial role. They have at best treated the human and social objectives of development in a rhetorical way and have not allowed this rhetoric to interfere with their basic support for the Western agricultural model in the LDCs. In spite of all declarations to the contrary, they have fostered the emergence and diffusion of high-technology, capital-intensive farming.

## Socio-economic Effects of the Dominant Model in the LDCs

The adoption, in whole or in part, of the dominant model by LDC governments, encouraged by international organizations and frequently under pressure from transnational corporation and 'aid' partners, has led to a series of disastrous consequences. The gravest among them is the accelerating dissolution of self-provisioning agriculture both as a major element in peasant farming and as a subsistence base of the poorer rural strata – the prime victims of hunger. Some of the other consequences are as follows:

- Relations of production and exchange, formerly oriented more directly to the maintenance of family livelihoods, become commercialized.

- Competition between peasants and entrepreneurial farms for the use of good quality land increases in direct response to higher demand for both food and export crops.

147

- The environment suffers as increasing numbers of families try to extract a livelihood from land that is diminishing in area and deteriorating in quality because of the over-use and improper husbandry they are obliged to practise for immediate survival.

- Agricultural 'modernization' strikes women particularly hard. They are among the first to be eliminated when commercialized farming overtakes self-provisioning, as the consecutive Indian censuses of 1961 and 1971 clearly illustrate. During that decade, two-thirds of all female cultivators ceased activity, while the number of female agricultural labourers increased by 50 per cent.

- Food 'imperialism' accompanies the introduction of the dominant model. The 'baby-foods scandal' provides a flagrant example, but other foods have received less attention. Some, like bread or soft drinks, may gain great prestige. Although the dominant model may promote commercial pseudo-variety (as in US-style supermarkets), true cultural variety inherent in the production, preparation and consumption of a broad spectrum of foods is markedly declining. This decline is accompanied by the deterioration of nutritional levels. Commercial promotion of Western processed foods downgrades not only local diets *per se* but also the symbolic value of traditional foods perceived, by comparison, as culturally inferior. Third World elites may take the lead in such consumption and are then imitated by their less privileged compatriots.

- Food aid plays a vital role in the introduction of new dietary habits. It can also create a bias towards foreign solutions of local problems: whereas nutritionists in Mysore State had developed suitable high-protein foods from local raw materials, their formula was rejected in favour of the corn–soya–milk blend provided by the US PL 480 Food Aid Program.

- Countries whose 'export-led' agricultural strategies cause them to emphasize the supply of foreign markets, and to forsake their peasantries' attempts to produce food for local consumption, grow increasingly dependent on massive cereal imports, tying them both economically and politically to privileged suppliers, more often than not the United States.

- Outside interventions and transfers of technology tend to reproduce the high-capital, low-labour-intensive characteristics of industrialized countries' food systems. This necessarily increases the *cost* of food, which must remunerate invested capital (e.g., centralized storage adds an estimated 20 per cent to the cost of grains sold in LDCs, according to an FAO expert). This, of course, places food beyond the reach of poor consumers and contributes to eliminating peasants who cannot compete in wholly mercantilized food systems.

## The Rapid Decline of Self-Provisioning

However deleterious these consequences of the introduction of the dominant model (the above list is far from complete) it must be stressed that the most serious among them is the marked decline of self-provisioning agriculture.

The drama of this process of decay lies in the fact that the 'umbilical' attachment of people to the land at the level of the family or kin-group is, with all its insecurities and natural hazards, the food system that has maintained humankind during most of its history. In the market-oriented developing countries, trends are encouraged that inevitably confirm or accelerate the decline of self-provisioning before other forms of economic activity are able to offer alternative means of livelihood to the displaced peasantry. As a consequence, marginalization and proletarianization are proceeding inexorably in Asia, Africa and Latin America, though at differing speeds and in different ways.

The full significance of this transformation is not entirely comprehended, but it seems to imply deterioration in the nourishment of the already poor as they are obliged to purchase food in unfavourable conditions from the market; massive migration to urban centres and a much higher level of conflict, disorder and repression. The removal of productive assets from women through new forms of division of labour in agricultural production may often result in a serious reduction of food provided to rural families.[2]

The actual producers of food – the overwhelmingly rural majorities of the Third World – are being progressively divested of their control over what they shall produce, by what methods, and of the resulting harvest. Imitation of the Western high-technology model and continued subservience to the needs of outside food systems cannot be expected to eliminate hunger – only to make it worse. The relevant questions in the 'hunger problématique' have become: 'Who controls the surplus?'; 'Who has the power to define what constitutes the "surplus" at the expense of the starving and malnourished?'

## Science, Scientists and the Hunger Problem[3]

The relationship between 'science' and 'development' is not a transparent one. A close and critical examination of this relationship may be itself a contribution to development and, ultimately, to science as well. Most Western scientists would see the following statements as unproblematic:

- Science is/should be 'value-free', 'objective'.

- The task of science is to discover *laws*.

- These laws should be as general as possible.

- The scientist (at least in his professional capacity) is a competent expert, tolerant, open-minded and politically neutral.

The label 'value-free' may hide a host of hidden values and assumptions of which the researcher may be unaware (although they may be obvious to others and surface in dialogue or confrontation). Scientific laws are conceived as reflecting a basically *unchanging* empirical reality. And in the notion of working towards 'general' laws, there is a clear norm of universalism. Behind laws lie *paradigms*, or generally accepted fundamental beliefs about phenomena, describing their nature but also defining the kinds of new investigations that can be undertaken without challenging the basic hypotheses.

The preceding set of propositions might be contrasted with a concept of science which would not hide values and assumptions but would try to make them explicit and subject to challenge and exploration. Such a science would be concerned not only with *seeking* invariances but also with *breaking* them; it would seek fewer universals and more insights relevant to the particularities of specific points in space and time. (Catastrophe theory is concerned with just such questions and is beginning to provide the mathematical structures for a science far more attuned to the qualitative and the discontinuous than to the quantifiable and the regular. It also stresses the irreversibility of certain phenomena and the impossibility of predicting them.)

The fundamental debate about Western science in general, and the positivist orientation in particular, has clear relevance for the discussion of any specific science, especially when the historical and socio-economic origins of these branches of knowledge are examined.

Much science is goal-oriented, and geared either to production or to social control. Science began to serve the now-dominant economic system around the seventeenth century, but since the nineteenth century this relationship has become more explicit. The maritime character of the British Empire was not without influence on the development of meteorology and naval astronomy; nor was the rational exploitation of colonial possessions unrelated to the establishment of agronomy, mineralogy, and tropical medicine as separate branches of knowledge. It is not surprising that the earliest agricultural research focused on cash crops to the exclusion of African or Asian food crops. Nutrition studies, as first undertaken in Europe, were designed to determine the minimum standards necessary for assuring the reproduction of the industrial labour force (particularly miners).

Present-day scientists may agree with Mao Zedong that science is the crystallization of knowledge developed through humankind's struggle for production, but it is also their duty to ask, 'Production for whom?' If science is to become relevant to the real needs of the Third World and to have any favourable impact on human and social development, it must undertake a fundamental re-examination of its goals and its methods.

What then are some of the issues and obstacles that must be faced by individuals and institutions seeking to help transform the hunger problématique through the use of the instruments of scholarship? We shall refer specifically here to 'research', but our remarks almost invariably apply to other activities carried out by intellectuals, like education and training.

## New Slogans versus Old Realities

There seems now to be near-universal recognition, at least at the rhetorical level, that 'growth models' and once-popular 'technological fixes' have not worked. Policies favouring capital-intensive, import-substitution industrial development have led to neglect of agriculture as a whole, and, within the agricultural sector, the wealthiest and most 'progressive' producers have received attention at the expense of small peasants and landless labourers. As we have stressed, these groups have become increasingly unable to produce enough or to buy enough food to meet their minimum needs. Such statements may now be regarded as truisms, but this does not mean that development agents and agencies are acting on their implications.

The proven ineffectiveness of liberal solutions for the pressing problems of the Third World has not even been accompanied by a genuine conceptual change of heart. Old slogans ('GNP growth', 'trickle down', 'take-off', etc.) wear out and are discarded, yet their replacements look suspiciously similar behind new façades. Concepts which may have been innovative when formulated by Third World leaders are deradicalized by the development establishment, or this establishment simply forges its own new 'appropriate terminology'. Two potentially radical concepts currently undergoing this watering-down process are the New International Economic Order and Basic Needs.[4]

So long as this establishment maintains the conceptual initiative and is able to impose its own terms of reference, it will hold an important tool for entrenching the status quo. Progressive scholars must attempt to regain the initiative in this area.

## Technical Solutions versus Politics

Although one now sees numerous references to the 'political will necessary' for carrying out the bland recommendations of international conferences, in practice development expertise generally confines itself to technical questions supposedly amenable to technical solutions. The all-important political dimensions in any real development (which always implies gains for some and losses for others) is left out.

The 'development intelligentsia' also treads carefully even where technical issues are concerned, avoiding examination of the social and political context in which they are placed. In designing projects, implementing scientific discoveries (e.g. Green Revolution seed varieties) or planning changes in technology, it usually ignores the following postulates which ought to be obvious to any neutral observer:

1. A project (scientific discovery, technological innovation, etc.) benefiting the least favoured classes will not be acceptable to the dominant classes unless their interests are also substantially served.

2. A project ... which benefits *only* the poor will be ignored, sabotaged or otherwise suppressed by the powerful in so far as possible.

3. A project ... which serves the interests of the dominant classes while doing positive harm to the poor may still be put into practice and if necessary maintained by violence so long as no basic change in the balance of political and social forces takes place.[5]

Development experts design programmes they claim will 'reach' the poor while offering no guarantees to that effect. The implementation of projects in which the poor stand to benefit may succeed so long as the area is saturated with capital and so long as these projects are administered over small areas by dedicated personnel having no particular interests to defend. It is, however, unrealistic to suppose that, beyond the pilot stage, market forces will not intervene and that the wealthier and more powerful elements of society will not appropriate whatever technical and financial benefits the project was designed to create.

## Systemic Adjustments versus Structural Change

Most research currently carried out by development agencies is concerned with face-lifting operations, not structural change, and starts from the premise that the present world system, given a few compromises, can be made to work for everyone, as it is claimed to have worked for everyone in the now-developed countries.

The Food Study Group does not believe systemic adjustments (e.g. the inclusion of more people in Green Revolution-type strategies), even if they occur, will change the status of the masses of hungry people more than marginally. Thus we cannot advocate research basically committed to tinkering with present structures. This is a waste of time if one's goals are really to benefit those who at present lack all control over the circumstances of their lives. Aside from what we consider the false premises and the self-serving nature of such scholarship, we might also point out that those seeking systemic adjustments rarely if ever consult the poor and powerless people their research is nominally designed to serve. Top-down research design and project implementation is still the rule.

We also take note that successful systemic adjustments in the past (successful, that is, in staving off acute social conflict) have to a large degree created conditions that make improvement in the status of the poorest members of society virtually impossible. One example submitted to the Group (by D. D. Narula) is that of the very limited land reform in India, which nevertheless extended rural control from 1–2 per cent of the landholders to 18–19 per cent today. It will be far more difficult to dislodge this recently created class than the previous feudal one without profound and painful social change.

Much research sponsored by major donors is also directed towards helping people *to make do with less* rather than aiding them to obtain more. Efforts are directed to 'getting the most from' an environment already depleted by the greed of national or international interests which have reduced the quantity and quality of resources available to the poor. Little work is devoted to strategies for regaining even those rights that theoretically belong to the most deprived, much less for demanding new ones.

How should one approach research basically concerned with such stop-gaps? There are delicate moral problems involved here:

one cannot avoid the problems of immediate survival facing the poor *today*, nor discount the possibility of perhaps saving a few lives through palliative measures that may help the powerless temporarily and in limited ways. Thus we would not state categorically that one should not engage in alleviating, wherever possible, the miserable conditions of the hungry. But this sort of work is, like it or not, on the level of 'systems tinkering' and basically accepts the status quo. It should not therefore be a priority for those who hope to do relevant work against the mainstream.

## Conflict with the Dominant Research Establishment

As in other areas of human affairs, the area of research is a terrain for conflict – at least when anything of importance is at stake. When there is general agreement on what constitutes the proper province of scholarly objectives and activities, one may assume that those who have an interest in maintaining the existing balance of power do not feel themselves threatened. Progressive scholars should thus welcome conflict as an admission that their work is doing powerless people some good, or might aid them in the future. This is a serious responsibility and places upon such researchers the burden of being more rigorous than their detractors and opponents while at the same time avowing and defending their 'value-loaded' approach.

The most immediate conflicts for progressive intellectuals and institutions will occur with the dominant research establishment which will quite naturally seek to maintain and increase its control over scholars and scholarship.

This establishment has a number of ways of ensuring its hegemony. One of the simplest and most effective, as some Third World Food Study Group members have brought out, is merely to occupy the terrain. Western foundations, universities, aid agencies, etc., appear in force in country X and immediately enlist the cooperation of all, or nearly all, the available scientific manpower, expertise, laboratories and institutions available. In most Third World countries, indigenous scientific capacity is underfunded to begin with, so it is materially feasible to put whatever capacity exists to work on spurious projects – or even on projects that quite candidly serve the needs of donor countries (as is the case with US 'Food for Peace' counterpart funds spent on agricultural or 'market development' research carried out in aid-recipient countries by indigenous scientists).

Any project proposed independently and designed to be of real assistance to the poorest and least influential groups, or one which might lead to a change in existing social relations, is, in effect, placed in direct competition with handsomely funded programmes which generally appeal to governments as much as they do to large and powerful donors. As one of our members says, speaking of the obstacles encountered in trying to start a small project targeted to the poorest people in a country heavily populated by development experts, 'I found the patterns of allocation of resources and grants strongly biased towards these well-established and dominant research institutions whose main objective seems to be confined to their own reproduction and development. In this respect the role of international agencies was determinant.' If by some freak occurrence an innovative project does get underway, according to this same participant, 'it becomes the focus of attention of international donors and observers visiting the country, receives a lot of publicity and diverts attention from the real [overall development prospects] in that country'. Such innovations, if they cease to be invisible to planners, take on an alibi status; in both cases they can be made to serve the system's needs. It is unwise for a local scientist to protest such an orientation of the scientific capacity of his country: 'The only two scientists who contested the way in which research was undertaken in the major ... institution were fired from their assignments.'

Another member points out that a position in the international research establishment is richly rewarded – the highest priority for Third World intellectuals apparently being at present expert status with the World Bank. This is also why they strive to obtain diplomas from prestigious Western institutions – these are much more highly rewarded than degrees from Third World universities.

A third member analyses the social realities of research carried out in underdeveloped countries as follows.

Most funds for research come from outside the country (from industrialized-country sources) so it is understandable that the objectives, the methodologies and the terms of reference also be dictated from the outside. Some work by Ph.D. candidates is done for established professors with their own theories to defend. Younger scholars must conform to the professors' guidelines if they want to find a job in academia later on. Scholarship may also serve to support the foregone conclusions of decision-makers or of the international development-planners who so frequently dictate the choices of national planners.

Scholars are virtually told what their findings are expected to be. Such work obtains recognition for the intellectual in government and/or academic circles, whereas independent, progressive researchers are rarely promoted. It is no wonder that their number is infinitesimally small compared to the numbers of 'yes men' (and 'yes women'). The near-total irrelevance of most social science curricula to the value systems, perspectives or historical evolution of Third World people has also been stressed by Food Study Group members.

## The Dominant Research Model: Prestige without Accountability

We have attempted to show how the dominant Western agricultural model is being propagated in the Third World with harmful consequences. (The same could be said for other areas – e.g. health care, industrial development under the aegis of transnational corporations, etc.) That there is also a dominant model in research, accepted and admired by most Third World intellectuals and seen as prestigious by their governments, cannot be over-stressed.

This prestige is not fortuitous. As Pierre Spitz points out, the dominant research establishment is actually engaged in two kinds of work. The first is empirical and operational and hews very close to reality because it is concerned with a more efficient manipulation and management of that reality. The audience for which this work is prepared is a limited one; much of it is confidential and restricted to the commissioning agency. It must, in fact, be largely confidential *because* of its adherence to reality, because most reality *is* oppression.

The second kind of work is more closely related to ensuring this model's dominance through the production and dissemination of an ideology destined for the broadest possible audience, spread by a variety of media and institutions, including universities. The practitioners of the first kind of scholarship should have no difficulty identifying the interests they are serving: they share these interests to the degree that they are rewarded by them. Scholars in the second group may not always understand the role they are playing. If so, they are themselves victims of the dominant ideo-logy – naïve but not dishonest; if not, then cynical or motivated by gain. Both kinds of work may, of course, be done at different times by the same persons.

Almost all research is geared either to production or to social control and is carried out for institutions (e.g. transnational corporations, leading foundations, lending agencies like the World Bank) which exercise power without any mitigating accountability. 'Production' in this context means production of goods and services which are wanted and can be paid for by consumers with purchasing power. This aim automatically precludes research and development addressed to satisfying the needs of those who live in poverty. The bodies which impose these goals on present research are answerable to no one – except a self-selected board – and the Food Study Group considers it fruitless to ask, or to expect, them to change their aims. They are not to be persuaded, but rather confronted and exposed.

That members of the power structures are willing to devote substantial resources to research indicates that the latter is not a luxury good but an important input to control: it helps to strengthen the power of those who exercise it while simultaneously contributing to thickening the ideological smokescreen behind which this power is exercised.

## Some Elements of a Progressive Approach to Research

### Research on Research

One immediately necessary task for progressive scholarship is to confront the dominant research establishment on its own ground. The sheer weight of resources devoted to spurious or irrelevant projects in the Third World ensures that the enormous body of work turned out will have a wide influence. (One may, for example, recall the success of the 'overpopulation-is-the-cause-of-hunger' school.) The Food Study Group's refusal to condone or participate in this kind of scholarship thus carries an important corollary: we see it as one obligation of intellectuals to carry out 'research on research' if they hope to undermine the dominant model's influence and compete for its audience in both developed and underdeveloped countries. It is important to examine *what* establishment research covers and *why* particular projects (and, of course, particular countries) are of special interest to bilateral and multilateral funders at particular times. It should be a relatively easy task to ascertain which social groups stand to benefit from the choice of certain projects rather than others.

### Studying the Powerful

Related to this target (examining power by examining its uses of the instruments of scholarship) is the importance of studying the dominant social and political forces both spatially and temporally. The Food Study Group believes that the reasons for poverty and hunger are not to be found mainly *within* the class of the poor and hungry but in their *relationships* with the rest of society (from the local to the national to the international level). The most important focus for research on poverty, which itself causes hunger, can be summarized in the single word 'power': power as it is expressed in social classes and through the institutions that serve them at every level.

In *The Crisis of Democracy* the Trilateral Commission castigated 'value-oriented intellectuals' who 'devote themselves to the derogation of leadership, the challenging of authority and the unmasking and delegitimization of established institutions' including those responsible for 'the indoctrination of the young'.[6]

We would assert that intellectuals should not only be value-oriented but indeed devote themselves to just those tasks decried by the Trilateral Commission. This can be achieved in different ways at different levels.

As Pierre Spitz again notes, there is a hierarchy in research (which is not to imply that one kind has more intrinsic worth than another): (1) factual or empirical work, in which the researcher's values naturally determine the topics pursued and the facts sought; (2) research designed to verify a hypothesis clearly defined at the outset and in which facts serve this aim; (3) epistemological research concerned with the very concepts and paradigms that underlie research and the tools it uses. At each of these levels, dichotomies (and conflicts) between the dominant and the dominated classes are, or should be, apparent. One of the tasks of research is to unmask the interests involved at every level – interests which will also determine the clientele for, and the uses made of, research. We do not wish to give the impression that research can be separated from its applications, particularly from its role in the creation of a dominant ideology and its dissemination through the mass media or educational and training institutions.

*Multidisciplinary Studies*

There has been a general recognition, at least in the progressive scholarly community, that single-discipline research for rural development is not the road to success. Although single-discipline work still prevails in the far greater part of scholarly output, there are numerous signs that a multidisciplinary approach is becoming fashionable. This itself will not constitute a panacea. If the disciplines, whatever their nature and number, still revolve around the old paradigms and tackle the wrong problems (or the right problems in the wrong ways) they might easily do more harm than the previously more limited approach. Multidisciplinary work could, however, become an important instrument if it were to take on the issue of power as it expresses itself at the global, regional/national and local levels.

*Creating and Using New Stocks of Knowledge and Innovative Methodologies*

Beneath the 'growth model' that dominated development thinking for so many fruitless years lay the assumption that there was a unique stock of knowledge (science and technology), that this was the exclusive preserve of the industrialized countries, and that it needed to be transferred along with capital if Third World nations were ever to 'bridge the gap'. But a concept of human development cannot mean 'Western' or 'elitist'. Does anyone really believe that insight is so asymmetrically distributed that billions of men and women deeply engaged in food production, preparation, distribution and consumption know nothing at all, whereas a few selected researchers (nutritionists, social scientists, agronomists, *et al.*) know everything? Thus stated, most would agree that there must exist huge stocks of knowledge beyond the confines of 'official' science and technology, but that they have gone largely uncollected, untapped and unutilized. There may be, in fact, four separate stocks of knowledge, of which two are as yet largely uncreated:

1. Western, positivist, mechanistic science and technology;

2. traditional, empirical, operational stocks of knowledge, stored by peasants and closely adapted to survival skills within the constraints of a wide variety of environments;

3. knowledge which might come from interaction between (1) and (2), if only self-satisfied 'experts' can be persuaded to listen and learn, and peasants, so long disdained, can be persuaded they have something to teach;

4. knowledge which might come from the significant demand in many *developed* countries for a simpler, more humane lifestyle.

New nature/human/technology 'mixes' are needed, including many that have not been imagined yet, but which might be part of that 'Third Science' stemming from a real dialogue between North and South, peasants and experts. This would necessarily imply sharing decision-making power as well as knowledge; as mass consciousness increased, elites would find their power diminishing.[7]

Methodologies of the social sciences in particular (but also of nutrition) developed during the late nineteenth and early twentieth centuries in an urban, industrial, masculine, Western context. They are thus more apt to be good at defining – and answering – questions posed by urban, industrial, masculine, Western societies. Research has not only treated people like objects, but has suffered from environment-blindness, sex-blindness and age-blindness. Nutritional science, for example, knows relatively little about traditional mixes and sequences of foods making maximum use of the environment. When it does take an interest in such matters, it is often to discover that Western inroads are destroying dietary practices with a sound scientific basis (e.g. food combinations ensuring optimum balance of amino acids). The invisibility of women in most development-planning can be corrected only when women themselves take an active part in the planning process. Something is known about infants and children under five (unfortunately, mortality statistics form a large part of this knowledge) but very little work has been done on old people. Third World people may have lower life-expectancies, but they also age more quickly. In fragile food systems, children and old people suffer disproportionately; just as they, along with women, are the first to be eliminated from productive work when control shifts from local communities to outside forces.

People have their own ways of stocking information, but these are rarely the ways that figure on social scientists' questionnaires. If peasants are asked, for example, how large a yield they produced, or how much they spent on cloth last year, or even how large their plot of ground is, they may have difficulty answering, but this does not mean that they are ignorant. Their measurement and information system merely uses other criteria: e.g. the 'quantity price', or amount that can be bought with one unit of currency at different times of the year; or the 'commodity basket' of purchases that are approximately the same every week or month; or the number of months they and their families were able to live off their own harvest without having recourse to purchased food. Questions asked inside the people's terms of reference will receive useful answers.

Surveyors who have rarely ever been hungry themselves can perhaps not be expected to realize immediately that *annual* data about food intake would seem strange indeed to peasants and their families whose problem is survival tomorrow, next week and next month, especially during the lean season. Surveys could, however, very usefully look at fluctuations rather than averages for various socio-economic groups. A survey of a village one month before and one month after harvest would give entirely different results.[8] This means that projects would have to last longer and that the 'people's methodology' would have to be adopted in order to learn something worth knowing.

## The 'Objects' of Research Must Become Its Subjects

Those for whom progressive research is purportedly being done –

the poor and hungry – must be consulted about their needs and helped by the researcher to define those needs. We believe that the worst-off know very well why they are poor, at least on the immediate local level, and that this knowledge represents one starting point for improving their status. This can come about only through various forms of organization in which the researcher should take as active a role as is warranted by the expressed desire of the community in question. We are not sure whether there are any serious thinkers who still believe in scholarly neutrality, but, if so, we would like to paraphrase Orwell and point out that 'all researchers are neutral, but they are more neutral towards some social groups than towards others'.

It is here that the problem of the accountability of the researcher should be posed. Intellectuals working at the 'micro' or community level should be accountable to that community, and the worth of their work determined by the degree of relevance to its felt needs. (Scholars concerned with 'macro'-level issues might well be judged, on the other hand, by the degree of controversy and confrontation their work gives rise to.)

Real development is incompatible with methodologies which envisage only the collection of data by an 'objective, impartial' scholar using a pre-designed survey questionnaire. There must also exist a commitment on the researcher's part actively to foster social change in the desirable direction. The intellectual must feel a sense of identity with the situation and, perhaps most difficult, must accept being changed by the research process; as of course the *researched* will also change if there has been real interaction. 'Participatory' or 'dialogic' research emphasizes the holistic approach, i.e., for food problems the researcher would enter into a dialogue with the people about life in the community as a whole, because food, nutrition, health, etc., are not viewed separately but as parts of life. The people's identification of the problem, their assessment of the obstacles to solving it and their proposals for doing so in spite of the obstacles should form the total process leading to meaningful action. Interaction between 'expert' and people should upgrade traditional knowledge as well as create new knowledge to be integrated into community practice.

The important point is that any research project is *itself a part of the power structure*; a progressive project should thus be concerned either with (1) denouncing with factual proof present power arrangements and their harmful effects on the poor – or at least showing the gap between rhetoric and reality in the way power speaks about itself (the 'discourse') or (2) strengthening the capacity of the poor to organize and free themselves from oppression. It is likely that most projects would not be able fully to combine these two aspects, and that one person would not be able to do both kinds of work, but both are important. An unresolved problem is how to establish fruitful collaboration and continuing contact between scholars engaged in type (1) or (2) so that their work becomes mutually reinforcing. A progressive research/educational institution could play a very important role in facilitating and maintaining such contacts. It might be particularly helpful to groups in the Third World to be able to make their needs known to scholars in the developed countries, where access to documentation on the power centres is easier.

## Research Outside the Dominant Food-System Model

We have attempted to make clear the concept of a food system and to suggest that there are large systems, or cycles, spanning countries, continents or the whole globe, which are gaining in importance; while small food cycles – self-provisioning on a family, community or regional level – are declining. This is perhaps an inexorable and irreversible movement; we cannot say. We believe, however, that it is the duty of the researcher and the development-planner to protect, to strengthen and to enhance the smaller cycles in all possible ways; to resist the encroachment of the large ones which are leading to increased hunger in the world.

*It is particularly urgent that scientific research outside the dominant agricultural model be undertaken without delay.* Without wishing to appear apocalyptic, we would still like to point out that a new world food crisis may be looming which could make the crisis of 1972–4 seem pale by comparison. The World Food Conference of 1974 predicted that the developing countries would be importing around 85 million tons of food in 1985. By 1978–9, the figure had already gone beyond 70 million tons (as compared to 50 million tons in 1976–7). After several years of abundance in the late 1970s, the stocks of the major grain exporters (particularly the United States) were being intentionally drawn down, with the result that a bushel of US wheat which sold for $3.12 in late August of 1978 is worth $4.43 at this writing (November 1979), and had gone as high as $4.60 in July before the first new harvests came in. The food dependency of most importing countries is increasing, not declining, and the failure of governments to conclude a new International Wheat Agreement in February 1979 is another ominous sign. Most observers believe that developed countries will continue to devote even greater amounts of grain to feeding animals in their own countries, thus further limiting available supplies.

The equilibrium of international food markets, with their reliance on the US and, to a lesser extent, on a handful of smaller exporters such as Canada, is so precarious that any relatively minor shock – climatic or commercial – could set off a disproportionate market reaction for which the Third World would have to pay. Outsized purchases by a major importer such as the Soviet Union or China; blight, or failure of the monsoon in Asia; a drop in US production; any or all could trigger an uncontrollable upward spiral in prices as speculation took hold. Food aid cannot be expected to palliate such conditions: the historical record shows that aid decreases as commercial purchases increase in the context of tight markets.

Only those countries deemed politically vital would continue to receive a significant supply of food aid in a period of scarcity. To these disquieting factors must be added the increasing reliance of

Third World food systems, imitating the dominant system, on energy-dependent inputs like fuels, fertilizers and other petroleum-based chemicals. This comes at a time when even increased OPEC-country aid cannot compensate for their mounting costs, particularly since Western transnational corporations largely control the marketing of these products.

Many Third World governments seem to be living in a sort of fool's paradise, lulled by several years of good weather and resultant good harvests – and perhaps by a belief in the benevolence of their traditional aid partners and suppliers of major food grains. The present food system, with its reliance on high-energy, high-technology imputs, is growing more vulnerable daily, to the point where it is not unrealistic to speak of an eventual systemic breakdown.

If systems breakdowns do occur (and, to many of us, this outcome appears to be only a matter of time) then we will long for the days when a different kind of complexity – biological, not industrial – made our farming systems more resilient and disaster-resistant.[9]

The higher the level of complex industrial technology in a given system, the more fragile and less capable of withstanding crisis it becomes. From this point of view, the systems in the industrialized countries are the most exposed to breakdown, whereas in the Third World there is still time to preserve and to improve the traditional farming practices which have provided the basis for human survival through several millennia. This, however, with rare exceptions is not being done.

On the contrary – not surprisingly, given the intellectual prestige and financial backing of the dominant model in both agriculture and research – most resources are being devoted to fine-tuning the dominant model itself to fit a greater variety of local conditions. Adolfo Mascarenhas reports, for example, that in Tanzania there is an area where peasants are capable of identifying and cultivating twenty-four different varieties of rice. Yet there is no Tanzanian (much less outside) research team monitoring their practices with the aim of understanding them in a more codifiable and 'scientific' way. On the other hand, research grants are being awarded for work on imported varieties of hybrid rice.

One encouraging example of research outside the dominant agronomic model which has come to our attention is the work being done by a team at Heidelberg University. This group takes an 'archaeological' approach to land-use practices of traditional farmers (e.g. the Kikuyu farmers in the Kilimanjaro region of Kenya) in order to understand the functional principles involved. The Kikuyu system is multi-faceted and includes various tree crops, bushes, standing crops and 'weeds' (which play a positive protective role); a system characterized by high species diversity, stability and complexity able to withstand the particular hazards of the local environment. The Kikuyu peasants exhibit great skill in arranging the species so that they interact with one another; they have also perfected anti-erosion and waste-using techniques, demonstrating a high level of scientific sophistication. Some of the lessons learned in Kenya have subsequently been used by this Heidelberg team in designing a minimum-physical-inputs system for farm improvement in Rwanda. They have also developed a similar approach in Mexico, using Mayan cultivation practices as a starting point.

In the context of a traditional system, generally a very efficient user of energy, it is entirely possible to integrate technological elements from outside the original system at fairly low cost. This can be desirable so long as it is the *farmers themselves* who determine what new technologies are opportune and so long as they retain control over the system as a whole. Thus we are not advocating a museum-conservation approach to traditional systems, however good, nor a goal of simply replicating them, but rather a creative blending of local expertise with Western scientific knowledge.

Or, as the UN Research Institute for Social Development has put it,

We do not suggest ... that modern production techniques should be rejected as such or that self-provisioning agriculture must be maintained or restored as a necessary basis for food systems and rural livelihood. What is suggested, however, is that the transition to higher levels of technology, increased capitalization and further economies of scale can only be achieved by means of firm and carefully prepared policies and programmes with the active participation of the different social groups concerned, and that much of the knowledge essential to the adequate preparation and execution of such policies is not available. In addition, the political will for such programmes and policies can hardly be expected to appear spontaneously in social structures that provide poor peasant groups with little power or influence. The worst danger is the precipitate uprooting and marginalization of rural majorities and nomadic fringe groups before alternative sources of livelihood are available to them.

Research beyond the confines of the dominant agricultural model could reduce such dangers to the degree that it strengthened traditional food systems, thus making the communities practising them more resistant to outside pressures. The knowledge that lies behind traditional systems is not always readily accessible to outsiders and can be acquired only through cooperation with peasant practitioners – easier said than done, especially for Westerners.

The Food Study Group has concluded that a major responsibility incumbent on institutions consciously directing their work against mainstream research and aspiring to help solve the food/hunger problem is to support 'creative dissidents', who should find an important place in future research.

## Summary and Recommendations

1. Research should be undertaken on the impact of *global* power structures at national and local levels in underdeveloped countries. Politics of particular actors (for example, trans-

national corporations, multilateral agencies, industrialized States, etc.) should be examined to ascertain their effects on food/hunger in the Third World.

2. Research at the *national* level should include an action/participatory component and should incorporate findings from the global level. The object of such work should not merely be to collect data but to initiate social change. It should also aim at upgrading and conserving traditional farming systems in each country.

3. Research is also required at the *epistemological* level, and would include 'research on research', examination of paradigms, creation of new knowledge stocks and methodologies; the placing of research and development systems in historical perspective. The creative dissidents span all these elements and contribute to their evolution. This epistemological component is not some sort of 'philosophical window-dressing' but a vital contribution to regaining what we have called the 'conceptual initiative'. Until the terms of reference can be changed, research and development programmes will remain in the usual technocratic ruts.

4. The ultimate *goal* of all this work should be to educate, train, sensitize and remould national elites and to raise mass consciousness for social change. Assuming that governments and other elites *want* to contribute to solving the food/hunger problem, they will need not only data on the interests which currently prevent this, but also a decolonized conceptual approach that relativizes and delegitimizes the dominant model(s) in any number of disciplines. Such a decolonized approach should be transmitted through educational and training institutions which should help people to recapture and liberate their own creativity – as individuals and as nations. Although this report has concentrated more on the theoretical elements of a hunger problématique, research critique, and proposals for

change, we believe that most of our observations apply to education and training as well. In other words, there are dominant models in curricula, pedagogical methods, etc.; these models are instituted and maintained by particular classes whose interests they serve; there are also creative dissidents working outside these models who need support. One form of support is the provision of alternative curricular tools. Participatory research is a form of education which raises mass consciousness, just as the exposure of present repressive power structures is one necessary step towards freeing creativity.

## Conclusion

Ideally, people should be in a position to make a choice as to the kind of food/agricultural system they prefer and to carry it out, based *on their own design*, but we are very far away from that goal. The Food Study Group is aware that all its recommendations run counter to currently observable trends: more centralized State bureaucracies, growing power of transnational corporate capitalism, etc. Greater popular control over food-producing resources and food itself seems, however, the only viable long-term strategy against hunger. Useful research will foster this strategy and will not only try to help the now-powerless to formulate what they want and need, but also attempt to provide them with useful information about the power structures that work against them so that they may frame more realistic strategies.

It is obvious that these strategies, like those of any real human and social development, will involve political conflict; this cannot be avoided. We are not, however, engaged in waiting for the revolution, which has little more to recommend it than waiting for the afterlife. We do believe that with the cooperation of men and women of goodwill everywhere – North or South, intellectuals or peasants – it is possible to build up countervailing powers, to work for slow revolution, to discover available political spaces and to create new ones within which it is possible to struggle against the economic and class interests which have no scruples about eliminating millions of people. As John Berger has written,

> The peasantry as a class is the oldest in existence. It has shown remarkable powers of survival – powers which have puzzled and confused most administrators and theorists. In fact ... the essential character of the peasantry ... despite all the important differences of climate, religion, economic and social history ... actually derives from its being a class of survivors. It is often said that the majority of people in the world today are still peasants. Yet this fact masks a more significant one. For the first time ever, it is possible that the class of survivors may not survive.[10]

We see it as the task of intellectuals to recognize our debt to this class of survivors, our common interest not only that they endure but that they prosper. We must be prepared to move forward with them; to do so, we must be prepared to abandon our comfortable hypotheses, our scientific certainties, our favourite wisdoms – including, perhaps, those set forth in this paper.

# 8
# THE SNOB THEORY OF UNDERDEVELOPMENT

*Comic relief time. Or at least a satirical tone for a serious subject. This piece appeared in* Development Forum, *June 1982, 'the single regular publication of the United Nations system in the field of economic and social development', under the title 'An Invitation to be Offended'.* Development Forum *does not require permission to reprint, but I thank them anyway and change the title back to 'The SNOB Theory of Underdevelopment'.*

> 'Of course, poor Mr James never *did* meet the right people.'
>> English dowager, commenting on Henry James, upper-class American anglophile novelist who took British nationality

> 'Breastfeeding is for savages.'
>> African doctor

I hope to be among the first to alienate nearly all my friends by bringing up in the most public and tasteless manner a subject not discussed in well-bred 'development' intellectual circles, except in whispers and with intimates, after midnight.

If you too are a believer, but are afraid to come out of the closet, perhaps this may give you the courage to talk openly about SNOB. The acronym stands for Social Naïveté of Behaviour or Simple Necessities of Business, depending on which side you're looking at. Those who espouse the SNOB theory hold dear the motto, 'Nothing So Blind as a Colonized Mind'.

SNOB is an idea whose time has come, because exploitation in the postcolonial world is a tricky business. No more rounding up the natives and telling them to produce, or else. No more dumping cheap goods on vassalized countries' markets to ruin local cottage industries. Tough times for business, these. But hardly desperate. There's more than one way to skin a cat – or a Third World country and its citizens. The SNOB method, properly employed, not only yields higher profits but provides more perverse satisfaction to its practitioners than common or garden domination.

The theoretical underpinnings of SNOB have been known for centuries and its practical applications are universal. SNOB's guiding principle is that human beings tend to imitate those they perceive as their social superiors. Adepts regard Molière, immortal author of *Le bourgeois gentilhomme*, as their greatest ancestor. Literati would add Proust, creator of Madame Verdurin and other unforgettable characters, to the Pantheon; while academics may recall Gabriel Tarde, early sociologist and neglected author of *The Laws of Imitation* (1895). Americans, more succinctly, may recite, if pressed, 'Oh carry me back to Boston / The home of the bean and the cod / Where the Lodges speak only to Cabots / And the Cabots speak only to God.'

SNOB in its early expressions was thus an intra-cultural phenomenon, operating within closed frontiers. Those who attempted to cross rigid class barriers were objects of ridicule because they tried so earnestly to imitate their 'betters' and did such a rotten job of it.

With the rise of consumer culture, advertisers and merchandisers were quick to see the goldmine SNOB promised. Calvert whiskey's 'Men of Distinction' campaign of the 1950s was a classic that changed the image of a decidedly lower-class brand. With transnational capitalism, SNOB began to creep across frontiers and now flourishes wherever insecure people gather: for example, one can sell *very* expensive raincoat to Americans, using pictures of Lady X and Lord Y strolling across lawns obviously trod by the same family for the past 500 years.

Harmless, you may say, and a further illustration that a fool and his money are soon parted. So, alas, are a fool and his culture. As SNOB steals from North to South; from the ex-colonists to the ex-colonized, it erodes the cultural topsoil and washes it away to sea, leaving barren ground that will readily soak up a variety of products profitable to their purveyors, if not to their purchasers.

The goal of the practising corporate (or development agency) SNOB is to enrol Third World bourgeoisies in the brotherhood: they can be counted on to carry along their own masses. In winning hearts and minds, modern SNOBs wouldn't dream of using bombs and napalm when training programmes, foundation grants, marketing experts and mass media work so much more effectively. The fun of the game is to make the victim *want* your ————. The blank may be filled in with 'dangerous pharmaceuticals', 'plastic shoes', 'infant formula', 'soft drinks', *ad libitum*; and easily extended to include 'hospital-based health care', 'educational system', 'agricultural techniques', etc.

This has proved almost too simple. The only element that adds spice and subtlety to the mind-colonizing game is this: the target population must be encouraged to abandon its own authentic culture in favour of a lower-middle-class, Western, wholly commercialized ersatz. Third World elites must not, with very rare exceptions, be allowed to witness or to participate in the culture of Western *upper* classes, for the very reason that this upper-class culture is often *uncannily close* to the one the conditioned victim must learn to despise as 'backward' and 'inferior' in his own country, for obvious commercial reasons.

The point can be illustrated in an area which is at once a basic need and an intensely cultural activity: food and eating. Witness the sleight-of-hand involved in the shift from an authentic Third World culture to raw Western consumerism aped by Third World bourgeoisies and back full circle to the values of the Occidental upper crust.

*Breastfeeding*

- 'Savages' breastfeed, as the quoted African doctor puts it.

- Western masses and *nouveaux riches* (and not-so-*riches*) Third Worlders bottlefeed with infant formula.

- Upper-class, educated Western women breastfeed.

*Shapes and Sizes*

- 'Natives' are thin because they work hard and often go hungry.

- Lower- and middle-class Westerners are often obese – as are rich Third World wives – living proof that their husbands can afford to stuff them.

- Rich Westerners are slender – indeed they may spend as much money losing weight as putting it on.

*State of the Plate*

- Peasants eat, necessarily, whole unprocessed food because they can ill afford anything else.

- *Hoi polloi* in the rich countries and the rich in poor countries are great customers for junk food, as transnational food-processing companies have learnt to their advantage. Here, too, Third World bourgeoisies have played their destined role of bringing much of the rest of the (far poorer) population to the joys of commerciogenic malnutrition.

- Upper-class Westerners now pay premium prices for whole, unprocessed foods.

*Meals versus Food Contacts*

- Peasants serve their fare in hand-crafted clay, wooden or metal utensils, and they eat as a group – family or clan.

- Plastic and Pyrex prevail among the commoners who, in the West, may rarely enjoy a family meal. In the United States, 'eating' is now sociologically described in terms of 'food contacts' – as many as fifteen to twenty a day in the snack civilization.

- Avant-garde Westerners seek out hand-crafted utensils and are the only ones who can still afford the time for leisurely dining and commensality (a variant of this is the business lunch). If they are especially chic, some of the food will come from their own gardens, just like Third World peasants.

It would be nice to make a similar case for peasant polyculture (mixes of different kinds of crops and animals) as opposed to standardized, vulnerable Western monoculture and back – but the environmental movement has not yet forced industrialized countries to recognize the importance of biological complexity in farming systems. The Third World, naturally, is working flat out to transform its polycultural systems into much riskier, monocultural ones.

Time-lags complicate the whole SNOB issue. Third World bourgeoisies also imitate Western styles of ten or fifteen years ago, now totally *passé* in their places of origin. Look at the young blades in Asia who think they are fashion-plates in bell-bottom trousers no Western kid (even a lower-class one) would be caught dead wearing today.

I believe SNOBism is here to stay. That is why I propose, on the principle, 'if you can't beat 'em, join 'em,' that we *encourage* Third World imitation of Western mores, but that we make some effort in the direction of social equality. Like poor Henry James, Third World elites never *do* meet the right people. Perhaps the United Nations could open a new agency, designed to receive Third World opinion-makers, with branches in the more desirable Western countries.

It would be partially staffed with volunteers from the best families and would devote itself to the display of authentic upper-class Western lifestyles. Trendy New York hostesses could lecture on how they serve unpolished rice and perfect vegetable terrines (nothing quite so *déclassé* as a steak nowadays) at their most fashionable dinners. Their husbands would explain that 'nobody' watches American series on television or buys *anything* plastic when a natural substance is available. Elegant Britishers would put down polyester and nylon; Scandinavian industrialists' daughters would carry on pleasant conversations while breastfeeding their babies. French intellectuals would take participants to film festivals to watch aesthetic movies about workers and peasants. The possibilities are endless . . .

Who knows? Western corporations could lose a few marginal markets, but Third World elites might begin to feel secure in their own traditions.

# 9
# THE KNOWLEDGE OF HUNGER

*In 1981, Nicole Ball published a remarkable critical bibliography entitled* World Hunger: a Guide to the Economic and Political Dimensions* *to which she kindly asked me to write a foreword. As soon as I saw the text, I realized that whatever needed to be said about hunger itself had already been said by Ball. The only path left open to the writer of a foreword was to make something of the fact that the bibliography's 3,000 and some entries actually existed – i.e., that hunger has been, to say the least, a problem very much in the academic limelight in recent years. Thus I tried to talk about the peculiar ambiguity of the 'hunger-and-development' scholar, his/her place in the power structures, and how we might 'apply ourselves to transforming the contents of future bibliographies into explosive devices and instruments of liberation'. This foreword, which is reprinted here with the kind permission of the publishers, also appeared in the Institute for Policy Studies' collective volume entitled* First Harvest, 1983.

Inclusion of this bibliography on world hunger in the War/Peace Bibliography Series published by ABC-Clio is a clear recognition that hunger and underdevelopment are forms of violence

---

*Libraries in particular should be urged to purchase Ball's work: available from ABC-Clio Press, Riviera Campus, 2040 Alameda Padre Serra, Box 4397, Santa Barbara, CA 93103.

and sources of conflict. Nicole Ball, who prepared this outstanding instrument for researchers, the first of its kind, subtitled her work *A Guide to the Economic and Political Dimensions*. This in itself is a step forward for scholarship. Indeed, until recently, hunger was generally regarded as a technical problem, amenable to technical solutions, or at most as the temporary malfunctioning of an essentially viable world economic system. Ball, both in her general introduction and in her headings for subsections, correctly guides the reader towards those studies which examine hunger as a function of poverty and poverty as a function of fundamentally inequitable power structures both within and between nations. She has done this as competently as she has collected the source materials – which is saying a great deal – and this foreword need not restate her fully justified conclusions.

Ball has also given us an important tool for examining how the allocation of power influences scholarship itself. A bibliography is not merely a convenience to the general reader and a time-saver for academics in libraries. It is also, particularly in the present case, a contribution to the sociology of knowledge – a documentary record of the ways in which scholars and institutions have viewed one of the great issues of their time. If we try to analyse this bibliography as an object in itself – concentrating not, as most of the following entries do, on poverty and hunger, but on what has been said about them – we may ask a few basic questions conducive to healthy critical thinking.*

First question: Who is doing the talking? Which is to say, who is in a position to publish books, monographs and scholarly articles on various aspects of world hunger and underdevelopment? Despite Ball's careful inclusion of many Third World sources and

---

*This is the approach taken by Pierre Spitz, to whom I am much indebted, in 'Silent Violence: Famine and Inequality', a study of the significance of the views on inequality within and between nations, especially the views of those in a position to institutionalize violence against the poor and to deprive them of their right to food.

authors (a rarity in the bibliographical genre), she herself would be the first to admit that those who publish are mostly Westerners. In other words, certain groups have the power to make their views known. Whatever their personal hardships may have been, chronic hunger has surely not been among them. Just as there were no Third World peasant representatives at the 1974 World Food Conference or at the 1979 World Conference on Agrarian Reform and Rural Development, so there are no hungry people speaking from direct and painful experience in these pages. Although it is perhaps not necessary to have known physical or social deprivation to write about them, one should still note that the works listed here proceed from a particular kind of external knowledge and that a collection of people with university educations, frequently Ph.D.s, are, by any standards, part of a privileged minority. This does not, of course, predestine them to adopt the point of view characteristic of the group to which they belong, but, statistically speaking, they are likely to share common intellectual or class biases and to ignore certain problems, not out of personal malice but because these problems may appear unworthy of notice or remain wholly invisible. Non-Western authors are not exempt from such tendencies, particularly when they have received their education under Western auspices.

These observations may become more persuasive when we ask a second question: What – and whom – are these authors talking about? The subject matter of most 'development' writing is more circumscribed than such a copious bibliography suggests. The disregard for the specific problems of Third World women in the male-dominated literature is one striking example; the absence of consideration for peasants' specific agricultural knowledge as opposed to that of 'scientific experts' is another. Cause for even more serious concern is the proportion of research devoted to the study of poor and powerless groups. This choice of subject is generally accompanied by a lack of interest in the doings of the rich and powerful in the same society. Research directed exclusively towards the victims of hunger, rather than towards their relationships with the powerful (locally, nationally and internationally), helps to mask the basic reasons for the poor's lack of access to food. Such a focus may help to explain the success of the 'overpopulation-is-the-cause-of-hunger' school. (Here, had Ball wished to provide an exhaustive bibliography, she might have needed roughly a third of the pages of this volume.) By placing the hunger problem squarely in the laps, figuratively and literally, of the people having the babies, scholarship has deflected attention from the responsibilities of the 'haves' to the plight of the 'have-nots', thus obviating the need for any changes in present power arrangements. The sheer weight of the literature devoted to topics that are at best marginal in explaining, much less attacking, the root causes of poverty also stifles academic and public debate and creates confusion in the minds of the general public. And yet, in spite of such obvious cases of scholarly bias or blindspots, a significant portion of the academic establishment would still have us believe that the social sciences are objective or, in the jargon of the trade, 'value-free'; that the social scientist is an impartial, politically neutral expert. Here a paraphrase of Orwell seems called for: All social scientists are neutral, but they are more neutral towards some social groups than towards others.

Third question: What goals does research serve, and whose goals are they? At one level, not so trivial as it might first appear, it serves the interests of the people publishing. All of us listed in these pages must live with the uncomfortable truth that at least a part of our own livelihood derives from the existence of the suffering of others. Our published works and inclusion in catalogues like this one may help us gain income or prestige and a higher rung on the career ladder. This in itself should cause us to feel in some way accountable to the Third World countries and people who provided raw material for our research or at least to our colleagues on the three poor continents. This, unfortunately, is not often the case. As of 1979, a massive publication on the Sahelian countries, compiled by a prestigious US university team, was unavailable to scholars in Upper Volta. This is not merely a lack of academic courtesy, but a demonstration of the social and political priorities and loyalties of mainstream scholarship.

What of the goals of research and the accountability of intellectuals at a more general level? Just as most work done in the physical and natural sciences ultimately serves production, so much social science eventually contributes to social control.

Research is intellectual production and, like other kinds of production, must be paid for. The government or international agencies and large foundations which fund scholarship have their own economic and political vision of what constitutes the desirable society. Viewed in this light, it is doubtful that (as Ball states in her introduction) 'foundations sponsoring the HYV research and the plant scientists whom they employed *could have chosen* to address the question of developing "peasant-biased" high-yielding varieties of seeds rather than the "landlord-biased" varieties which ultimately became the basis of the "seed-fertilizer [green] revolution"' (emphasis added). This revolution was, in fact, an alternative to agrarian reform, which implies redistribution of power: it was a means of increasing food production without upsetting entrenched interests (as well as a means of providing increased revenues to the Western firms supplying industrial inputs). The choices made by research sponsors were, from their point of view, altogether logical ones; the alternative of peasant-biased varieties was probably not even imagined, much less given serious consideration. Academic defenders of the Green Revolution – and they were and are legion – rarely bothered to ask 'Production by whom? and for whom?'; questions which have now been answered, for example, in the case of India where substantial grain reserves exist partly because half the population is too poor to buy them.

Knowledge costs money, and money is not thrown away by those who dispose of it. It is no accident that our libraries are filled with studies on the hungry and poverty-stricken of the Third World. Cynically but realistically put, the more one knows about those who may, in desperation, become restive and dangerous, the better tools one possesses for keeping them in check. Scholarship may also, wittingly or unwittingly, serve purely commercial interests. One fears, for instance, that the current vogue for studying 'appropriate technology' may become a vehicle for introducing new dependency-creating products in societies where incomes are inadequate for the purchase of expensive high-technology goods, but which can contribute to Western corporate interests at their own level.

Finally, social scientists can also function as promoters of particular ideologies and help to create a climate in which development strategies devised by the powerful may be pursued without hindrance or criticism. Intellectuals, as Noam Chomsky has put it, are 'experts in legitimation' and in packaging concepts so that they will sell, even if the wrappings conceal shoddy and adulterated merchandise.

There are basically three paradigms or models in the literature of development and hunger alleviation. The first is the 'growth/trickle-down' model, more fully described by Ball, which seeks the increase of gross national product through industrialization and by concentrating on those elements of society supposedly most 'modern' or 'entreprenurial' (poor peasants, in contrast, are 'backward' or 'traditional', although it is no longer considered fashionable to say so). The accumulated wealth of these 'modernizing elites' will, eventually, also benefit the worse-off. This model encourages the import of foreign capital and technology (as well as the implantation of multinational corporations) and assumes that the development process in the Third World should imitate the one that occurred in the now industrialized Western countries. Economic and social control is concentrated in the hands of the classes which act as motors of growth. This paradigm presupposes harmony: harmony at the national level (the elites will somehow want to share their advantages with their poorer compatriots, towards whom their attitude is essentially benevolent); harmony at the international level, also called 'interdependence' (the present world system is beneficial to all nations which should trade according to the principles of 'comparative advantage'). Due to its generally recognized failure, this first model has lately been perceived as badly in need of a facelift. This has been undertaken but is largely rhetorical. New keywords are *basic needs* and *participation*, but, as defined by experts, mostly from developed countries. Deprived people are neither to be consulted as to their needs nor allowed to participate to the extent that they might demand fundamental changes in existing patterns of income or power distribution.

The second model is based on 'dependency theory' which holds that there is a centre (the rich countries, with the United States as the centre of the centre) and a periphery (the Third World); and that the former has consistently exploited the latter since colonial times. The goal of development is thus to correct this historic and ongoing imbalance through the use of measures summed up in the New International Economic Order (NIEO) strategy: fair and stable prices for Third World raw materials, free access to northern markets for industrial goods, State control over multi-national corporations' practices, alleviation of debt, etc. This model also rests on an assumption of global interdependence, but stresses that serious adjustments will have to be made in the world system so that all nations can benefit and achieve that mutuality of interest which does not yet exist. This is the stance from which nearly all Third World governments (the so-called Group of 77) argue in international negotiations.

The third model does not deny the need for an NIEO, but tries to enrich this concept with a class analysis. The world is not merely divided into rich/powerful and poor/relatively powerless nations: all countries, including the rich ones, are characterized by a dominating and a dominated class (each, of course, with its own subdivisions). The NIEO is an incomplete solution to the problems of hunger and underdevelopment because nothing guarantees that increased national revenues will benefit the poor more than marginally. In the third model, the goal of development is not merely greater equality between States, but the decent livelihood and dignity of all human beings. Unlike the first model, this approach assumes not harmony but conflict. Third World elites will not give up their privileges without a struggle and will meanwhile prevent any substantial advantages from trickling down. Rich nations will continue to exploit poor ones, but industrialized country elites will also support their Third World counterparts so that this exploitation may more conveniently continue.

Advocates of the third model see hope for the Third World not in the greater integration of the less developed countries into the world system but in their greater independence from it. They call for self-reliance – the full use of all local material and human resources – before asking for outside help and for a fundamental redistribution of power as the only way to end hunger and misery. *Basic needs*, yes, but as defined by the communities concerned; not so much *participation* as empowerment – the capacity to control those decisions which most affect one's life.

Has scholarship anything to contribute to the emergence and the enforcement of the third model (for which my own bias will be obvious)? Development students, researchers and writers must address the needs of the most deprived and must be accountable for the work they produce. Students who see such accountability as an intellectual and moral imperative can begin by approaching the material listed here with their critical faculties on full alert and by asking the kinds of questions we have sketched here: Is the study part of the 'conventional wisdom', or does it try to take an opposing or unpopular point of view? Where does it stand in relation to the above three models, i.e. to power? Does it presume harmony and proceed in a social and political vacuum? Could the work contribute to increasing the knowledge – and thus the manipulative capacity – of national or international elites?

The reader, and especially the writer, should not forget that researchers, too, stand somewhere in the power structure. Their work can be used by the rich against the poor, but also, one may hope, vice versa. Why not turn our sights towards those who hold control, with a view to giving a clearer understanding of their activities to those whose lives they affect? This is often a difficult task, for the well endowed are less vulnerable to scholarly scrutiny than those who have no choice but to let themselves be studied; we should accept this as a challenge.

The mass of scholarship listed here represents an incalculable number of hours devoted to examining various aspects of world hunger, and while all of us have been writing, the relative and absolute numbers of hungry and destitute people have vastly increased. It is time we asked ourselves why, as scholars, we are still discussing poverty and want, and applied ourselves to trans-forming the contents of future bibliographies into explosive devices and instruments of liberation.

# 10

# UTOPIA, THE UNIVERSITY AND THE THIRD WORLD:
## AN IMAGINARY COOPERATION PROGRAMME

*The after-dinner speech is not a genre I've often practised. When your subject is almost invariably hunger and poverty, it's not a great feeling to stand up after a banquet and talk about them. If you do, you must first take infinite precautions, moving the audience away from its own guilt, a destructive emotion that does nothing for understanding and nothing for the hungry themselves.*

*The conference during which this dinner took place was organized in Guelph by the Universities of Guelph (Ontario, Canada) and Wageningen (Holland) in August 1983 on the theme of 'The Role of Universities in Integrated Rural Development'. Speechwriting is good discipline for making yourself think seriously about a problem. I tried to do that here, keeping in mind that I was still supposed to be the intellectual equivalent of brandy and cigars.*

*The network of people who met at this conference is still going strong, thanks to the efforts of Professors Tony Fuller and Wout van den Bor who edit the* Rural Development Notes *newsletter from their bases at Guelph and Wageningen. Many of us met again at Guelph in October 1989.*

Surely we who labour in the vineyards of Third World rural development are often tempted to dream, to fantasize and to play the 'absolute power' game; the game that allows us to run the world the way it ought to be run. Most of us have been frustrated by a project somewhere, sometime, that should have gone right and went wrong. Or, according to our different temperaments, we may become enraged or shrug our shoulders in disgust when reading the annual reports of certain official aid organizations, or just the daily newspapers. How, we may ask, is it possible to spend so much money for such paltry, or even negative, results? Occasionally, we may even be rewarded by participating in a project which goes according to plan and really benefits the needy people for whom it was intended. When this occurs, and after the initial flush of pride, we may find ourselves even more frustrated, and wonder why *everyone* doesn't see the wisdom of acting in just such a way *everywhere*. People whose daily lives revolve around the problems of develop- ment know – or at least believe they know – what needs to be done; they do not need an after-dinner speaker to tell them. All of us feel, consciously or unconsciously, that the problems are soluble: what we need is that some superior Being give us abso- lute power to get them solved.

Tonight, the organizers of the Guelph-Wageningen Conference on *Universities and Integrated Rural Development* have given me a splendid opportunity. They have handed me what amounts to *carte blanche* to play the 'absolute power' game in public. I intend to play it in somewhat the same way that André Malraux composed his 'Imaginary Museum': no problems of money, personal or national susceptibilities, or obstacles engendered by any powers-that-be are going to get in the way of my particular utopia. I will not be upset if you decide to say about me what William Lamb is reported to have said about Lord Macaulay: 'I wish I were as sure of anything as he is of everything.' The aim of utopias, from Plato to Thomas More and onwards, has always been to make political points which at some periods in history could not be made in any other way without fear of reprisal. Here, among colleagues, I do not fear reprisals: hence my aim will also be to provoke each of you to envisage his or her own utopia.

Perhaps, through a collective effort of imagination in our coming days together and after we separate, by juxtaposing and confronting and arguing about our utopias we may come closer to a genuine politics, in the noblest sense, of successful integrated rural development, and have a clearer idea of how we as scholars and practitioners might work in order to make that politics a reality, inside and outside the University, in both North and South.

Before I use the opportunity given me, let me make a disclaimer, then situate my utopia in relation to current trends in development theory and practice as I perceive them. First, the disclaimer. I am not especially well qualified to speak about integrated rural development, and I say this without false modesty. I have never spent six months living in a Third World village, nor have I ever had to deal with the nuts and bolts of a project: I therefore speak from the particular point of view of someone who does not work in the field, as many of you have done, unless it is the field that has come to be called 'development education'.

Second, my utopia will not be set in a vacuum. Part of the crisis in development thinking – and I believe we shall all agree that a crisis exists – stems from deep yet often unspoken divergences in our definitions of 'development'. What does the word mean? To oversimplify, one could say that there are basically three definitions, or models, or paradigms, or even factions where development is concerned, and most of us, myself included, are committed to one or another of these models, largely on *ideological and political grounds*. The first duty of people involved in development is to lay their cards on the table and make those political grounds explicit. This I shall attempt briefly to do.*

The first paradigm could be called the 'GNP growth plus trickle-down model', although the question 'Growth for whom?' is

---

*These three models appear in the preceding piece as well, but I have left them here because they don't take up much space and they help to situate Utopia University.

rarely asked. Where rural development is concerned, this model stresses 'technological fixes' like the Green Revolution or Post-harvest Technology; it tends to concentrate on the entrepreneur class of farmers in the better-endowed areas and it claims that greater national production will automatically benefit poor and hungry people living in the same national space. This model also tends to give priority to cash crops, to encourage transfers of Western technology, and to welcome the presence of trans-national agribusiness corporations. Basically, this model assumes that the rural development process in the Third World should be in large measure imitative of the one that took place in the now-industrialized countries. It presupposes – although this is rarely stated outright – a world ruled by *harmony*. 'Trickle-down' will work because the attitudes of elites towards their poorer and hungrier compatriots are essentially benevolent. At the global level, nations are interdependent and should exchange raw materials, goods and services according to the principles of comparative advantage in a world system which is supposed to be ultimately beneficial to all.

In this first model, though growth may indeed take place, power does not change hands. Control over resources not only remains where it was (with the privileged few in the First and Third Worlds) but is actually reinforced by the development process itself. Most observers are at last willing to recognize that development practice based on model one is a patent failure. Third World societies are, if anything, more polarized between small elites and destitute masses than ever before.

The second paradigm – again very briefly – rests on the theory of dependency, or of the centre countries versus the periphery. According to this dependency model, the centre has exploited the periphery since colonial times and the goal of development is thus to correct an historic and ongoing imbalance of unequal exchange which continues to impoverish Third World societies. This unjust situation can be altered by applying the measures variously referred to as the New International Economic Order, the

UNCTAD basket of recommendations or, most recently, the Brandt Report Programme: fair and stable prices for Third World products, debt relief, easier access to northern markets for finished goods, massive transfers of aid in the style of the Marshall Plan, etc. This paradigm also rests on the assumption of global interdependence, but stresses that serious adjustments will have to be made in the world system before all nations can benefit and achieve real reciprocity and harmony which does not yet exist. This, of course, is the stance from which Third World governments in the Group of 77 argue in international negotiations – and small wonder, since the model concerns States, and States alone. Ten years of spurious North–South 'dialogue', carried out at enormous cost in resources the Third World could have invested better elsewhere, have not brought us one inch closer to world harmony as defined by model two.

Even if it had been achieved, power relations might ideally change *between* countries, but not necessarily *within* them. In the House of the G-77 are many mansions: Pinochet's Chile and Marcos's Philippines, so to speak, call for the same measures as Zimbabwe or Nicaragua.

As you may have guessed already, my particular utopia is not to be found within the frontiers of either of these models, but rather in the largely unexplored territory of the third paradigm, where human rights, human dignity and human needs are the touchstones of theory and the goals of action. This territory may very well be inaccessible and beyond the realm of reasonable politics. That is precisely why it seems worth asking how we may come a little closer to it and how university cooperation programmes may help us to do so.

Indeed, when we seek to describe the third model, we have already reached the outskirts of utopia. Of the three possible paradigms I am suggesting, this one has been the least well articulated theoretically and is certainly the least practised. Just by trying to give it a name, I reveal my own bias in its favour, but I would call it the model of 'authentic' or 'liberated' development.

What might it look like? The third model would not deny the need for some sort of New International Economic Order, but it would be wary of locking Third World countries into the international market as a primary means of development. In fact, it would try to help them to disengage from this market as one way of refocusing attention on their internal needs before catering to the needs of foreigners. It would certainly try to enrich the State-to-State relationships of model two with a class analysis, demonstrating that the world is not merely divided into groups of rich and powerful nations versus poor and relatively powerless ones. All countries, including the industrialized ones, have their own centres and their own peripheries, or their dominant and dominated classes, if you prefer a different vocabulary. For proponents of the third model, the Brandt programme is a partial, even illusory, solution to underdevelopment, because nothing guarantees that increased national revenues will benefit the poorest people more than marginally, especially those who live in the countryside.

Authentic development means more than greater equality between States: it demands a decent livelihood and basic rights for all human beings. This paradigm, like the other two, also rests on an unspoken assumption. Unfortunately, this assumption is not very palatable to governments, international organizations or, for that matter, to many individuals. That notion is, of course, *conflict*. Elites will not often give up their privileges without a struggle and will usually prevent whatever they can from trickling down. The dominant classes of rich, strong nations will continue to exploit poor and weak ones, but they may sometimes give extra support to their Third World counterparts so that this exploitation may more conveniently continue. Such support may range from outright military presence to various kinds of economic aid and cultural ties between the elites, each of which gets something from the bargain. Allow me to add that this is the case whether we are speaking about the Western or the Eastern bloc.

Thus model three cannot really work in most societies unless there is some redistribution of power, both between and within countries – including the industrialized countries. Any development project should thus contribute to this end.

So should university cooperation programmes. Thus I'll start building my utopian programme in the land of model three. By virtue of the absolute power conferred on me tonight, I'll begin by changing the terms of reference. In utopia, we won't ask how northerners might contribute to 'integrated rural development' in the poorer countries of the South, but rather decode the officialese. This rather barbarous term, 'integrated-rural development', was invented by powerful financial institutions for their own purposes. In plain English it means an adequate livelihood and human dignity for the vast majority of the landed or landless peasantry who are presently deprived of both. The first question to ask is not, therefore, 'What can we contribute to integrated rural development?', but rather 'Why are so many millions of people prevented from enjoying both a decent livelihood and a modicum of dignity, and what, if anything, may we do about it?'

The reasons these millions of people live in deprivation lie partly in the developed countries, partly in the Third World itself and partly in relationships between the two. Although universities do not have the power to make State policy, nevertheless the concepts and intellectual attitudes elaborated in academia do have a way of trickling down – or up. Let's give the universities a utopian opportunity to influence official attitudes and look in turn at what northern universities, southern ones and a partnership between them might do to improve the lot of the poor majority.

In Utopia University-North, scholars concerned with rural development are constantly criticizing their own models, concepts, curricula and scientific systems. The first principle they all agree on is that no science is socially neutral. Once when I asserted this in front of an eminent American professor, he replied that he could think of lots of socially neutral sciences – poultry science, for example. I was glad he had picked such an easy example to shoot down! The chicken which grows from an imported day-old chick, is genetically engineered to eat an imported corn–soya mixture, and is sterile and thus non-reproducible is obviously not the same bird as the one which can be raised on local feedstuffs and can lay eggs that will produce other chickens *ad infinitum*. The social – not to mention financial – consequences of the two chicken-raising systems will not be at all the same either.

At Utopia U, every practitioner of a 'hard' or 'soft' science enjoys studying the historical and social conditions in which his or her discipline developed. Sociologists recognize that the methodology of their discipline was elaborated largely at the end of the nineteenth century in an urban, northern, white, masculine context. So they're aware that it may not be very good at asking and answering questions posed by rural, southern, non-white societies in which women play a vital role. They seek to counteract these deficiencies. Our biologists at Utopia-North know and deplore that virtually every branch of their science has been used at one time or another, including the 1980s, to promote the claim that North Americans and Europeans are superior to everybody else.

Utopia U-North agronomists, to take another example, know that their training was concerned with getting the most production per *person*, not per unit of land, for the very good reason that North America always had a huge frontier and relatively few people to work it. They understand that this is not the Third World's problem, where relatively large numbers of people must try to earn a living on relatively small amounts of land. In Oklahoma, what's wanted is optimum production from optimum resources. In Orissa a system that reduces costs and especially risks for the farmer is much more important, even if it's not quite so highly productive.

Out there in the real world, our occidental models have been dominant in so many disciplines for so long that we tend to think they are not just unique but inevitable as well. Yet even in the so-called 'hard' sciences, even in mathematics, the most advanced thinkers now recognize that there are many ways of looking at reality and that the social, political and economic climate of the times has a great deal to do with the ways chosen by scientists. This proposition is, of course, far more evident in the social sciences.

At Utopia University-North, I am therefore founding the Institute for the Deconstruction and Relativization of Elementary and Advanced Models – whose acronym is, of course, I-DREAM. At the I-DREAM, philosophers, historians and social scientists will work with their colleagues in the physical and natural sciences to examine the origins, development and curricula of the various disciplines; their function in the societies where they are practised and the particular interests they have served and continue to serve. At the I-DREAM, researchers will be concerned with taking apart mathematical, physical, biological and social models and putting them back together in novel and interesting ways – or at least proving that other ways exist.

Of course the Institute will also work in practical disciplines like medicine, architecture, engineering, agronomy or city planning. I suspect that researchers at the I-DREAM may discover, for example, that centralized, hospital-based curative medicine and the highly industrialized, expensive food systems used in Western societies are certainly not the only ways (and perhaps not the best ways) to care for people's health or provide them with a varied and nourishing diet. I'm almost sure that these researchers will find that the United States needs land reform as much as does Latin America, and that the assembly-line system in our factories was designed for the benefit of people like Henry Ford, not for the workers. They may further determine that solar energy is preferable to nuclear power in every respect except that it is decentralized by nature and cannot be tightly controlled by the State. Thus it will not be adopted in most countries.

In short, these research workers will concern themselves with understanding what political, economic and social power has to do with the development of science, technology and the several arts.

The Institute for the Deconstruction and Relativization of Models will not be merely a research institution. It will dispense one general, compulsory course, for all the students in the university, wherever they come from, whatever their chosen area of study.

This course will start with the deconstruction of models in the more technical and easily understood disciplines and work upwards towards models in biology, physics and mathematics. Furthermore, each advanced undergraduate student will be expected to attend a seminar at I-DREAM related to his or her major field of study. Anyone who intends to deal professionally with a non-occidental society will get a double dose. Third World students who come to our university for training, and who tend to admire us more than we deserve, will be required to spend some of their time at the Institute. They will also be expected to enrich its work, through communications describing how their own societies have solved various basic human problems.

I am not entirely sure what to do with the general university faculty, beyond the walls of the I-DREAM. Will they accept recycling? Will they take part voluntarily in the Institute's work? I particularly fear non-cooperation from monetarist economists and sociobiologists, and I warn them tonight that even in utopia we are not above subtle forms of coercion!

Third World students will come to Utopia U for work on advanced degrees, but we will recommend that they do their undergraduate work in their own countries or regions. I doubt whether the crimes of the past are still being perpetrated in most northern universities. Still, who has not heard stories like the one about the Indian soil scientist doing his Ph.D. in the US on moon soils – or the African architect learning in Canada how to construct buildings to withstand snowfalls of several metres. Our faculty advisers will all be attuned to the special needs of their Third World students – sometimes beginning with special language needs – and the students' dissertations will all reflect concern with the problems that their own societies need to solve.

Thus may our University help to encourage critical thinking about Western models and to stem brain drain.

On the campus of Utopia University-South will be founded a sister Institute to the I-DREAM. For want of a better name, I shall call it the Institute for the Decolonization of the Mind. Here again compulsory courses will be taught to all the students: courses concerning the values and achievements, past and present, of the civilizations born on the three so-called 'poor' continents.

The Institute for the Decolonization of the Mind will, like its sister Institute, undertake studies in the practical disciplines as well as the arts and sciences. This will be called the Birthright Programme. Researchers will learn to make maximum use of the renewable resources of their environment. Subjects like the curative powers of plants, the beauty and practicality of earthen or wooden architecture, and the rationality of peasant systems of cultivation will be studied scientifically. The Birthright Programme's aim will neither be to enforce traditional practices nor to place them in some sort of museum; even less to persuade Third World societies that they should make do with second-rate technology. Instead, the programme will try to discover the scientific principles underlying traditional solutions so that these practices can be improved rather than destroyed, as is so often the case today.

Because we have no financial restrictions at Utopia University North or South, or at our sister Institutes, exchanges between their students and faculty will be intense and definitely run on a two-way street. Though the North specializes in deconstructing and multiplying models and the South in restoring Third World accomplishments to their rightful status and perfecting them, they share a communications network. Video conferences, computer linkages and personal visits keep them abreast of each other's work.

Frequent joint meetings of Northern and Southern Utopians will also lead to solving some practical problems which are in effect political problems. At present, most University cooperation is arranged, like it or not, on a State-to-State basis. Third World governments are usually the ones to decide which students will get a chance to study abroad. With the help of their Utopia South colleagues, northern university people may be able respectfully to suggest that these governments offer such an opportunity to a much larger proportion of women who, for example, are now fewer than 10 per cent of the francophone Third World students in France.

Because Utopians recognize that knowledge is not neutral, they also realize that research itself is necessarily situated somewhere in national and international power structures and that it does not necessarily serve all classes of society without bias. Experience tells them that all States requesting university cooperation programmes do not, alas, take a deep interest in the needs of their own poor, rural populations – the very people most in need of 'development'. Utopian Universities entering into cooperative arrangements thus have the right to establish a list of priority countries – those whose leaders have demonstrated 'political will, honesty and true respect for the population', as French Ambassador-at-large Stéphane Hessel recently put it.

To state matters bluntly, no scholar from Utopia U North or South will ever be asked to contribute to, say, nuclear research in a repressive country where half the population is malnourished. Such scholars might, however, perfectly well undertake research needed or requested by peasant associations or non-governmental organizations in the same country. In other words, Utopia U personnel will seek out partners for research cooperation beyond governments, and they will make substantiated judgements, political judgements, about States, based on their human rights record.

Let's assume that Utopia University in the North has received a request from a Third World government for cooperation in a rural health care programme. Will it hand the problem over to the medical school and have done? Certainly not. In our University, we have long since recognized that something labelled 'health' cannot be conveniently situated within the limits of medicine or biology. Health implies nutrition, and nutrition implies the equitable distribution of food, which in turn depends on agrarian structures, the relative power of landowners, and rural people's access to land and to jobs. A healthy population also needs clean water, which raises problems of engineering for wells and dams – but also such social problems as who will fetch and carry the water. In most places, women will; and, if the clean water well is too far away, they may prefer the brackish pond. One could go on lengthening the list of factors that must be considered if the health programme is to work, but the need for interdisciplinary thinking should be apparent.

Utopia seems to be a necessary prerequisite for even the most basic improvements, if one is to judge by what occurs in the real world. Consider the apparently simple matters of the exchange of knowledge and academic courtesy. Arguably, one of the reasons why so much research work is done on poor communities is because researchers feel they need not ask the permission of such communities to examine them. People are observed, whether they like it or not. In Utopia we are first going to find out what these communities themselves believe needs to be researched, and we will make our results available to them as we go along. It is likely that what they need is not more research on their own practices, which they understand perfectly well, but research on the doings of moneylenders and the workings of commodities markets. Utopians will spend much of their time learning about the rich and powerful, in order to convey this useful knowledge to the poor and powerless, in hopes of altering the balance.

In the real world, if you want to do a dissertation on the Rockefeller or the Tata dynasty, you will be given limited opportunity for direct observation, or you will have to grovel to obtain their consent; and then you may risk having to write a hagiography. Why do most researchers feel no accountability to the subjects of their work, provided those subjects are in no position to control or to protest? These same subjects will help to assure the scholar of university tenure and a comfortable income for the rest of his days, yet he seems willing to give them little in return.

Does this sound like an exaggeration? Why, then, did a Latin American Development Studies Institute offer space, counsel and every courtesy to over 300 North American Ph.D. candidates and receive in return – how many copies of their dissertations would you guess? I hope you will be as incredulous as I was when you learn the number, which I discovered from the Director of the Institute in question. Exactly twelve. Why, again, was a massive study on the Sahel, undertaken by the University of Michigan and published in the US by USAID in 1977, unavailable to scholars in Upper Volta as of 1979?

These examples do not reflect a lack of academic courtesy alone but also a demonstration of the priorities and loyalties of mainstream scholarship. At Utopia U, students who do not supply at least three copies of their work to institutions of their choice in the country where the research was carried out will receive diplomas entirely unsuitable for framing, because they will be emblazoned with a scarlet letter: 'F', perhaps, for 'Freeloader'.

I'm tempted to continue playing the absolute power game, but this excursion to Utopia has been long enough. You will doubtless come up with many ideas for improving my ideal university cooperation programme – or revamping it altogether. Perhaps you will have found many of my recommendations obvious – but for me Utopia is also a place where no one needs to fear making a fool of himself (or, in this case, herself) by asking naïve or obvious questions. If these remarks help in any way to make all of us participating in this conference more creative individually and collectively, I shall be well content, and I thank you warmly for your attention.

# II

# ORDERING THE WORLD:
# FROM ICIDI TO ICIHI

*The Independent Commission on International Humanitarian Issues*
*– ICIHI – grew out of UN resolutions concerning the 'International*
*Humanitarian Order', but its real impetus and dynamism came from*
*its co-chairman, Prince Sadruddin Aga Khan (former UN High Com-*
*missioner for Refugees), who shared the chairmanship with Hassan*
*Bin Talal, Crown Prince of Jordan. The twenty-four additional com-*
*missioners were 'eminent persons' from all over the world. Some of*
*ICIHI's members had already served on the Brandt Commission in*
*the late 1970s–early 1980s. The Brandt Commission's formal name*
*was the Independent Commission on International Development*
*Issues, or ICIDI, though I doubt whether anyone ever actually called*
*it that.*

*During its three-year lifespan (1983–6), ICIHI commissioned*
*independent research on three major topics: humanitarian norms in*
*the context of armed conflicts; natural and man-made disasters; and*
*vulnerable groups (refugees, children, indigenous peoples, etc.). It also*
*held consultations, one of them on food security issues which I*
*attended in July 1984 with a few other 'experts' and a couple of the*
*commissioners.*

*ICIHI's report* Famine: a Man-Made Disaster? *(Mark Malloch*
*Brown ed., Pan Books, London, 1985) was an excellent and forthright*
*statement, possibly because it was a report to, not a report by, the*
*Commissioners. It thus avoided the consensual demands and blandness*
*of the Brandt Commission reports. Subsequent ICIHI publications also*

*appeared, on deforestation, desertification, etc. I prepared a couple of background papers for the Commission at the request of its then Secretary, Brian Walker; but, aside from these and my attendance at the above-noted consultation, took no part in its work.*

*This letter to the participants in the consultation is included here because it raises important points about our choices of political categories and highlights some of the shortcomings of the Brandt Commission.*

*Page references in the text are to the first and second reports of the Brandt Commission:* North–South: a Programme for Survival *and* Common Crisis, *both published by Pan Books, London, 1980 and 1983.*

---

A personal memo to the participants in the Geneva meeting of 27 July 1984

Beyond the pleasure I had in participating, our meeting left me with two major impressions. First, the Independent Commission on International Humanitarian Issues (ICIHI), or at least the part of it that I met, genuinely wants to go beyond the conclusions of the Independent Commission on International Development Issues (ICIDI), better known as the 'Brandt Commission'; ICIHI seeks to break new ground and to make meaningful recommendations. Second, the Secretariat was somewhat disappointed that its invited 'experts' had no ready-made blueprints to offer in the food/hunger area, where lies our presumed expertise.

On reflection, perhaps our greatest problem was one of classification: what to put in and what to leave out. We got a bit bogged down in the 'seamless web' syndrome where everything is connected to everything. Well, everything *is* connected to everything, but, as Joan Robinson said, 'To know anything one must know everything. But to talk [and, may I add, to write] about anything, one has to leave out a great deal.'

Since progressing 'beyond Brandt' and classifying seem to me intimately related, let me try to sort out (i.e. to classify – one can't escape) some thoughts to show why that's so.

If we didn't have categories, we couldn't possibly organize our daily lives, much less write long reports. The categories we choose are, however, another matter. In *Les Mots et les Choses*, Michel Foucault led off with the classification of animals in Jorge Luis Borges' imaginary Chinese encyclopedia. In this (mythical) work, the categories of animals are

> (a) belonging to the Emperor, (b) embalmed, (c) tame, (d) suckling pigs, (e) sirens, (f) fabulous, (g) stray dogs, (h) included in the present classification, (i) frenzied, (j) innumerable, (k) drawn with a very fine camelhair brush, (l) *et cetera*, (m) having just broken the water pitcher, (n) those that from a long way off look like flies.

Foucault was trying to provoke in us the shock of recognizing the arbitrariness of our own categories, to bring us up against a totally alien way of organizing the world. This list induces vertigo, a sense of things falling apart. What if our own categories were as fragile, or as crazy? People become frightened when their systems of classification are threatened, and small wonder!

Here, now, is another system – this time a real one; the brainchild of the General Commissioner of the Paris Universal Exhibition of 1900. Monsieur Picard divided his exhibits into eighteen groups and 121 classes. He wrote that 'The objects must be on display to visitors in a logical order, their classification must correspond to a simple, clear and precise conception which carries in itself its philosophy and its justification, so that the basic idea [*l'idée mère*] is revealed without effort.' Picard's 'logical order' is the following:*

1. Education and Teaching (because, 'through them, man *enters* life')

2. Works of Art (because they must keep their 'place of honour')

*For Picard's classification, I am indebted to George Perec, 'Penser/Classer' in *Le Genre Humain* N. 2 (quarterly review published with the cooperation of the Maison des Sciences de l'Homme, l'École des Hautes Études en Sciences Sociales and the CNRS, Fayard, Paris, 1982). Perec, however, did not draw the political implications of this list.

3. Instruments and Methods of Arts and Letters

4. Mechanics

5. Electricity

6. Civil Engineering and Transportation

7. Agriculture

8. Horticulture and Orchards

9. Forests, Hunting and Fishing

10. Foods

11. Mines and Metallurgy

12. Decorations and Furnishings of Public Edifices and Private Houses

13. Threads, Textiles and Clothing

14. Chemical Industry

15. Various Industries: paper, cutlery, jewellery, goldsmithing, watchmaking, wickerwork, knick-knacks ('*bibeloterie*'), etc.

16. Social Economy, Hygiene, Public Health, Medicine and Surgery (this category is truly harrowing: here are displayed strait-jackets for the insane, beds for the handicapped, crutches and wooden legs, military surgeons' battlefield kits, Red Cross first-aid equipment, apparatus for resuscitating the drowned and the asphyxiated, etc.). Social Economy, according to Picard, 'should come naturally after the various branches of artistic, agricultural or industrial production because it results from them as well as being their philosophy'. (???) NB: The passage is no clearer in French: '... *elle en est la résultante en même temps que la philosophie*'.

17. Colonization, a category which did not figure in the Universal Exhibition of 1889. This new category is 'amply justified by the need for colonial expansion felt by all civilized peoples'.

18. The Army and the Navy

This may seem a very roundabout route indeed to take towards our common pursuit, but, whatever the appearances, I am not merely trying to amuse you on a dull August day. Picard's way of ordering the world – remember that his exhibition was 'universal' – may seem at first glance almost as bizarre as the Chinese animals. I am prepared to award a handsome certificate to whichever of you proposes the best explanation of what his 'idée-mère' actually was. My own interpretation is that it is no accident that categories 1 to 16 lead us, however tortuously, to the 'need' to subjugate ignorant peoples through the use of military might, since this is obviously the only normal and civilized way to behave when one has electricity, horticulture and decorated public edifices. Picard's classification indeed follows a 'logical order', if only because he eventually arrives at the 'right' conclusions, i.e. the conclusions desired by the powerful elites of his own time. He provides them, as promised, with a 'philosophy' and a 'justification'.

The Brandt Commission showed a suitable concern for the problems of Third World peoples and I do not wish to impugn the motives of its Commissioners, least of all those of Brandt himself. The ICIDI was, nevertheless, a spin-off of the World Bank (proposed by McNamara, working under the direction of a former high World Bank official), and one may suppose that the Bank had something to say about the selection of the northern and southern participants.

When people share major assumptions – those categories which are to some degree prior to thought because they are simply *given* – their geographical origins matter very little. The power to decide what the categories are going to be, or to arrange things so that no real discussion about them even takes place (much the best method), is a very real power. Policing the borders of the classification system has been an important task of ruling classes since the beginnings of history, and I see no reason why the World Bank – which is just a metaphor for those who think like the Bank – should relinquish this power willingly.

ICIDI, like any individual or body, had its own prior assumptions and classification system, of which I will give just a few examples. One of the Commission's most revealing assumptions is its tacit rejection of history. Poverty and underdevelopment in the South are just *there* – no attempt is made to explain how such conditions may have come about, possibly because such an analysis would imply a recognition of the North's responsibility in this state of affairs (not only during the colonial period, but throughout the entire post-war era as well). So, to begin with, all the categories in the Brandt system are flat and two-dimensional at best, with no historical depth.

ICIDI also fully shares the general UN-system myth that all governments, especially those in the Third World, are representative of their people (i.e. their poor majorities) and can consequently be counted upon to act in their interests. Although Chairman Willy Brandt says in his introduction to *North–South* that 'We in the South *and* the North should frankly discuss abuses of power by elites . . .' (p. 10, his emphasis), the Commission itself never proceeds to act on this suggestion. From its Report, one would never guess that governments represent, on the whole, the interests of those who keep them in power and that they themselves are interested in remaining in power. Thus the category of the benign State is also a constant.

From this assumed harmony at the national level, it is a natural step to assuming harmony – potentially anyway – at the international level. Of course there are problems between the North and the South, but 'none of [them] can effectively be solved by confrontation: sensible solutions can only result from dialogue and cooperation . . . *development means interdependence . . .*'

(pp. 22–3, my emphasis). Having gone to great lengths to point out what could be the happy consequences for all of a recognized interdependence, the Commission then asks, 'if these mutual interests exist, why have the measures that embody them not been implemented long ago? Are people and governments not aware of the mutuality of interests?' ICIDI's answer is essentially that there is not enough public knowledge of the facts; or that, in negotiations where both sides stand to gain, 'either may feel unwilling to give in because they are not gaining enough or because the other gains too much. This is especially true in negotiations between unequals . . .' (p. 66).

In the Brandt world-view, then, there is nothing fundamentally wrong with the global economic system: with a bit of goodwill on both sides (there *are* only two sides – North and South) it could be made to work for everyone in the South as it is assumed to have worked by now for everyone in the North. In fact, it is precisely because we must save this global economic system that common sense and cooperation are necessary.

Thus in the course of Brandt's argument for 'massive transfers' (of money and other resources from North to South) we learn that the 'dynamic developing countries' are a 'new economic frontier' where investments will prosper because these countries have 'fewer of the . . . social and political constraints operating in the North' (p. 67). What does this mean? No effective trade unions and a cheap, docile labour force? ICIDI doesn't say. One does, however, know from experience that northern investors do indeed prefer countries without such 'social and political constraints'.

In the same vein, trade should be expanded, protectionism is always wrong, even for infant industries; all countries should participate as fully as possible in world markets. Unfortunately, the discussion on access to those markets (p. 69), while deploring trade barriers, is quite separate from the discussion of transnational corporations (p. 73) which happen to control two-thirds of world trade. As to the TNCs, 'a very substantial mutual interest lies in harnessing the economic strength and experience of the multinationals for development'. We are not, however, told how this is to come about in a world where the TNCs are profit-seeking entities and actors on their own, not subject to the dictates of nations or of international bodies.

In the Bank's-eye, Brandt's-eye view of the world, 'trickle-down' (rebaptized for the occasion 'massive transfers') will somehow work this time around, although it is easy to show that it has not worked over the past thirty years. For ICIDI, there is no contradiction between, on the one hand, full participation in and concentration on world markets and, on the other, self-reliance, in spite of the demonstrated impoverishment such participation has brought to the LDCs, with the exception of the NICs.

In the area of food and agriculture, which interests us in the context of ICIHI, 'modern' agricultural technology and large-scale development schemes are never called into question by the Brandt Report. Some samples: 'At the moment there should be no clear danger of a worldwide shortage of fertilizers, nor is there yet an urgent need to introduce plant varieties less dependent on chemicals. Modern high-yielding plants are efficient converters of nitrogen into food with the minimum non-food content and making efficient use of sunlight' (p. 100).

This short passage is a splendid concentrate of unstated assumptions. Because the category of 'modern agriculture' clearly has a totally favourable connotation, the Report does not (indeed *could* not) ask (1) *which* people in the Third World can afford to use 'modern high-yielding plants' cultivated with chemicals, (2) whether the vast majority of the world's peasants do not need 'low-risk, stable yield' systems more than 'high-yielding' ones, and (3) whether the 'non-food content' (straw, etc.) of plants does not have its place in the peasant's survival economy (you will perhaps recall my story about people freezing to death in Bihar from lack of straw to cover themselves).*

*In 1980 in India, I learned from a high official of the Indian civil administration that for the first time people in his country were dying from exposure. Why? Because straw had been a free good and the poorest people used it to keep warm.

Brandt is for nothing if not for growth, and here it seems that agriculture is a real drag: 'Virtually all these [low-income] countries have two-thirds or more of their workers in agriculture and all of them rely heavily on exporting raw material. These are among the chief economic causes of their slow growth' (p. 51). Some countries, like India and the Philippines, have, however, seen the light and have adopted the 'new crop varieties of the Green Revolution [which] produced substantial agricultural growth ...' (p. 52). Again, we do not learn that there was also substantial (and substantiated) criticism of the Green Revolution which could certainly have been made available to the Commissioners, many of whom were probably not aware of this literature. They might then have been less eager to praise growth for growth's sake and might have pondered the fate of the millions who are excluded from this kind of agricultural productivity.

But in Brandt's ordering of the world this is not possible because there is no history. We look only at the fraction of the peasantry using the Green Revolution *now* and at its total output. There is no particular connection between the countryside and the city either, so we do not witness out-migration from rural areas. The Report does not even contain a section on urban problems *per se*. In other words, the particular set of categories chosen (or, rather, assumed) renders invisible the poor people who suffered from intensified competition for land and employment, induced by the Green Revolution, and were forced to settle in shanty-towns, or who simply lost their livelihood and died. Similarly, we do not

When short-straw varieties came to dominate agriculture, reducing overall quantities of straw, and as industrial paper production also began to use straw as a raw material – decimation of forests having made wood-pulp-based paper expensive – straw became a commodity people could not always afford.

My lack of ecological sensitivity in 1984, not to mention that of the Brandt Commission, shows in this passage. Another unstated assumption of ICIDI that I should have caught is its belief that chemical fertilizers do not undermine natural soil fertility, do not pollute drinking water from streams or ground water through run-offs, do not kill fish, a major source of protein, etc.

learn about the appalling living conditions of the Filipino peasantry, nor the 48 per cent of the Indian rural population still living below a very stringently determined 'poverty line'.

The power to define categories is *ipso facto* the power to include and to exclude. Bank-type, Brandt-type logical ordering leaves Bank-type initiatives out of all the more painful equations. Thus intervention by outside agencies, particularly international ones, cannot, by definition, make the plight of poor people worse and development spending always automatically results in development. Profligate use is also made in Brandt of what I like to call the 'ubiquitous we': 'We are arming ourselves to death' ... 'Mankind still behaves as if all these resources – up to now so abundantly wasted – were renewable' etc. All of which is true but gives the impression that grandmothers and Upper Voltaics bear as much responsibility for this state of affairs as missile corporations and owners of Rolls-Royces.

Some progress is made in the second Brandt Report. Published in 1983 after Cancún had well and truly disposed of the myth of the New International Economic Order, *Common Crisis* contains some hopeful signs. Timid murmurs of criticism are heard concerning some international institutions.

'[Cancún called] for a review of agricultural and food agencies working within the framework of the United Nations,' says Report No. 2. 'While we are aware of excellent work being done by sections of several institutions, there has been criticism of other activities, of overlapping functions and inadequate coordination. *We support an urgent review of this kind*' (p. 32, emphasis in the original).

The IMF (which we targeted at our meeting as one of the chief contemporary factors reducing poor people's food security) also attracts mild criticism: 'There is typically more than one way of achieving external equilibrium, but the Fund generally assumes a very limited range of possibilities ... in particular it should avoid advocating policies for a number of countries which, when carried out by all of them together, will reduce world income and employment at a time when expansion is needed' (p. 62).

The *Common Crisis* report also comes close to saying (p. 36) that if Western countries like the US had taken the slightest interest in Afghanistan during the decade before the Soviet invasion – when this miserable country was a rock-bottom aid recipient relative to its size and poverty – they would have helped to reduce East–West tensions before the fact: 'Certainly the situations of that country and many others now call forth military expenditures well in excess of anything that was ever provided to promote their development – development which might have forestalled political crisis.'

So there's a good deal one can build on in Brandt 2, and even in Brandt 1. Since I'm trying here to discuss for a very small audience the epistemological problem of world-ordering, I've stressed the (negative) aspects which clearly support my case. One could doubtless make the same points more gently, to ICIHI's Commissioners for example, some of whom overlap with Brandt's. The signal weakness of the Independent Commission on International *Development* Issues, ICIDI, remains, however, its basic view of development as something that is done *to* people *by* governments or by UN agencies or by something called the 'international community', which takes responsibility for trade policy, high finance and the like. The people themselves are invariably regarded (if they are present at all) as objects, as obstacles or as victims, never as actors.

The enormous opportunity of the International Commission on International *Humanitarian* Issues, ICIHI, lies in its very mandate, which demands that people be placed at front and centre stage. If it carries out this mandate with imagination and if it is willing to cast a critical eye on its own world-ordering categories, it can actually turn ICIDI inside out.

Many of the recommendations I would personally like to see emerging from the ICIHI process can be read *en filigrane* or as the mirror image of the criticisms set forth above, so I'll not repeat them systematically here. What does seem urgent is that a credible body state clearly that the emperor has no clothes on. The official development strategies practised up to now simply haven't worked.

Non-Governmental Organizations are already saying this as loudly as they can, but they get no help from any body even remotely attached to the United Nations. It is often felt that the UN system wants NGOs to parrot its own views to their constituencies, not to make serious inputs to the system itself.

One could conceivably argue that things might have been even worse without the 'development' interventions of past decades, but surely this is cold comfort. We need a frank admission of failure and a recognition that nearly all the strategies that *have* worked have been smaller-scale, pragmatic, non-technocratic and community-based. In the UN system itself, the work of Unicef, IFAD and the High Commission for Refugees stands out in this regard.

A humanitarian commission must come out on the side of human beings, but this apparent tautology implies some formidable political hurdles. The first one is ideological – to alter the present dominant categories and to insist on new ones. Instead of a simplified 'North–South' view, one must recognize and explore the class relations in both central and peripheral countries and their international connections.

As was cogently pointed out at our meeting, neo-classical economics manages to divorce 'production' (agricultural or otherwise) from 'distribution', that is, people's access to food. Within this neo-classical framework, a certain gentleman (one of ICIHI's Commissioners from a northern country) can indeed claim that criticizing the Green Revolution for not having solved inequalities is like 'accusing a fork of being a poor knife'. (Actually critics of the GR usually say it has made such inequities worse, but this gentleman's response would be the same: those problems have to be solved by someone else, for example the State, which invariably governs with a view to social justice and equality, as we all know.)

In a humanitarian world-view, the categories of production

and distribution, or access, would be interdependent, not separated, so that one would always be required to ask 'production by whom and for whom?'

Before making recommendations for improving the lot of ordinary people, one must first come to terms with the State. In the Brandt world-view as in the UN system, development is exclusively channelled through governments. Helping rural people to produce more food – and in particular helping them to hold on to enough of it for their own adequate consumption – means on the other hand strengthening popular organizations like peasant cooperatives, women's groups, etc., which the State may often see – correctly – as directly opposed to its own priorities, one of which is usually to extract as much wealth as possible from the countryside.

We also need a critique of the multilateral agencies, too timidly addressed by Brandt. The problem is to carry it out in such a way that it does not bring grist to the mill to the likes of Reagan!

If ICIHI decides to stick mainly to the *gaps* that exist in other (official or quasi-official) bodies' work on food security, then a quick list would further include:

- *Food aid*. To my knowledge, no respectable body has gone further than saying 'food aid *can* be harmful but doesn't need to be'. There is so much evidence that a lot of it *has* been harmful that official reports are now obliged to make this minimal admission, while never going so far as to explain how one avoids negative impacts. It would not be difficult to make specific recommendations in this area.

- *'National Food Strategies'* (as proposed by the World Food Council and taken up by the EEC Development Commission *inter alia*). These so-called 'strategies' are the latest fashion, but are unlikely to do countries much good so long as they remain limited to their announced scope – i.e. national. All countries' food systems have become profoundly integrated into the world economy and it is fruitless to examine or try to improve them outside this context. This is a further example of the importance of the choice of categories.

- *The international agricultural research network*, including the CGIAR (Consultative Group on International Agricultural Research) and the major institutes. More support for alternative agricultural research is desperately needed – on polycultural, risk-reducing systems in particular, as well as on choices of agricultural technology appropriate to such systems, individual natural and social environments, etc.

- *Transnational agribusinesses*. My personal boredom with the subject notwithstanding, it's worth repeating that TNCs are not around to provide food or employment but to make profits, full stop. Nor, in my view, can they be 'harnessed', as Brandt would have it; they must rather be confronted and exposed, as the Nestlé campaign proved. Some support from a respectable body for such campaigns would be most helpful – beyond the grudging recognition finally granted the Nestlé campaign by WHO under strong NGO pressure.

Finally, I'll repeat my own plea for a two-way North–South people's research and monitoring system. Northern participants would provide the kind of information to which they have the easiest access (on TNCs, contracts, State or multilateral agencies' policies and the like); southern participants would provide case-studies on what actually takes place when the Bank, the FAO or a TNC implements a project in a specific area. Such a system would not need to be limited to NGOs – many individual scholars would also want to participate if they were given expenses and minimum remuneration to do so. A North–South research network would allow southern entities to commission work directly useful to them. For example, I once did a study for Nicaragua on potential markets for basic grains in surplus. Though nominally a 'Nicaraguan' study and a contribution to their National Food Plan, most of the research was done in Washington and could not have been accomplished in Managua.

Above all, in order to make a strong impact on public opinion and to attain a higher intellectual standing than Brandt – the two are linked – ICIHI must think seriously about a new 'categorical imperative'. May the Commission seize the conceptual initiative and render the poor visible and audible!

# PART IV

# HUMAN RIGHTS

# THE RIGHT TO FOOD AND
# THE POLITICS OF HUNGER

*This is the text of the 1985 Yvon Beaulne Lecture on the International Protection of Human Rights, delivered in March 1985 at Ottawa University and sponsored by the Human Rights Centre there. This was not, I am pleased to say, a 'memorial lecture' and Mr Beaulne, former Canadian Ambassador to the United Nations and one of the framers of the* Universal Declaration of Human Rights, *was in attendance with Mrs Beaulne.*

*Although not chronologically quite the last paper in this collection (both 'Food, Famine and Service Delivery' and 'Food Strategies for Tomorrow' were given later), I'm putting it at the end of this new edition of* Ill Fares the Land *because it links this book to* A Fate Worse than Debt, *which I had by then begun to work on. Since* Fate *appeared, I've pursued the human rights theme and written a paper dealing specifically with its links to Third World debt.*

*I happen to be writing this introduction on 22 August 1989. Two hundred years ago, between 20th and 26th August 1789, the* Declaration of the Rights of Man and the Citizen *was elaborated and adopted by the French Constituent Assembly. Article 15 of this Declaration states, 'All public officers are accountable to society for their administration.' Two hundred years later, we have not made much progress in implementing Article 15, particularly at the international level. The public officers of the World Bank and the Inter national Monetary Fund who devise the 'stabilization' and 'structural adjustment programmes' to deal with Third World debt have an enormous negative impact on the lives of millions. No one elected them; they are not accountable to the societies of the North or of the South.*

*For understanding, for dramatizing, the human consequences of debt (including increased hunger), human rights criteria seem to me even more relevant than they were four years ago. We could start by trying to put Article 15 back on the political agenda.*

---

No human right has been so consistently enshrined in international legal instruments as the right to food. This right figures specifically in Article 25 of the Universal Declaration. Both International Covenants (the one on Economic, Cultural and Social Rights as well as the one on Civil and Political Rights) declare that 'in no case may a people be deprived of its own means of subsistence'. Article 11 of the Economic, Social and Cultural Rights Covenant makes quite long and specific provisions intended to guarantee the 'fundamental right of everyone to be free from hunger' and to 'ensure an equitable distribution of world food supplies in relation to need'.[1] Other articles declaring that 'everyone has a right to life' or proclaiming the 'inherent right to life' would be meaningless if they did not presuppose people's right to the food that sustains life.

Governments too have constantly reaffirmed this right. Ten years ago, governments represented at the World Food Conference again solemnly committed themselves to eradicating hunger. They promised that 'Within a decade, no child will go to bed hungry, no family will fear for its next day's bread'; a promise which rings very hollow indeed in this year of massive famine.

Universal Declarations, International Covenants and World Conference Resolutions notwithstanding, no human right has been so frequently and spectacularly violated in recent times as the right to food. Surely all of us vigorously oppose torture, disappearances, arbitrary imprisonment and other flagrant infringements of human rights, as we must do; but none of us could claim that all these combined deprive more people of life itself than the absence of food. Even war comes a poor second. The toll of hunger on human life is equal to a Hiroshima explosion every three days.

We are not, however, going to indulge in quantification tonight. Is Unicef right in claiming that 40,000 children die daily due to hunger or hunger-related illness? When FAO says that 500 million people suffer from hunger and malnutrition, is it being more or less accurate than the World Bank, which speaks of one billion people in those circumstances? In a sense, without being callous, we can answer, 'Who cares?', since even one death from hunger, even a single person suffering from malnutrition, is a scandal in a world which has vanquished food scarcity, where more than enough food exists for everyone. The most recent US Department of Agriculture estimate says that our 1984–5 global harvests will exceed 1.6 billion tons of cereals, up 8 per cent from last year.

I could prove to you with simple arithmetic that if 15 million children are now dying from hunger every year, they could be saved with less than a two-thousandth of the world's harvests (0.002 per cent), even assuming you gave them an adult ration and that there was absolutely no food available to them locally – not even breast milk. There may once have been people who took comfort in the Malthusian view, which assured us that the number of mouths to feed would inevitably and necessarily outstrip the supply of food. It may have been morally easier to look at the persistence of hunger as a natural law, since this automatically absolved human society and human organization of any responsibility. However convenient, this view is no longer tenable.

Even when they know that there is plenty of food available in global terms, the numbers' approach, the quantification of hunger, tends to make people numb. How can an individual contemplate doing anything at all about a scourge that strikes

223

between half a billion and a billion people? Worse than that, the numbers' approach makes us focus on the victims. I did it myself a moment ago when I spoke of how little food proportionally would be needed to save 15 million children, as if it were up to some vaguely defined group called 'us' – in Canada, the United States, Europe and other rich countries – to feed another, quite different group called 'them' – the poor and famished in the Third World. It's not that the victims are unimportant – far from it – but if we focus *only* on them, we risk blinding ourselves to the true causes of hunger. Since faulty analysis leads to faulty action, we shall stray even further from a solution.

No: we must find another way forward. Here I believe that human rights can be an invaluable instrument. Well-meaning people sometimes claim that the human rights approach to hunger is not only wrong but positively harmful. What is the point, they ask, of proclaiming principles that are completely unenforceable? Such critics point out that every time these principles are undermined – and, in the case of hunger, this happens millions of times every day – the very concepts of international law and norms of behaviour are flouted. All you have ac- complished with the human rights approach, they say, is to encourage disrespect for your own standards and create an un- bridgeable credibility gap.

I do not share this view for at least three reasons. The first is that the human rights stance reminds us of what we are in constant need of hearing: there is no group called 'us' and none called 'them'. We are all fragile, extraordinary human beings, with our dignity and our defects, our hopes and our struggles to attain them. Accidents of birth and geography have placed some of us in more favourable positions than others. We to whom such accidents have granted particular privilege should never confuse our duty to help alleviate suffering with some imaginary, inherent difference between ourselves as 'haves' and others as 'have-nots'. Taking human rights seriously helps to avoid a 'them' and 'us' mentality.

The second reason which makes the human rights approach valuable is precisely *because* it can be described as 'utopian'. We need utopias. Today's seemingly unreachable goals are tomorrow's triumphs. One hundred and fifty years ago, it was utopian to think of ridding the United States of slavery. Utopias mobilize people's energies. Which do you prefer: the cry of '*Liberté, Égalité, Fraternité*' or a sober analysis of the reasons why you will never be able to bring down the French monarchy and the established order? So it must and will be with ending hunger.[2]

The final reason for using the human rights approach is an eminently practical one and brings me to the heart of what I hope to say tonight. When we speak of rights, *human* rights, in the same breath we must speak of violations. When we speak of violations, we have in mind *human* institutions, *human* agents as violators. How does it sound to you if I say, 'Drought has violated several million Ethiopians' right to food'? Or, 'Floods have violated Bangladeshis' rights to food'? Or, 'Africans are presently violating their right to food by having too many children'? Such propositions are barely grammatical, much less intellectually convincing.

At this point you are entitled to ask whether every case of hunger truly implies a wilful violation of the right to food. It's true that acts of God like drought and flood or population pressures can aggravate hunger. But climatic extremes and environmental destruction can often be traced to human action or inaction. Pushing this statement to its limits, I will even say that there *are* no ecological problems, only the social and political problems that invariably underlie and cause ecological damage.

As for demographics, Third World parents know that having many children may be the only way to maximize gains for the family today and ensure some security for themselves tomorrow. Wherever and whenever hunger occurs, I'm convinced that human agencies and agents are at work; that hunger is basically a reflection of inequity at the local, national and international levels. This is why, ethically speaking, the correct response to hunger, and the cardinal virtue we need to respond to it, is justice, not charity. Again the relevance of the human rights approach is clear. The notions of rights and of justice are inseparable.

All this being said, if I were allowed to change the language of the Universal Declaration and the International Covenants, I would certainly speak of people's right to *feed themselves* rather than of the 'right to food'. After all, animals in zoos, patients in hospital and prisoners in jail have a right to food. Surely we need a less passive, more dynamic concept. If not properly qualified, the 'right to food' sounds almost like a right to hand-outs. I believe the framers of the basic human rights documents understood this perfectly when they declared that 'in no case may a people be deprived of its own means of subsistence'. What they surely meant was that human communities develop ways of coping with their environments in order to provide their members under normal circumstances with a decent livelihood, including food. Given a chance and a modicum of justice, people *will* feed themselves – they will not need 'us' and they will not ask for hand-outs. But when justice is absent, they can be and often are deprived of the right to their own means of subsistence.

Who then – what human institutions – are preventing people from feeding themselves? Why is it that late in the twentieth century more people are going hungry than ever before? Why is there a worldwide crisis in agriculture, stemming paradoxically from both over-production and under-production? These are all political questions. Let's start by reviewing a few recent headlines: 'Farms wither in Middle America' ... 'For millions of Africans, destiny is starvation' ... 'Chicago becomes city of hunger' ... 'In Ethiopia, the Dark Ages continue' ... etc. etc. – you could all supply your own additions from any perusal of this week's or last month's press. The newspapers no longer say much about hunger and malnutrition in Asia, or north-eastern Brazil or Haiti or so many other places, but this does not mean it has gone away. Can we make any sense out of these and other headlines? Can we find any connections between hunger in American cities and African savannahs, between massive farm failures in Iowa and the near-total collapse of the Ethiopian peasantry? Is it worth seeking any common explanations?

We all know it's rash to explain complex phenomena by simple causes and that no single factor is uniquely responsible for hunger. Still, I'd like to take a stab at a short explanation, even if it's inadequate. On the food production side, it is that *non-producers are gaining greater and greater control over producers*. Or, put in terms closer to our concerns this evening, non-producers are depriving producers of their means of subsistence, which is to say, depriving them of their human rights. This, of course, leads directly to more precarious food consumption. Every family that loses its land, every person unable to find work, becomes a candidate for hunger.

Non-producers come in a variety of shapes and guises. They may be absentee landlords and local usurers, or corporations and banks, or governments and State bureaucracies or even development aid agencies. In the United States where hundreds of farms are now failing every week, agribusiness corporations determine how much farmers must pay for their inputs and often what they will receive for their output. Farmers' costs of production now frequently exceed what they receive for their crops and animals. Banks decide whether farmers get loans, how much interest they will have to pay for them and when to foreclose on their mortgages. The government in turn judges which categories of farmers should receive help, if any.

My own (perhaps cynical) view is that the present American administration is wilfully allowing the demise of a huge fraction of the agricultural sector because it *wants* a much smaller number of farmers to deal with. Agricultural exports are vital to the US, just as they are to Canada; world market prices are low because production in relation to commercial demand has been too high and stocks are plentiful. The dream of US agricultural policy has always been to control supply more closely. This will become possible only when the government can negotiate with a more limited number of producers. Already just 1 per cent of US farmers receive over half of all the farm income. This top slice will be encouraged and nurtured; the other food producers will disappear because they have lost all control over their costs and revenues.

As farmers disappear, food output will be more closely controlled and food prices will rise. Meanwhile agribusiness corporations have also gained more control over consumers. The US Department of Agriculture itself says that consumers are being overcharged an average 10 per cent more for all food items than they would pay if real marketplace competition existed. Fewer than 8 per cent of the items available in US supermarkets are unprocessed – everything else has gone through the companies' shiny machines and been made more expensive.

Government also plays a role in denying the right to food to vast numbers of citizens. During the Reagan era, millions have seen their food-stamp benefits curtailed or totally cut off. So it is no surprise that the independent Physician Task Force on Hunger in America reported last month after a year-long investigation, 'Hunger is a problem of epidemic proportions across the nation ... Clearly lack of food is not the cause of hunger in America ... The recent and swift return of hunger can be traced in substantial measure to clear and conscious policies of the federal government.'

What of food producers and consumers in the Third World? The World Bank tells us that 90 per cent of the world's hungry live in the countryside. This percentage may change as more and more people lose their land and livelihood and migrate to cities; but at present, and strangely, the people most deprived of food are overwhelmingly rural. They are people who do produce or who could produce food. The industrialized nations have contributed to their dispossession. For example, we have encouraged the transfer of the Western food system model to these poor and radically different societies. Because our model (the one used in the US and Canada) seems to be marvellously productive, modern and efficient, many Third World countries have enthusiastically tried to copy it. What we have all forgotten is that this model is *meant* to function with a lot of expensive capital inputs and to give work to as few people as possible. This model is no longer logical even in North America with its vast expanse of land and small rural populations – as we can readily tell from the farm failures it spawns. In land-poor countries, where millions seek their livelihood in farming, this model is a recipe for disaster. So-called 'Green Revolution' techniques have displaced peasants beyond counting and have frequently made food more expensive in the bargain. In the Third World as in the United States, a combination of corporate interests and State policies has helped to create hunger and outmigration from the countryside.

Many of the same corporations that purvey expensive processed-food products in the rich countries are now also introducing the poor to the joys of commerciogenic malnutrition. Soft drinks, snack foods and chewing gum devour a big piece of many poor families' food budgets. They may even sell the few nutritionally valuable foods they have on hand, like fruit or eggs, in order to buy junk food. First came colonization, now coca-colanization. The baby foods scandal is too well known to bear repeating tonight, except that it should remind us that it's often the weakest – in this case, infants – whose human rights are most easily disregarded by the strong.

Other non-producers which have gained a tight grip over food supplies in poor countries are the big international financial institutions, both public and private. The crushing burden that international debt lays on peasants and urban workers has not yet been properly recognized. During the 1970s, Third World elites borrowed heavily from Western banks, which were going all out to recycle petro-dollars. Generally those elites used the money to buy Phantom jets and other costly toys, as well as so-called 'development' projects, which benefited only themselves or became white elephants. Sometimes they simply sent suitcases full of money north to private bank accounts. An officer of the Bank of International Settlements says that capital flight has been taking place on 'a massive scale': $55 billion left Latin America alone in this way between 1977 and 1983. That amounts to a third of all borrowing during the period, and the official in question admits this is a 'conservative estimate'.

Now the loans are comi_g due, the chickens are coming home to roost and the banks are afraid that some of their clients may renege on their loans. By common and tacit consent of banks and OECD governments, the International Monetary Fund has been called in to make sure the debtors pay up. The IMF's role is to devise what it calls 'adjustment' programmes; the recipients are more likely to call them 'austerity' programmes. In all cases, standards of living are drastically reduced and prices for basic goods rise, while wages are usually blocked and all consumption subsidies removed. Naturally it is the poorest and most vulnerable classes which are expected to do the belt-tightening, not the elites who squandered the original loans in the first place.

Here are just a few examples drawn from countries now under IMF tutelage:

- In Brazil, cancellation of subsidies has led to dramatic food price increases, especially for staples which the poor depend on most. In 1983, the price of beans went up 769 per cent and rice 188 per cent, while the minimum wage, for those lucky enough to have paid employment, was adjusted by only + 142 per cent during the same period.

- In the Philippines, there have been three devaluations in a year and a half, each accompanied by increases in the cost of living. Inflation is still running at 40 per cent a year, the minimum wage is $2 a day, unemployment is now well over 20 per cent and malnourishment and infant mortality are on the rise.

- In the Dominican Republic, IMF-induced price-hikes of 40 per cent for bread and flour and 100 per cent for cooking oil brought thousands out on to the streets in demonstrations in April 1984. In the ensuing repression, 186 were killed and hundreds more wounded or arrested.

- In Peru, many people in the Lima slums now exist on a steady diet of a fish-meal-based chicken-feed called Nicovita, which is produced in unsanitary conditions and causes parasitical diseases. Infant mortality in some neighbourhoods is 50 per cent.

The IMF also insists that countries export more to earn hard currency. Frequently, all they have to export are agricultural products. Export crops are thus pushed at the expense of food crops, which receive little or no investment. Brazil, for example, is the second largest agro-exporter in the world, although three Brazilians in five suffer from some degree of malnutrition. Everywhere soils, waters and forests are 'mined' to increase exports. Wanton destruction of these resources will of course weigh heavily on future food production.

One could go on citing further violations to people's right to food perpetrated by an alliance of the banks, the IMF, the debtor elites and the OECD governments protecting their own banking networks. Perhaps the best summary is provided by an example of black humour currently circulating in Peru:

> OFFICIAL:  You'll have to tighten your belt.
> CITIZEN:   I can't. I ate it yesterday.

Most countries where large numbers of people suffer from serious hunger are in the market economy orbit, but not all. A smaller group of countries has chosen to imitate the Soviet model and its disastrous institution of collective farming with central planning. Here the non-producers ruining the prospects for producers are the obtuse State bureaucracies and the leaders so imbued with ideology that they cannot even see how their own peasants react.

Mozambique, after several years of disappointing agricultural development and lately a food crisis second only to Ethiopia's on the African continent today, has finally decided to stop putting its agricultural investment into State farms. The government has announced that from now on it will give greater incentives to independent peasant producers, and high time!

The case of Ethiopia is complex, hideously so, and made worse by war and drought. Even though the present Marxist military government (the Derg) carried out sweeping land reform ten years ago, it too chose to invest nearly all its agricultural development budget in collective agriculture. Of the 5,000 large estates which were turned into State farms a decade ago, not one is financially viable today. These farms buy more machinery than they can maintain and rely on other expensive capital inputs.

Ethiopia is nothing if not an agrarian society – almost nine-tenths of the population are peasants – yet the new party whose advent was celebrated with such expense and fanfare last autumn is called the 'Workers' Party'. This seems to be more than a symbolic choice of language. The present economic plan provides for only 12 per cent of the national budget to be spent on agriculture, and nearly all of that will go to the collectives, and to irrigated agriculture. State farms occupy only 4 per cent of the cultivated land but get most of the attention. Smallholders, the seven million peasants who work 94 per cent of the land, are the lowest priority of all. Further collectivization is still one of the main government objectives despite its proven inefficiency and unpopularity with the peasantry.

The Ethiopian peasantry might still have been able to cope in spite of drought, erosion, deforestation and government policy, had it not been for ceaseless wars. It is no accident that the worst horrors of the current famine began in the north where the central government is trying to stamp out revolts. Call them rebels or secessionists, call them freedom fighters or whatever you like: the fact remains that while the famine has now spread beyond the region, the victims are still overwhelmingly from the northern provinces, where 85 per cent of the territory is in the hands of liberation movements.

Ethiopia now boasts the largest army in Africa (over 300,000 men) on which it spends $440 million a year. To put down rebellions, the country has borrowed some $3 billion from the Soviet Union for arms purchases on which it reportedly must pay interest of $200 million a year. Just one or two per cent of this huge military budget could have prevented the famine from getting out of hand, if it had been spent in time and if the government had wanted to help victims in the rebellious provinces.[3]

You have all heard a hundred and one comparisons of armaments budgets and development spending, so I'll try not to bore you with the hundred and second. I would simply like to point out that it's not just in Ethiopia that the military violates the people's right to food. The Third World now imports about $25 billion annually in military hardware from the major industrialized countries. This of course prevents the same money from being spent on food production or other development, so one can say that arms kill, whether they are used directly against people or just grow old gracefully in depots.

As serious and less well known is the fact that an increasing proportion of the imported weaponry is designed to control hungry and angry citizens. Now that the poor in many countries are rising up against impossible living conditions, governments respond with riot weapons, crowd-monitoring devices, computerized intelligence networks, prison and torture equipment. Twenty-five countries, which have had to reschedule their foreign debts since 1981, spent $11 billion in the preceding five years on equipment like this to repress their own hungry citizens.[4]

Powerful and unholy alliances between the elites of capitalist or socialist countries and their Third World counterparts thus act in many ways to deprive people of the right to feed themselves. There is, however, a further dimension to violations of the right to food. The power to deprive also exists at the village level, even at the family level.

Alas, one group whose rights are the most systematically – almost automatically – ignored is the largest group of all. I am, of course, speaking of women. Women, according to UN figures, own just 1 per cent of the world's property. This means that women cultivators rarely control their means of subsistence, that they can't obtain credit for land or for farming inputs. Women receive only 10 per cent of the world's income. Men tend the export crops and take the proceeds. Women frequently take care of the food crops but get no reward – even though sixteen out of every twenty-four hours worked are worked by women. This means that women are working two hours for every one hour worked by a man – almost all these hours without pay. An ILO study published in 1979 showed that, in Africa, fourteen out of seventeen agricultural tasks fell entirely to women. Do you still wonder why African women want large families? How could they manage without them?

Naturally, when scarcity or famine strikes, women – along with children – are the first to suffer. Even under supposedly 'normal' conditions, they fare less well than men. Studies of the household distribution of food in many countries show that girls are fed consistently less than boys. Even pregnant and nursing mothers do not get their fair share of the family food. Women are biologically hardier than men – the proof is that in the industrialized countries there are 1,066 women for every 1,000 men. As for members of the second sex in the Third World, constant deprivation and overwork result in a ratio of only 969 adult women for every 1,000 men.[5]

Women may be often written off when there is not enough food to feed the whole family adequately. So a poor woman or a poor female child is always at the bottom of the heap. However, the poor as a class, both women and men, throughout the Third World are engaged in a constant struggle with those in positions of power in their own villages and neighbourhoods. Landlords and usurers do not hesitate to deprive the poor of land or of food whenever such actions can increase their own power and privilege.

There's nothing new about this. The Finance Minister to Louis XVI, the former Geneva banker Jacques Necker, was constantly warning the king about the need to protect his poor subjects against the rapacity of the rich. The king, we must conclude, did not listen carefully. Necker, on the other hand, survived the Revolution and, a year before his death in 1804, was still reflecting on the vital subjects of food-prices and the poor's access to food. Let me quote him in his own elegant language:

Lorsque les propriétaires haussent le prix (du pain) et se défendent de hausser le prix de la main d'oeuvre des hommes industrieux, il s'établit entre ces deux classes de la société une sorte de combat obscur, mais terrible, où l'on ne peut pas compter le nombre de malheureux, où le fort opprime le faible à l'abri des lois, où la propriété accable du poids de ses prérogatives l'homme qui vit du travail de ses mains.

[When the owners raise the price (of bread) yet refuse to raise the wages of working men, a kind of shadowy (obscure) yet terrible combat is established between these two classes of society in which one cannot count the numbers of the wretched: the strong oppress the weak under the protection of the law and property crushes under the weight of privilege the man who lives from his labour.]

Necker goes on to explain that when the price of bread goes up, poor people can no longer save. Sometimes they can barely eat enough to keep on working. The owner, on the other hand, grows richer and can force down wages because his workers have no food reserves. 'They must work today,' says Necker, 'so as not to die tomorrow.'[6]

Necker, though a man of means, was way ahead of Karl Marx in recognizing 'this shadowy yet terrible combat' between classes. He also saw through the method used by the property-owning class to get the better of the workers: to deprive them of bread by raising its price. When they lost their bread, they lost their bargaining power as well.

This shadowy and terrible combat goes on every day in thousands of villages, where the small peasantry is almost always on the losing side. Land is becoming concentrated in ever fewer hands, so large segments of this peasantry become landless or near-landless. Rural people also have fewer opportunities for earning some income – in cash or food – as landlords mechanize and produce less for local needs than for the market. Without land, without income, millions are sinking into hunger.

This state of affairs is not only deeply shocking – it is a quite recent development. Third World societies used to have support systems which allowed the peasantry to survive in all but the most dire circumstances. So did Necker's pre-Revolutionary France, for that matter. I have friends in India who have told me how their fathers kept food in store for emergencies, which could be distributed to 'their' peasants. Poor people had gleaning or gathering or grazing rights, or rights to hunt or cut firewood. Revolutions could and did occur when these rights were rescinded. They had patrons, or extended families, or neighbourhood and community mutual-help networks. The Chinese had elaborate systems to combat famine involving the central government, provincial administrations and local rich families.[7] African societies had rules for producing and consuming food in highly egalitarian ways.

I am not saying that no one ever died of hunger in so-called traditional societies, and I'm not trying to hold a brief for feudalism or paternalism. I simply want to point out that poor people's support systems are breaking down under outside pressures. Profits take precedence over human and village relationships. Nothing takes the place of the customary support networks;

resiliency disappears, people become suddenly subject to a dog-eat-dog dependency on the market for work, for credit, for food and the other necessities of life. The so-called free market may provide them only with the freedom to starve.

As people's reserves dwindle and their means of subsistence become more precarious, the tiniest change in their level of resources may spell disaster. A distinguished member of the Indian Administrative Service told me some years ago that, for the first time in Bihar, people were beginning to die of exposure. I asked how this was possible. Very simple, he said. The poorest people used to cover themselves with straw at night, and straw was free. Now straw has a price – a very small one, but a price just the same – which the poor cannot afford. So they die. Why has straw become a commodity? Partly because Green Revolution cereal varieties are short-straw plants, so there's less available. Partly because the forests that used to provide woodpulp for paper have been cut down, and straw is now used in papermaking. One can always find excellent economic reasons for other people's deaths.

What is true for the individual's slim survival margin is also true for whole communities. When they have already been brought close to the brink, the smallest push can send them over the edge. In Northern Ethiopia today, agriculture has for the most part simply stopped. The story told by Kiros Gebre Mikael, a refugee at Makalle camp, is typical: 'How can I go back? I have nothing to go back to. Once I had a good store of seed grain, but there was no rain, the crop did not grow and the seeds rotted in the ground. Once I had four oxen for ploughing, and of these, when there was no food left to eat, I sold two and slaughtered two for meat. So you see, I cannot go back. I have eaten my future.'[8]

Another bizarre shift has occurred. States and communities often used to *define* themselves and their members according to those they would feed and care for and those they wouldn't. 'Bread and circuses' were due to real Romans, though not to outsiders. I recently saw a document from Shakespeare's town, Stratford-upon-Avon, dating from 1598, just after the serious food scarcities of the 1590s. A man is called before the local council and upbraided for harbouring a strange woman in his house. The town fathers seem to care very little about his morals – what worries them is that the lady in question is pregnant and that, if the baby is born within the town's precincts, Stratford will be responsible for seeing it fed until it comes of age.

Today the State more often than not protects not the right to food but *those who violate* the right to food. This is the case in countries in the First or Third Worlds which are governed on behalf of banks, corporations or the landholding classes; where the rights of property always supersede the right to eat.

What paths might we follow towards the utopia where food rights will at last be respected, protected and cherished? Let me recommend several. Food aid in emergencies is absolutely vital, but when it becomes entrenched and institutionalized it undermines people's right to feed themselves. It does this by competing with local producers, by creating tastes for foods such as wheat that can't be grown locally, by absolving recipient governments of the responsibility to devise coherent food policies. Every developed country without exception needs to review thoroughly its food aid policies.

In the case of Ethiopia, most Western governments have been pushed by their own citizens into delivering emergency relief, but they refuse to envisage longer-term development aid in order to help millions of peasants like Kiros Gebre Mikael find a future. The West must also push for a negotiated solution between the Ethiopian government and the liberation movements, without which no development can ever take place and the tragedy will be compounded.

We must protect those rare successful experiments where a government *does* undertake to guarantee its citizens the right to feed themselves. This is true of Nicaragua today, and I am extremely pleased to note that Canadians have continued to support the Nicaraguans despite unrelenting propaganda, hostility and pressure from their powerful neighbour to the south. Canada should try to do more and bring other, like-minded governments along with it. To Ronald Reagan and his contras we must say *No Pasaran.*

Because traditional support systems have broken down, because the State affords no protection and often makes things worse, because the conditions of life are becoming intolerable, poor people everywhere are inventing new ways of organizing themselves to ensure their right to food. Many Third World producer and consumer groups are being helped by non-governmental organizations in the industrialized countries; but many others are being severely repressed in their search for justice.

If we take seriously the right to food for everyone, we must ask ourselves equally serious questions about justice. Are we prepared to accept that the first right of those deprived of food is to organize resistance *against* those forces which violate their rights? Do we recognize that the right to food for all cannot be ensured without political conflict? Would we support the Bishop of Fortaleza in Brazil, who approved a starving mob that stormed a full granary, saying that the right to food supersedes the rights of property? Are we ready to stand up to the forces in our own societies that deprive people of food, even indirectly? The right to food and the freedom to resist injustice are inseparable. There is no freedom without bread, and no bread without freedom.

# NOTES AND REFERENCES

## 1 OVERCOMING HUNGER:
### STRENGTHEN THE WEAK, WEAKEN THE STRONG

1. World Bank, *World Development Report 1980*, Washington, DC, August 1980, p. 61. See also Marcelo Selowsky, *The economic dimensions of malnutrition in young children*, World Bank Working Paper 294, 1978, Table 1. Selowsky assumes, as we have done, 3,500 calories per kilo of grain.

2. John Ball, The Sermon at Blackheath, 1381, cited in Leonard Silk, *The Economists*, New York, Discus Books (Avon), 1978, pp. 230–31.

3. Personal communication from a member of the Indian Administrative Service, New Delhi.

4. See, for example, Dr Moises Behar (WHO), 'Nutrition of Mayan children before the Conquest and now', *Clinical Pediatrics*, Vol. 9, 1970, pp. 187–8, as well as contemporary testimony cited in Nicole Ball, 'Understanding the causes of African famine', *Journal of Modern African Studies*, Vol. 14, No. 3, 1976; Pierre Spitz, 'Silent Violence: Famine and Inequality', in *Violence and its Causes*, Unesco, 1980; Fray Bartolomeo de las Casas, *Très Brève Relation de la Déstruction des Indes*, Paris, Maspéro, 1979 (original 1552).

5. For some aspects of the breakdown of 'patron/client' relations, see Prof. Shigeru Ishikawa, *Labour Absorption in Asian Agriculture*, Bangkok, ILO (ARTEP), July 1978, sp. p. 96 f. and Appendix 3. Many instances of this breakdown are described in the series of volumes published by the UN Research Institute for Social Development under the general title 'Social and economic implications of the large-scale introduction of new varieties of foodgrains' but more simply described as the 'Green Revolution' series. The director of the project, the late Andrew Pearse, published

an overview volume containing many details on the 'crisis of livelihood': *Seeds of Plenty, Seeds of Want*, UNRISD and Oxford University Press, 1980.

6. World Bank, *Land Reform*, Rural Development Series, July 1974, sp. Tables 6, p. 55, and 11, p. 60. The Bank's figures are old; landlessness and rural dispossession have grown much worse during the past decade. One should also consult the collective volume *Poverty and Landlessness in Rural Asia*, ILO, 1977.

7. World Bank, *World Development Report 1979*, Ch. 4, 'Employment Trends and Issues', and the same report for 1980, p. 40. See also *Poverty and Landlessness*, op. cit.

8. For details on the population issue, see Susan George, *How the Other Half Dies*, Penguin, 1976, and Montclair, NJ, Allanheld, Osmun, 1977, Ch. 2.

9. National Research Council, *World Food and Nutrition Study*, Washington, DC, National Academy of Sciences, 1977, Table 1, p. 157.

10. World Bank, 1980, op. cit., p. 42 ('Small is productive'); also World Bank, 1974, op. cit., Table 2.2, p. 32.

11. In the 1960s between 30 and 70 per cent of the additions to urban population were migrants from rural areas. World Bank, 1979, op. cit., p. 55. Rural out-migration has accelerated since the 1960s under 'Green Revolution' and 'modernization' pressures: see the UNRISD series and the Pearse overview, op. cit.

12. World Bank, 1980, op. cit., p. 72.

13. Michael T. Klare, 'The international repression trade', *The Bulletin of the Atomic Scientists*, November 1979, and with Cynthia Arnson, *Supplying Repression*, Washington, DC and Amsterdam, Institute for Policy Studies, 1981.

14. The increase in Nicaraguan basic grain production is clear from figures the author consulted in January 1981 in Managua at the research centre attached to the Ministry of Agriculture (INRA-CIERA). Small peasants had, for the first time, access to land, credit, fertilizer, etc., and massively improved their food production. There is a drawback: since people are well fed for the first time in decades, they are much less anxious to earn wages by harvesting cash crops – this has posed a problem for the government.

15. Report of the Independent Commission on International

Development Issues – commonly referred to as the Brandt
Commission: *North-South: A Programme for Survival*, London, Pan,
1980.

16. FAO, World Conference on Agrarian Reform and Rural
Development, INF. 3, 'Examen et analyse de la réforme agraire et
du développement rural dans les pays en voie de développement...'
1979, Ch. 11, pp. 112–13.

17. FAO, *The State of Food and Agriculture 1979*, FAO, 1980,
pp. 1–54.

18. A growing literature on the environmental/energy impact of the
North American food system includes Robert van den Bosch, *The
Pesticide Conspiracy*, Garden City, NY, Doubleday, 1978; *Farmers'
Use of Pesticides* (in 1964, 1971, 1976), US Department of
Agriculture Economic Reports Nos. 145, 268, 418; David and
Marcia Pimentel, *Food, Energy and Society*, Resource and
Environmental Science Series, London, Edward Arnold, 1979; Gerald
Leach, *Energy and Food Production*, Guildford, Surrey, IPC Science
and Technology Press, 1976; Nicole Ball, 'Deserts bloom ... and
wither', *Ecologist Quarterly*, Spring 1978. The impact poor
conservation practices may have on US exports (and vice versa) is
examined in Lauren Soth, 'The Grain Export Boom: Should It Be
Tamed?', *Foreign Affairs*, Spring 1981.

19. See Sylvan Wittwer, 'Food Production Resources: land, water,
energy, fertilizer, capital and manpower', in *Plant and Animal
Products in the US Food System*, Washington, DC, National
Research Council, National Academy of Sciences, 1978, sp.
pp. 23–5.

20. Pierre Spitz has frequently insisted on the importance of peasants'
contributions to agricultural knowledge and 'scientific' neglect
thereof: see, *inter alia*, 'La recherche agronomique au service des
paysans pauvres du Tiers Monde', in *Revue Tiers Monde* (IEDES-
PUF), Vol. XX, No. 78, April–June 1979, and 'Livelihood and the
Food Squeeze', *Ceres*, FAO, May–June 1981.

21. See the UNRISD 'Green Revolution' series, op. cit.; and K. C.
Abercrombie, 'Agricultural employment in Latin America',
International Labour Organisation, *Review*, July 1972.

22. It is instructive to note that China has consistently *added* agricultural
labour at a rate of about 2 per cent per annum since 1952, while

the growth rates of net output per worker have climbed from 2.6 in 1952–7 to 8.3 in 1977–9. See World Bank, *China: Socialist Economic Development*, a 'Grey Cover', i.e., restricted report, No. 3391-CHA, Annex C, pp. 72–3, 1 June 1981.

## 2 DANGEROUS EMBRACE:
### CULTURE, ECONOMICS, POLITICS AND FOOD SYSTEMS

1. Ljubljana ECE-UNEP Seminar preparatory document: ECOSCOC/-ECE/SEM.11/PM/R.1, October 1978, para. 10, mimeograph.
2. An example of culture and ethics setting dietary practice is to be found in the Jewish dietary laws. They particularly serve to distinguish categories which are, and must remain, separate: through food, man is distinguished from God, one people from another, the clean from the unclean, etc. For the Hebrews, anything mixed or partaking of two natures is unclean and thus inedible – be it a wingless bird, a water creature without scales and fins, or an animal both herbivorous and carnivorous like the pig. The principle of separateness also applies to processes of food production, as in this passage from Leviticus: 'Thou shalt not let thy cattle gender with a diverse kind, thou shalt not sow thy field with mingled seed' (XIX: 19). See Jean Soler, 'The dietary prohibitions of the Hebrews', *The New York Review of Books*, 14 June 1979, pp. 24–30; and Mary Douglas, *Purity and Danger*, London, Routledge & Kegan Paul, 1966, Ch. 3.
3. Philip Stewart, 'Human Ecology: a new kind of knowledge?', paper presented at the colloquy, 'Homme biologique et homme social', Centre Royaumont pour une Science de l'Homme, December 1978, mimeograph. An obvious example is the impact of Hindu beliefs on the Indian environment (the famous 'sacred cow').
4. Lesley Gordon, *Green Magic*, London, Ebury Press, 1977, p. 87; and for the connection between cotton and the Civil War, Gavin Wright, *The Political Economy of the Cotton South*, New York, W. W. Norton, 1978, Ch. 5.
5. Pierre Spitz, 'Notes sur l'histoire des transferts de techniques dans le domaine de la production végétale', paper presented at the OECD seminar 'Science, Technology and Development in a Changing World', DSTI/SPR 74.75, April 1975.

6. Centre Français du Commerce Extérieur, *Le Développement de la Production du Soja au Brésil*, Collection 'Énquêtes à l'Étranger', November 1973, p. 49 f. See also UPI dispatches 'Rio beans shortage causes disorders' and 'Black beans the write-in choice of thousands who voted in Rio', in *The International Herald Tribune*, 13 October 1976 and 22 November 1976.

7. World Bank, *World Tables 1976*, Table 8, 'Foreign Trade Structures: Export Composition', and Economic Data Sheet No. 1, 'National Accounts and Prices'.

8. Pierre Spitz has discussed this question at length in 'Silent Violence: Famine and Inequality', *International Social Science Journal*, Vol. XXX, No. 4, 1978.

9. Dr Moises Behar, 'Nutrition of Mayan children before the Conquest and now', *Clinical Pediatrics*, Vol. 9, 1970, pp. 187–8.

10. Addis Hiwet, 'Ethiopia: from autocracy to revolution', Occasional Paper No. 1, *Review of African Political Economy* (London), 1975, cited in Nicole Ball, 'Understanding the causes of African famine', *Journal of Modern African Studies*, Vol. 14, No. 3, 1976, p. 522.

11. From French colonial archives in Laurence Wilhelm, 'Le rôle et la dynamique de l'État à travers les crises de subsistence', unpublished *Mémoire de Thèse*, cited in Spitz, 'Silent Violence . . .', op. cit.

12. Andrew Pearse, *The Latin American Peasant*, London, Frank Cass, 1975, p. 9.

13. M. Merlier, *Le Congo de la colonisation Belge à l'Indépendence*, Paris, Maspéro, 1963, cited in M. K. K. Kabala Kabunda, 'Multinational corporations and the installation of externally oriented economic structures in Africa', in Carl Widstrand, ed., *Multinational Firms in Africa*, Uppsala, 1975, pp. 305–6.

14. Le Gouverneur Blacher to the Administrateur du Cercle de Dosso, Niger, 16 June 1931, cited in J. Egg *et al.*, *Analyse déscriptive de la famine des années 1931 au Niger et implications méthodologiques*, Paris, Institut National de la Recherche Agronomique, July 1975, mimeograph, p. 37. Jean Suret-Canale in *Afrique Noire*, Vol. II, *L'Ère Coloniale*, discusses the use of taxation in detail.

15. Various aspects of the development of the US model will be found in Alan Olmstead, 'The mechanisation of reaping and mowing in American agriculture 1833–1870', *The Journal of Economic History*, Vol. 35, June 1975, pp. 327–52; and in this same *Journal*,

Vol. XXII, No. 4, 1962: a special issue on the 100th anniversary of the founding of the US Department of Agriculture. See especially Wayne D. Rasmussen (chief historian of the USDA), 'The impact of technological change on American agriculture 1862–1962', pp. 578–91; and Martin Primack, 'Land clearing under 19th-century techniques', pp. 489–97. A visit to the Smithsonian Institution permanent exhibition of agricultural technology is also highly recommended.

16. US General Accounting Office, *The changing character and structure of American agriculture: an overview* (Report CED-7-178), Washington, DC, December 1978, p. iii; and John E. Lee, 'Agricultural finance: situation and issues', *USDA 1978 Food and Agricultural Outlook Conference*, Proceedings, Washington, DC, November 1977.

17. USDA, *Alternative Futures for US agriculture: a progress report*, prepared for the Committee on Agriculture and Forestry of the US Senate, by USDA Office of Planning and Evaluation, Washington, DC, September 1975.

18. On the environmental impact of the high technology system, see Robert van den Bosch, *The Pesticide Conspiracy* (and the preface to it by Paul Ehrlich), Garden City, NY, Doubleday, 1978; *Farmers' use of pesticides* (in 1964, 1971 and 1976), USDA Agricultural Economics Reports Nos. 145, 268, 418; David and Marcia Pimentel, *Food Energy and Society*, Resource, and Environmental Science Series, London, Edward Arnold, 1979 (sp. pp. 137–9); Gerald Leach, *Energy and Food Production*, Guildford, Surrey, IPC Science and Technology Press, 1976; Nicole Ball, 'Deserts bloom . . . and wither', *Ecologist Quarterly*, Spring 1978.

19. National Academy of Sciences, *Genetic Vulnerability of Major Crops*, Washington, DC, 1972, p. 1. The best comprehensive report on reduction of seed variety, future germ-plasm resources and the danger of industrial takeover of seeds is Pat R. Mooney, *Seeds of the Earth: a private or public resource?*, London, International Coalition for Development Action, a special edition for the UNCSTD Conference, Vienna, 1979.

20. Cf. Erik Eckholm and Frank Record, *The two faces of malnutrition*, Worldwatch Institute Paper No. 9, Washington, DC, 1976; *Hearings* before the US Senate Select Committee on Nutrition and

Human Needs, Washington, DC, March, April and May 1973 (in four parts).

21. Nick Kotz, *Hunger in America: The Federal Response*, New York, The Field Foundation, 1979 (quote on p. 23).

22. Susan George, *Feeding the Few: Corporate Control of Food*, Washington, DC and Amsterdam, Institute for Policy Studies/Transnational Institute, 1979.

23. Andrew Pearse, 'Technology and peasant production: reflections on a global study', *Development and Change*, Vol. 8, 1977. All the UNRISD Studies on the Green Revolution, directed by Pearse, should be consulted on this subject. Definitive conclusions in Andrew Pearse, *Seeds of Plenty, Seeds of Want*, Geneva, Clarendon Press and UNRISD, 1980.

24. Martin Kreisberg, 'Miracle seeds and market economies', *Columbia Journal of World Business*, March/April 1969. Kreisberg is now the Coordinator for International Organization Affairs of the Economic Research Service, USDA. His more recent volume, *International Organizations and Agricultural Development*, USDA, Foreign Agricultural Economic Report No. 131, May 1977, is a compendium showing that donor agency aid goes to implementing the dominant model, e.g. 'The IBRD and IDB have put major emphasis on projects ... to purchase needed production inputs, particularly machinery', p. vii.

25. K. C. Abercrombie, 'Agricultural employment in Latin America', *International Labour Organisation Review*, July 1972; and Solon Barraclough and Jacobo Schatan, 'Technological change and agricultural development', *Land Economics*, University of Wisconsin, May 1973.

26. Garrison Wilkes, 'The world's crop plant germ plasm: an endangered resource', *The Bulletin of the Atomic Scientists*, February 1977; and Mooney, cf. note 19.

27. E. Reusse, 'Economic and marketing aspects of post harvest systems in small farmer economics', FAO *Monthly Bulletin of Agricultural Economics and Statistics* (a two-part article), Vol. 25, Nos. 9 and 10, September and October 1976.

28. *Multinational corporations in Brazil and Mexico: structural sources of economic and non-economic power*, Report to the Sub-Committee on Multinational Corporations of the US Senate Committee on Foreign

Relations (usually referred to as 'the Church Report' from the name of the Committee Chairman), Washington, DC, August 1975, Appendix A, Table 7.

29. See Susan George, 'Nestlé Alimentana, SA: The Limits to Public Relations', *Economic and Political Weekly*, Vol. XIII, No. 37, Bombay, 16 September 1978.

30. Details in Charles Medawar, *Insult or Injury?* 'An enquiry into the marketing and advertising of British food and drug products in the Third World', London, Social Audit, 1979.

31. Robert Ledogar, *Hungry for Profits: US food and drug multinationals in Latin America*, New York, IDOC, 1976, sp. Ch. 6; and Overseas Private Investment Corporation, *Annual Reports*, 1973 to 1978.

32. Taken directly or calculated from data in USDA, *US Foreign Agricultural Trade Statistical Report*, Calendar Year 1977, Washington, DC, June 1978.

33. See Maureen McKintosh, 'Fruit and Vegetables as an International Commodity', *Food Policy*, November 1977.

34. Cf. Susan George, *Feeding the Few*, op. cit., Part I, and 'Le Tiers-Monde face à ses riches clients', *Le Monde Diplomatique*, March 1979.

35. USDA, *Agricultural Outlook*, March 1979, p. 4. Wheat prices in relevant issues of *Business Week*.

36. 'Untying aid proves to be a slow process', *Ceres-FAO Magazine*, No. 69, May/June 1979, pp. 4–5 and graph.

37. See *Annual Reports*, P.L. 480 (US Food for Peace law); and OECD, *Development Cooperation*, Annual Report of the DAC Chairman, 1975, pp. 94–5. This concerns the second and third European Development Fund Commitments. In subsequent DAC reports, the contributions to industrial versus food crops are not broken down, so the situation may have changed since 1975.

38. Further details on the Industry Cooperative Programme in Susan George, *How the Other Half Dies*, Montclair, NJ, Allanheld, Osmun, 1977, and Harmondsworth, Penguin, 1976, Ch. 9.

39. Robert Hirsch, with Boubacar Bah, *Some thoughts on the situation regarding food supplies in the Sahel countries and on the prospects on the horizon for the year 2000*, CILSS, and the Club du Sahel, the Nouakchott Colloquy, July 1979, mimeograph. See pp. 20–2, 33, 38.

40. Effects of US food aid in Susan George's *How the Other Half*

*Dies*, op. cit., Ch. 8. A case study on how the cancellation of food aid immediately *improved* the nutritional situation in one country in Thomas Marchione, 'Food and nutrition in self-reliant national development: the impact on child nutrition of Jamaican government policy', *Medical Anthropology*, Vol. 1, No. 1, Winter 1977. See also Paul Isenman and Hans Singer, 'Food Aid, Disincentive Effects and Their Policy Implications', *Economic Development and Cultural Change*, Vol. 25, No. 2, January 1977.

41. 'A case for community based oil extraction units in small-farmer oil palm rehabilitation schemes versus the large-scale central milling approach in Nigeria', in *Proceedings* of West African Seminar on Agricultural Planning, Zaria, 1974, Ife, Nigerian Institute of Public Administration. The quote is in E. Reusse, op. cit., Part 2, note 27, and the study is apparently also by Reusse, of FAO, since no other author is cited.

42. World Bank, *Annual Reports*, 1975, p. 55, and 1978, p. 77.

43. e.g., the kind of work being done by UNRISD in the project *Food Systems and Society* could lay the ground for much better-defined development projects, but this kind of research cannot be done in the short 'kamikaze' expeditions favoured by most lending agencies.

44. For examples, see Khadija Haq, ed., *Equality of Opportunity Within and Among Nations*, Part IV, 'Women and Equality of Opportunity', New York and London, Praeger Special Studies, 1977.

45. SAREC (Swedish Agency for Research Co-operation with Developing Countries), Bo. Bengtsson, ed., *Rural Development Research: the role of power relations*, Sarec Report R4/1979, p. 38; and Adolfo Mascarenhas, Director of the Bureau of Resources and Land-use Planning (BRALUP), Tanzania, personal communication.

46. Michel Cépède, 'Acculturation "Aristophanique" des communautés rurales et groupes "Hésiodiques" dans les sociétés industrialisées', paper presented at the World Congress of Sociology, Uppsala, 1978, p. 3.

47. World Bank, *Land Reform*, Rural Development Series, Table 2.2.

48. Prof. Dr Kurt Egger (and team), *Agro-Technological Alternatives for Agriculture in the Usambara Mountains*, Botanisches Institut der Universität-Heidelberg, December 1976, mimeograph, p. 22.

49. Ibid., p. 5.
50. E. F. I. Baker and Y. Yusuf, 'Mixed cropping research at the Institute for Agricultural Research, Samaru, Nigeria', in *Intercroppping in Semi-Arid Areas*, Report on a Symposium, International Development Research Centre, Ottawa, 1976, p. 17 (emphasis added).
51. Mahbub ul Haq, 'Toward a Just Society', *International Development Review*, Society for International Development, 1976, No. 4, p. 4.
52. Jere R. Behrman, *International Commodity Agreements: an evaluation of the UNCTAD Integrated Commodity Programme*, Overseas Development Council Monograph No. 9, Washington, DC, 1977.

## 3 FOOD, FAMINE AND SERVICE DELIVERY IN TIMES OF EMERGENCY

1. Robert T. Snow, 'The Impact of Famine Relief: Unasked Questions in Africa', in Bruce Currey and Graeme Hugo, eds., *Famine as a Geographical Phenomenon*, Dordrecht, Holland, D. Reidel Publishing Company, 1984, p. 158.
2. United Nations Research Institute for Social Development: *Famine Risk and Famine Prevention in the Modern World*, UNRISD/76/c.19, Geneva, June 1976, p. 2.
3. Amartya Sen, *Poverty and Famines: an Essay on Entitlement and Deprivation*, Clarendon Press, Oxford, 1981.
4. Bruce Currey, 'Coping with Complexity in Food Crisis Management', in Currey and Hugo, eds *Famine as a Geographical Phenomenon*, op. cit., Table 1 on the sequence of information gathering, in the Bengal Famine Code, 1913, pp. 194–5.
5. Id., pp. 187–8.
6. Robert Chambers, Richard Longhurst, Arnold Pacey, eds, *Seasonal Dimensions to Rural Poverty*, Totowa, NJ, Allanheld & Osmun, 1981.
7. R. Dirks, 'Social responses during severe food shortages and famine', *Current Anthropology* XXI: 1 (1980), pp. 21–4.
8. e.g. Tony Jackson with Deborah Eade, *Against the grain*, Oxfam, Oxford, 1982.

## 4 FOOD STRATEGIES FOR TOMORROW

1. Although 'Third World' is no longer a very useful concept, I still

prefer this shorthand expression to the euphemisms of 'developing' or 'less-developed' countries. 'Dominated' countries would probably be the most accurate term.

2. The Common Agricultural Policy (CAP) places levies on agricultural imports to European Community (EC) countries to raise their prices to those of EC-produced commodities.

3. F. F. Clairmonte and J. H. Cavanagh, 'Transnational Corporations and Services: The Final Frontier', *Trade and Development: An UNCTAD Review*, No. 5, 1984, Table 9; figures for 1982.

4. This was written before Mikhail Gorbachev became General Secretary of the Soviet Union.

5. For example, 186 people were killed during the 1984 food riots in the Dominican Republic, and long prison sentences have been meted out to captured food rioters in Morocco. Other riots have occurred in Latin America and North Africa. One could add that the present perilous situation in Central America results basically from people rising up against an intolerable situation of hunger, land deprivation, displacement of the peasantry to make room for cash crops, miserable plantation wages and the like, all maintained by local oligarchies under the protection of the United States. Nicaragua, previously the worst-fed country in the region, has redistributed control over food and food-producing resources and is consequently under serious pressure. Nicaragua represents what an Oxfam publication calls 'the threat of a good example' (Dianna Melrose, *Nicaragua: The Threat of a Good Example?*, Oxfam, Oxford, 1985).

6. USDA, World Agricultural Supply and Demand Estimates (WASDE-180), 10 April 1985, Table 1; estimate includes wheat, coarse grains and milled rice.

7. FAO, *World Food Report 1984*, p. 13.

8. The Group of 77 denotes the caucus of all Third World nations in the United Nations. Originally the term applied to the 77 developing countries which formed a coalition at the United Nations Conference of Trade and Development in 1964.

9. The Lomé Convention is a trade and development agreement between the EC and African–Caribbean–Pacific (ACP) countries. The main points of the agreement are duty-free access on a non-reciprocal basis to all industrial imports and 96 per cent of

agricultural imports to EC countries from ACP countries, stabilization of export receipts for ACP countries, increased development aid for ACP countries, increased industrial cooperation between EC and ACP members and the creation of an institutional framework for the operation of the agreement. The agreement, first signed in 1975, was modified and extended by Lomé II and Lomé III.

10. The papers from these two sessions are C. Stevens, 'The Importance of Food Aid in Development Programmes: Evaluation and Prospects', and H. Schneider, 'Food Aid Issues from the Recipient Countries' Perspective' (C. Cosgrove and J. Jamar, eds, op. cit., pp. 83–121).

11. François Guillaume, French Minister of Agriculture in 1987 and president of the Fédération Nationale des Syndicats d'Exploitants Agricoles from 1979 to 1986, interview with the Agence France Presse, 31 August 1983, cited in SOLAGRAL, *L'Aide alimentaire*, Syros, Paris, 1984, p. 79. This short book is an excellent introduction to food aid.

12. Giles Merritt, 'Farm War: The Heavies Won't Suffer Alone', *International Herald Tribune*, 18 June 1985.

13. Cf. EEC Court of Auditors, *Special Report on Food Aid*, Brussels, 30 October, 1980; also Africa Bureau, Cologne, and Institute for Development Studies, Sussex, *An Evaluation of the EEC Food Aid Programme*, Cologne and Brighton, June 1982. In 1980 the European Parliament asked the Commission for a proposal on reforming food aid. This was eventually supplied (in April 1983) under the title *Food Aid for Development*. This document is one of the bases of the ongoing debate, part of which has also been carried out in *Food Policy* (special issue on food aid), Vol. 8, No. 3, August 1983, various authors.

14. SOLAGRAL, op. cit., p. 62.

15. 'EEC Arthritis', *The Economist Development Report*, March 1985.

16. SOLAGRAL, op. cit., p. 66.

17. See Pascal Érard and Frédéric Mounier, *Les Marchés de la faim*, La Découverte, 1984, esp. pp. 128–9.

18. *Some* disasters, because food may be the last thing needed in others. See Tony Jackson with Deborah Eade (*Against the Grain*, Oxfam, Oxford, 1983) who explain how Guatemalan peasants were

undercut by food aid shipments after the 1976 earthquake, which had not touched the local harvests.

19. Susan George, *How the Other Half Dies: The Real Reasons for World Hunger*, Penguin Books, Harmondsworth, 1976, Ch. 8, and for greater detail on PL 480 counterpart fund use, Susan George, *Les Stratèges de la faim*, Grounauer, Geneva, 1981, Ch. 6.

20. SOLAGRAL, a French research organization, has produced a guide (Jean-Marc Bêche, 'Étude sur l'utilisation des fonds de contrepartie', 1986), at the request of the French Ministry of Cooperation and Development, on the use of counterpart funds for development. This guide could doubtless serve the needs of other European countries and the EEC as a whole. The guide (in mimeographed form) is available through SOLAGRAL, 185 rue de Charonne, 75011 Paris.

21. Tony Jackson, op. cit., note 18.

22. Odette Mengin, writing in *Faim et Développement*, May 1983, cited in Érard and Mounier, op. cit., p. 109.

23. Piet Terhal and Martin Doornbos, 'Operation Flood: Development and Commercialisation', *Food Policy*, Vol. 8, No. 3, August 1983. A colleague has also been kind enough to communicate two (unsigned) confidential notes on Operation Flood emanating from the EEC secretariat; these reach similar conclusions.

24. OECD, *Development Cooperation 1983*, taken directly or calculated from Table C-2.

25. Europe Information Développement, *Les Stratégies alimentaires: Nouvelle forme de coopération entre l'Europe et les pays du Tiers Monde*, EEC, DE-40, December 1982.

26. An exceptionally good source on the issues raised (or not raised) by the Lomé Convention will be found in the series of *Lomé Briefings*, 22 issues from 1983 to 1985, prepared by various authors for the Liaison Committee of Development NGOs to the European Communities, rue de Laeken 76, 1000 Brussels. Anyone seriously interested in pursuing the question of European development strategies and Third World policy should have a complete set.

27. The Stabex (export receipts stabilization) system provides currency transfers to countries heavily dependent on single commodities for export earnings in years when export receipts drop significantly due to poor harvests or low world prices.

28. The administrative bodies of the EC are the European Parliament, the Council of Ministers and the Executive Commission. The Commission, which has the task of implementing treaties, operates through Directorates General (DGs). DG VIII is the Development Directorate.

29. The Ecumenical Report Joint Task Force has useful things to say in 'The Pisani Memorandum on the EC Development Policy: Assessment and Recommendation by the Churches' Joint Task Force on Development Issues', JTF/1983/25E, available from the Joint Task Force Secretariat, 23 avenue d'Auderghem, B-1040 Brussels.

30. Cf. Laurence Tubiana (INRA, Montpellier) and her paper, 'Les Pays du Sud de la Méditerranée et l'Europe des 12', for the Journées d'Etudes, *Stratégies alimentaires* (12 avenue de la Soeur Rosalie, 75013 Paris), 10–12 June 1985. Mimeo.

31. By 1986, the net transfers to the rich countries made by Latin America alone amounted to $106 billion.

32. Tony Hill, 'Lomé II Is Dead, Long Live Lomé III', *Lomé Briefing*, No. 22, 1985.

33. 'Value for Money', *The Economist Development Report*, April 1984.

34. Quoted in Tony Hill, op. cit., note 32.

35. Brian O'Neill, 'Small Is Beautiful: Micro-projects in the New Convention', *Lomé Briefing*, No. 21, 1985.

36. Ibid.

37. Cf. Jean-Marie Fardeau, 'Encourager l'initiative paysanne', in *La Lettre de SOLAGRAL*, July–August 1984.

38. I have dealt in detail with the question of food systems (and the penetration of Third World food systems by Western ones) in *Les Stratèges de la faim*, note 19, and in a shorter and more readable version in *Feeding the Few: Corporate Control of Food*, Institute for Policy Studies, Washington, DC, 1978, as well as several papers collected here.

39. Robert Chambers, 'Putting "Last" Thinking First: A Professional Revolution', in *Third World Affairs 1985*, Third World Foundation for Social and Economic Studies, London, 1985, p. 85.

40. Various methods for 'reading' the signs of impending famine are suggested by several authors included in the volume *Famine as a Geographical Phenomenon*, Bruce Currey and Graeme Hugo, eds, Dordrecht, Holland, D. Reidel Publishing Co., 1984.

41. If EEC people can read only one book this year, it should be this book (New York, Longman, 1983), in which they will find much wisdom.
42. The Physician Task Force on Hunger in America (whose chairman is Dr J. Larry Brown of the Harvard School of Public Health) reported in 1985 that: 'Hunger in America is a national health epidemic ... We believe that today hunger and malnutrition are serious problems in every region of the nation. We have, in fact, returned from no city and no State where we did not find extensive hunger ... It returned, we believe, because the programs which virtually ended hunger in the last decade have been weakened' (*Hunger in America: The Growing Epidemic*, Middletown, Conn., Wesleyan University Press, 1985).

## 6 BIOBUSINESS:
### LIFE FOR SALE

1. David Pramer, Ph.D., Director of the Waksman Institute of Microbiology, Rutgers University, 'Ensuring quality Education in Biotechnology', *BIO/TECHNOLOGY*, Vol. I, No. 2, New York, April 1983.
2. In a paper of this length, I do not have space to go into all the other determinants of scientific activity, including individual curiosity. I therefore hope that the reader's response to the emphasis laid here on the economic and political context will not be an automatic accusation of 'vulgar Marxism'. Besides, we shall find some far more specific links between business objectives and scientific activities as we proceed.
3. Pnina Abir-am, 'The Discourse of Physical Power and Biological Knowledge in the 1930s: a Reassessment of the Rockefeller Foundation's "Policy" in Molecular Biology', *Social Studies of Science*, Vol. 12, Sage, London and Beverly Hills, 1982, p. 345.
4. Edward Yoxen, 'Life as a Productive Force: Capitalising the Science and Technology of Molecular Biology', in *Science, Technology and the Labour Process*, Les Levidow and Bob Young, eds, CSE Books, London, and Humanities Press Inc., New Jersey, 1981. See especially pp. 87–91. Warren Weaver's skills were subsequently put to use in an important position in the US wartime Office of Scientific

Research and Development, which oversaw everything from the atomic bomb to anti-malarial drugs.

5. Watson's introductory remarks to the anniversary Conference are reported in *Nature*, Vol. 302, 21 April 1983, pp. 651 ff.

6. Professor Jonathan King, 'Erosion of Biomedical Research through Unregulated Commercialization', Paper presented at the American Association for the Advancement of Science (AAAS) Symposium (January 1982) on Commercial Genetic Engineering, organized by Professor Sheldon Krimsky.

7. Lewis Thomas, 'The Technology of Medicine', in *The Lives of a Cell: Notes of a Biology Watcher*, New York, Bantam, 1975, p. 39.

8. Susan George, *How the Other Half Dies*, Penguin Books (UK) and Allanheld, Osmun (USA), 1976/77, Ch. 5.

9. Jonathan King, op. cit., note 6.

10. James Watson's famed *The Double Helix* (1968) is not necessarily the best or most accurate of these histories, though it makes racy reading. Maurice Wilkins, who shared the 1962 Nobel Prize with Crick and Watson, once confided: 'If you read the book [it says] "I'm Jim, I'm smart; most of the time Francis is smart too; the rest are bloody clots."' I tend to agree with his assessment. A more useful layperson's history was first published in *The New Yorker* in its 'Annals of Science' series: Horace Freeland Judson, *DNA*, 27 November, 4 and 11 December 1978; subsequently published in book form. Also, *The DNA Story: a Documentary History of Gene Cloning*, by J. D. Watson and John Tooze, San Francisco, W. H. Freeman & Co., 1981; an exhaustive (and expensive) volume reproducing a huge number of documents on gene-splicing and the debate engendered by it.

11. For those who read French, an excellent summary of the biological skills involved in the development of recombinant DNA techniques is Jean-Claude Kaplan, 'Le Génie Génétique', in *Les Manipulations*, No. 6 in the series 'Le Genre Humain', Paris, Fayard, 1983. For those who don't, the most comprehensible summary I've come across is 'Shaping Life in the Lab', *Time Magazine*, 9 March 1981.

12. M. Kenney, F. H. Buttel, J. T. Cowan and J. R. Kloppenburg, Jr, 'Genetic Engineering and Agriculture', Cornell Rural Sociology Bulletin Series, Bulletin No. 125, July 1982.

13. 'Biotech Comes of Age', *Business Week*, 23 January 1984.

14. *Financial Times Survey*, 'Biotechnology', 3 May 1983.

15. *Business Week*, op. cit.
16. 'The Livestock Industry's Genetic Revolution', *Business Week*, 21 June 1982.
17. Harold M. Schmeck, Jr, 'Gene splicing called key to agricultural progress', the *New York Times*, 20 May 1981. The think tanks that did the study are called Policy Research Corporation of Chicago and The Chicago Group, Inc. They claim to have undertaken the study on their own, without outside financial backing, so they must be confident of finding paying customers.
18. Anne Crittenden, Interview with T. N. Urban in 'Talking Business', *New York Times*, 5 May 1981.
19. Mary-Dell Chilton, 'L'Introduction de gènes étrangers dans les plantes', *Pour la Science*, August 1983 (this is the French edition of *Science*: the same article certainly appeared in English, though perhaps at another date).
20. Anne Hughey, 'More firms pursue genetic engineering in quest for plants with desirable traits', *Wall Street Journal*, 10 May 1983. This article sums up a lot of other corporate activities in plant genetics, 'a burgeoning field'. See also 'The race to breed a supertomato', *Business Week*, 10 January 1983, and H. Garrett De Young, 'Crop Genetics: the Seeds of Revolution', *High Technology*, May 1983.
21. OECD, *Impact des Entreprises Multinationales sur les Potentiels Scientifiques et Techniques Nationaux*, Direction de la Science, de la Technologie et de l'Industrie, DSTI/SPR/79.23.MNE, August 1979. This report is unsigned but is the work of the excellent researcher François Chesnais.
22. See note 18.
23. Leon Wofsy, 'Biology and the University on the Market Place: What's for Sale?', speech at Berkeley, 16 March 1982, typed transcript.
24. Peter Behr, 'DuPont Gives Harvard $6 million', *Washington Post*, 30 June 1981.
25. Wofsy, op. cit., and Sheldon Krimsky, 'Commercial Genetic Engineering: Impacts on Universities and Non-Profit Institutions', introductory remarks for a Symposium of the American Association for the Advancement of Science, Washington, DC, 6 January 1982; cf. note 6.
26. David F. Noble, 'The Selling of the University', *The Nation*, 6 February 1982.

27. Victor Cohn, 'Profit seeking said to inhibit biology research', *The Washington Post*, 17 June 1981.

28. See Wofsy, op. cit., who spoke before the Pajaro Dunes Conference took place, and William Boly, who reported on it in 'The Gene Merchants', *California Magazine*, September 1982. This is an excellent, detailed article showing how biotech has developed and is affecting California.

29. Chief Justice Burger's opinion for the 5–4 Supreme Court decision is quoted in Edward Yoxen, *The Gene Business*, London, Pan Books, 1983, p. 98.

30. *Time Magazine*, cf. note 11.

31. Tom Kiley writing in the *New York Times* of 29 August 1982, p. 4 f., and quoted in *Rx for the Future: Biotechnology and Public Policy in California*, Office of Appropriate Technology, State of California, December 1982, photocopy of typescript. This document, unsigned but prepared by Nancy Pfund, summarizes Kiley's arguments, p. 35.

32. Professor Irving Kayton, Director of the Patent Law Program, The National Law Center, George Washington University, 'Does Copyright Law Apply to Genetically Engineered Cells?', *George Washington Law Review* (1982), 50, pp. 191–218; also summarized by the author in *Trends in Biotechnology*, Vol. 1, No. 1, Inaugural Issue, March/April 1983; Elsevier Science Publishers, Bio-Medical Division, Amsterdam.

33. Paul Berg *et al.*, the so-called 'Moratorium Letter', *Science*, 26 July 1974, p. 303.

34. Stephanie Yanchinski, 'Keeping the Gene Genie in the Bottle', *New Scientist*, 14 April 1983; also *Rx for the Future*, op. cit., note 31.

35. Philip J. Hilts, 'EPA to Regulate Gene Engineering', *International Herald Tribune*, 11 August 1983.

36. Philip J. Hilts, 'Clergymen ask ban on efforts to alter genes', *Washington Post*, 9 June 1983.

37. For a balanced discussion of what genetic research is already contributing to medicine and how genetic techniques can be used to predict and thus prevent individual susceptibility to certain diseases, see Dr Zsolt Harsanyi and Richard Hutton, *Genetic Prophecy*, London, Paladin Books, Granada Publishing, 1983.

38. Stephen Jay Gould has dealt with this theme in virtually everything he has written (notably in *The Mismeasure of Man*, New York,

Norton, 1981) and is highly recommended reading. A previous generation's formulation of this recurrent theme is particularly crass, considering who said it: 'No economic equality can survive the working of biological inequality': Herbert Hoover, *The Challenge to Liberty*, 1934, Ch. 3. A philosopher's view in 'The Genetic Adventure', *QQ: Report from the Center for Philosophy and Public Policy*, University of Maryland, Vol. 3, No. 2, Spring 1983.

39. 'Morgan Stanley taps Middleton as President of new venture unit', *Wall Street Journal*, 2 May 1984.

40. David Fishlock, 'Government Initiatives in UK Biotechnology', *Financial Times*, 11 May 1984.

41. Steve Lohr, 'Japan closing biotech gap', *International Herald Tribune*, 21 March 1983, and Harold M. Schmeck, 'Japan rivaling US in Biotechnology', *International Herald Tribune*, 28–29 January 1984.

42. Both quotes cited in David Noble, op. cit., note 26.

43. Nelson Schneider of E. F. Hutton, interviewed in the Central Television–Channel Four film, *The Gene Business*, 1984 (directed by Alan Bell, presented by SG).

44. Frederick H. Buttel, Martin Kenney and Jack Kloppenburg, Jr: 'From Green Revolution to Biorevolution: Some observations on the changing technological bases of economic transformation in the Third World', *Cornell Rural Sociology Bulletin Series*, Bulletin No. 132, August 1983.

45. Id. See also Martin Kenney, 'Is Biotechnology a Blessing for the Less Developed Nations?', *Monthly Review*, April 1983. On the perverse social effects of the Green Revolution, Susan George, *How the Other Half Dies*, cf. note 8.

Since this paper was written, an excellent book on 'The Political Economy of Plant Biotechnology' (the subtitle) has appeared: Jack R. Kloppenburg, Jr, *First the Seed*, Cambridge University Press, 1988. I regret not having had the benefit of his remarkable research.

Another recent and excellent source is the special number of *Development Dialogue* (1988: 1–2) entirely devoted to biotechnology: Cary Fowler *et al.*, *The Laws of Life: Another Development and the New Biotechnologies*, Dag Hammarskjöld Foundation, Ovre Slottsgatan 2, S-752 20 Uppsala, Sweden.

## 7 DECOLONIZING RESEARCH

1. On this and other questions in this report, see 'Toward a World without Hunger: Progress and Prospects for Completing the Unfinished Agenda of the World Food Conference', a report by the Executive Director of the World Food Council, WFC/1979/3, 23 March 1979; e.g., 'To get additional food into the diets of those [hundreds of millions who are chronically hungry] involves much more than increasing food production ... Greater production does not ensure that the increased food available will reach large numbers of hungry and malnourished people, nor can selective programmes for nutrition intervention – useful as they are – meet the needs of large malnourished populations afflicted by a shortage of food energy or calories ... Basically, the main obstacle to meeting the nutritional needs of large populations is one of poverty or lack of "effective demand" ... [Solutions] must be sought in development policies which increase employment for the rural landless and the urban poor and stimulate increased production by small subsistence farmers.' Paras. 121, 123.

2. These two paragraphs are taken from the United Nations Research Institute for Social Development's project report, *Food Systems and Society*, with whose analysis the FSG is in full agreement. The Group wishes to draw particular attention to this study: UNRISD/78/-C.14/Rev. 1 (quote from p. 21).

3. Questions discussed in this section are more fully treated in the Food Study Group's *Issues Paper* (Susan George, Rapporteur): HSDRGPID-2/UNUP-54, United Nations University, 1979.

4. With the exception of President Nyerere's speech, the proceedings of the recent World Conference on Agrarian Reform and Rural Development (WCARRD, Rome, July 1979) were a striking example of unanimous participation in conceptual deradicalization.

5. cf. a similar analysis in Richard Franke and Barbara Chasin, 'Science versus Ethics', *Science for the People*, July 1975.

6. Crozier, Huntington, Watanuki, 1975, Noam Chomsky, in *Intellectuals and the State* (Het Wereldvenster Baarn, the Netherlands, 1978) provides a brilliant analysis of intellectuals as 'experts in legitimation' and of the institutions they serve as disseminators of the 'state religion'. His comment on the Trilateral study: 'The crisis

of democracy to which they refer arises from the fact that, during the 1960s, segments of the normally quiescent masses of the population became politically mobilized and began to press their demands, thus creating a crisis, since naturally these demands cannot be met, at least without a significant redistribution of wealth and power, which is not to be contemplated.' On 'value-oriented intellectuals': 'Speaking of our enemies, we despise the technocratic and policy-oriented intellectuals as "commissars" and "apparatchiks" and honour the value-oriented intellectuals as the "democratic dissidents". At home, the values are reversed.'

7. Ponna Wignaraja should be credited with conceptualizing the separate knowledge stocks and the perspective of new 'mixes'.
8. Details of a seasonal methodology can be found in Pierre Spitz, 'Drought, Stocks and Social Classes', UNRISD, 1979.
9. cf. the presentation by Elise Boulding at the MIT Workshop.
10. John Berger, 'Towards Understanding Peasant Experience', *Race & Class*, Vol. 19, No. 4, Spring 1978.


12 THE RIGHT TO FOOD AND THE POLITICS OF HUNGER

1. United Nations, *Human Rights: A Compliation of International Instruments* (ST/HR/1/Rev.1), New York, 1978. An interesting analysis will be found in Philip Alston, 'International Law and the Right to Food', *Food as a Human Right* (Asbjorn Eide *et al.*, eds), United Nations University (HSDB-11/UNUP-503) 1984, p. 162.
2. Forcefully argued by Pierre Spitz, who uses the French Revolution example, 'Right to Food for Peoples and for the People: a Historical Perspective', in P. Alston and K. Tomasevski, eds, *The Right to Food*, International Studies in Human Rights, Martinus Nijhoff Publishers, for SIM, Holland, 1984, p. 170.
3. Some of the information on Ethiopia from Colin Legum's *Third World Reports*, of 7 February 1985 (Richmond, Surrey, mimeo) and from Graham Hancock, *Ethiopia: The Challenge of Hunger*, London, Victor Gollancz, 1985.
4. Figures from 'World Military and Social Expenditures 1983', *World Priorities*, Washington, 1983; conclusions from the figures drawn in Nigel Twose, 'Cultivating Hunger', a paper for Oxfam and the World Food Assembly (Rome, November 1984), mimeo.

5. For two excellent summaries, see Georgina Ashworth, 'Women are not half human: an overview of women's rights', and Jocelyn Kynch, 'How many women are enough?: Sex ratios and the right to life'; both in *Third World Affairs 1985*, published by the Third World Foundation, London, 1985.
6. Necker, 'Sur la législation et le commerce des grains', in *Manuscrits de Monsieur Necker Publiés par sa Fille*, chez J. J. Paschoud, Libraire à Genève, An XIII (1804); (not to be confused with the book of the same title, published in Paris in 1775).
7. R. Bin Wong, 'Les émeutes de subsistances en Chine et en Europe occidentale', and Pierre-Etienne Will, 'Le stockage public des grains en Chine à l'époque des Qing (1644–1911). Problèmes de gestion et problèmes de contrôle'. Both articles in *Les Annales (Economies, Sociétés, Civilisations)*, March–April 1983. The article by Robert Chambers, 'Putting "last" thinking first: a professional revolution', in *Third World Affairs 1985* (cf. note 5), is excellent on vulnerability and resilience of poor people's support systems.
8. Graham Hancock, op. cit., note 3, pp. 92–3.

# FOR THE BEST IN PAPERBACKS, LOOK FOR THE 🐧

In every corner of the world, on every subject under the sun, Penguin represents quality and variety – the very best in publishing today.

For complete information about books available from Penguin – including Pelicans, Puffins, Peregrines and Penguin Classics – and how to order them, write to us at the appropriate address below. Please note that for copyright reasons the selection of books varies from country to country.

**In the United Kingdom:** Please write to *Dept E.P., Penguin Books Ltd, Harmondsworth, Middlesex, UB7 0DA*

If you have any difficulty in obtaining a title, please send your order with the correct money, plus ten per cent for postage and packaging, to *PO Box No 11, West Drayton, Middlesex*

**In the United States:** Please write to *Dept BA, Penguin, 299 Murray Hill Parkway, East Rutherford, New Jersey 07073*

**In Canada:** Please write to *Penguin Books Canada Ltd, 2801 John Street, Markham, Ontario L3R 1B4*

**In Australia:** Please write to the *Marketing Department, Penguin Books Australia Ltd, P.O. Box 257, Ringwood, Victoria 3134*

**In New Zealand:** Please write to the *Marketing Department, Penguin Books (NZ) Ltd, Private Bag, Takapuna, Auckland 9*

**In India:** Please write to *Penguin Overseas Ltd, 706 Eros Apartments, 56 Nehru Place, New Delhi, 110019*

**In Holland:** Please write to *Penguin Books Nederland B.V., Postbus 195, NL–1380AD Weesp, Netherlands*

**In Germany:** Please write to *Penguin Books Ltd, Friedrichstrasse 10–12, D–6000 Frankfurt Main 1, Federal Republic of Germany*

**In Spain:** Please write to *Longman Penguin España, Calle San Nicolas 15, E–28013 Madrid, Spain*

**In France:** Please write to *Penguin Books Ltd, 39 Rue de Montmorency, F-75003, Paris, France*

**In Japan:** Please write to *Longman Penguin Japan Co Ltd, Yamaguchi Building, 2–12–9 Kanda Jimbocho, Chiyoda-Ku, Tokyo 101, Japan*

## PENGUIN PHILOSOPHY

### I: The Philosophy and Psychology of Personal Identity   Jonathan Glover

From cases of split brains and multiple personalities to the importance of memory and recognition by others, the author of *Causing Death and Saving Lives* tackles the vexed questions of personal identity. 'Fascinating ... the ideas which Glover pours forth in profusion deserve more detailed consideration' – Anthony Storr

### Minds, Brains and Science   John Searle

Based on Professor Searle's acclaimed series of Reith Lectures, *Minds, Brains and Science* is 'punchy and engaging ... a timely exposé of those woolly-minded computer-lovers who believe that computers can think, and indeed that the human mind is just a biological computer'.– *The Times Literary Supplement*

### Ethics   Inventing Right and Wrong   J. L. Mackie

Widely used as a text, Mackie's complete and clear treatise on moral theory deals with the status and content of ethics, sketches a practical moral system and examines the frontiers at which ethics touches psychology, theology, law and politics.

### The Penguin History of Western Philosophy   D. W. Hamlyn

'Well-crafted and readable ... neither laden with footnotes nor weighed down with technical language ... a general guide to three millennia of philosophizing in the West' – *The Times Literary Supplement*

### Science and Philosophy: Past and Present   Derek Gjertsen

Philosophy and science, once intimately connected, are today often seen as widely different disciplines. Ranging from Aristotle to Einstein, from quantum theory to renaissance magic, Confucius and parapsychology, this penetrating and original study shows such a view to be both naive and ill-informed.

### The Problem of Knowledge   A. J. Ayer

How do you *know* that this is a book? How do you *know* that you know? In *The Problem of Knowledge* A. J. Ayer presented the sceptic's arguments as forcefully as possible, investigating the extent to which they can be met. 'Thorough ... penetrating, vigorous ... readable and manageable' – *Spectator*

## PENGUIN POLITICS AND SOCIAL SCIENCES

### Comparative Government   S. E. Finer

'A considerable *tour de force* ... few teachers of politics in Britain would fail to learn a great deal from it ... Above all, it is the work of a great teacher who breathes into every page his own enthusiasm for the discipline' – Anthony King in *New Society*

### Karl Marx: Selected Writings in Sociology and Social Philosophy
### T. B. Bottomore and Maximilien Rubel (eds.)

'It makes available, in coherent form and lucid English, some of Marx's most important ideas. As an introduction to Marx's thought, it has very few rivals indeed' – *British Journal of Sociology*

### Post-War Britain   A Political History   Alan Sked and Chris Cook

Major political figures from Attlee to Thatcher, the aims and achievements of governments and the changing fortunes of Britain in the period since 1945 are thoroughly scrutinized in this readable history.

### Inside the Third World   Paul Harrison

From climate and colonialism to land hunger, exploding cities and illiteracy, this comprehensive book brings home a wealth of facts and analysis on the often tragic realities of life for the poor people and communities of Asia, Africa and Latin America.

### Housewife   Ann Oakley

'A fresh and challenging account' – *Economist*. 'Informative and rational enough to deserve a serious place in any discussion on the position of women in modern society' – *The Times Educational Supplement*

### The Raw and the Cooked   Claude Lévi-Strauss

Deliberately, brilliantly and inimitably challenging, Lévi-Strauss's seminal work of structural anthropology cuts wide and deep into the mind of mankind, as he finds in the myths of the South American Indians a comprehensible psychological pattern.

# FOR THE BEST IN PAPERBACKS, LOOK FOR THE 🐧

**Political Ideas**  David Thomson (ed.)

From Machiavelli to Marx – a stimulating and informative introduction to the last 500 years of European political thought.

**On Revolution**  Hannah Arendt

Arendt's classic analysis of a relatively recent political phenomenon examines the underlying principles common to all revolutions, and the evolution of revolutionary theory and practice. 'Never dull, enormously erudite, always imaginative' – *Sunday Times*

**The Apartheid Handbook**  Roger Omond

The facts behind the headlines: the essential hard information about how apartheid actually works from day to day.

**The Social Construction of Reality**  Peter Berger and Thomas Luckmann

Concerned with the sociology of 'everything that passes for knowledge in society' and particularly with that which passes for common sense, this is 'a serious, open-minded book, upon a serious subject' – *Listener*

**The Care of the Self**  Michel Foucault
**The History of Sexuality Vol 3**

Foucault examines the transformation of sexual discourse from the Hellenistic to the Roman world in an inquiry which 'bristles with provocative insights into the tangled liaison of sex and self' – *The Times Higher Educational Supplement*

## A Fate Worse than Debt

How did Third World countries accumulate a staggering trillion dollars' worth of debt? Who really shoulders the burden of reimbursement? With solid evidence and verve, Susan George answers these questions.

Debt-induced economic austerity is destroying the lives of countless Third World people who derived no benefit from the borrowed millions but must now make great sacrifices to bail out their élites. Northern economies stagnate and unemployment soars as the South serves the banks first and slashes imports. Nature pays too, as natural resources are cashed in to service debt. Yet the crisis *could* be a fantastic opportunity to create greater economic justice. With enough popular pressure in both North and South, the 3-D solution – Debt, Development, Democracy – could make debt an instrument not of oppression and despair but of liberation.

'She writes trenchantly and with conviction. Her commitment to the poor and her determination to expose the injustices of the international system which ensure continuing poverty shine through all her writings' – Brian W. Walker, Former Director General of Oxfam.

## How the Other Half Dies

'Hunger is not a scourge but a scandal': this is the premise of Susan George's classic study of world hunger. Contrary to popular opinion, malnutrition and starvation are not the result of over-population, of poor climate or lack of cultivatable land. The reason hunger exists on such a vast scale is because world food supplies are controlled by the rich and powerful for the wealthy consumer.

The multinational agribusiness corporations, Western governments with their food 'aid' policies and supposedly neutral multilateral development organizations share responsibility for the fate of the underdeveloped countries. Working with local élites, protected by the powerful West, the United States paves the way and is gradually imposing its control over the whole planet.

*How the Other Half Dies* was written after the World Food Conference in 1974 and now has a new foreword in which recent changes in the situation are reviewed. Yet the needs remain the same and the book's relevance, its ability to shock and its power to enrage have in no measure diminished.